Breathless Memories

One American's Memoirs:

Jim's Life Journey

James Kenneth Patrick Graham J. D.

Copyright © 2011 by James Kenneth Patrick Graham J. D.

Library of Congress Control Number: 2010913554
ISBN:	Hardcover	978-1-4535-6760-9
	Softcover	978-1-4535-6759-3

All rights reserved. No part of this book may be reproduced or transmitted in any form or by any means, electronic or mechanical, including photocopying, recording, or by any information storage and retrieval system, without permission in writing from the copyright owner.

This book was printed in the United States of America.

To order additional copies of this book, contact:
Xlibris Corporation
1-888-795-4274
www.Xlibris.com
Orders@Xlibris.com
53842

October 24, 2011

Breathless Memories

*To our friend Helen Ward.
Please share our "Breathless Memories" journey of life.
All the Best,
Jim & Cindy
Graham*

Mr James K Graham
1744 Heron Ridge Dr
Bloomfield MI 48302

Contents

1. Heritage and History of the Graham/Boyle Family 19
2. Childhood 63
3. Schooling 73
4. Marriage and Children 105
5. Military Service 157
6. Working Career Summary 165
7. Charitable Endeavors and Political Associations 205
8. Friends 223
9. Deaths (Eulogies) 245
10. Retirement and Remarriage 273
11. Financial Accomplishments 303
12. Travel 321
13. Hobbies 383
14. Discipline 389
15. Spirituality and Core Values 391
16. Loyalty—God, Family, and USA 395
17. Luck—(Blessings) 403
18. Diet—Physical Fitness 405
19. Life's Strengths and Shortcomings 411
20. Favorite Sayings 415
21. Sense of Humor 419
22. Staying Alive at Seventy-five 421
23. Summary and Conclusions 461

Appendix
A1. My Whimsical Words—Sometimes in Rhyme 467
A2. Little Pleasures I Enjoy! 541
A3. Bibliography of Life 545
A4. Scottish Clans and Tartans 549
A5. Graham Family History 553

Dedication

It hardly seems possible that five years have passed
since this autobiographical project
began in January 2005.

The dictionary defines the word *"dedicate"* as
*"to address a book to a friend or loved one
as a mark of affection or respect . . ."*
It is that, and much more. This Dedication is the defining summary
for this labor of love that chronicles the historical segment of one
loving family's earthly journey from the 1840s to 2010.
My motivation was to record the achievements of many fine family
members through the memories and records of six generations—
in other words, the anthology of how the
Graham-Boyle
came to be, within the centuries stated above.

Thanks to my son, Kevin, and my daughter, Jennifer,
for their idea that I write a history of my life.

Special remembrance to my deceased loved ones:
Mom, Dad, sister Catherine, brothers William and Robert,
and late wife, Betty.

Deep appreciation to my wife Cindy
for her timeless essential work in computerizing, collecting,
managing, researching, categorizing, and transcribing this literary
labor of love for the past, present, and future generations.

Finally, to family
who contributed long-lost photos and memorabilia
of our heritage:
Brian Jordan, Nan Jordan, Cathy Alexander, and Margaret McDevitt,
and my brother Bill Graham's family tree.

Thank You, One and All!

While the family history is of interest to those who live in 2010, hopefully, it will be of some historical interest to future generations of our family.

As it is written,
"You cannot know where you are going,
if you don't know where you have been."

Finally, the expression,

"It is not the breaths in life you take that matter, but the moments that leave you breathless, that count,"

carried great significance in our family's history.

The path from the Emerald Isle, to Bonnie Scotland,
to America the Beautiful,
encompassed many "breathless" times in our genealogical journey. My sincere thanks for the breathless occasions, especially those included in this autobiography, that have blessed me in my life.

Slainte
—James K. Graham J. D.

From

The Emerald Isle

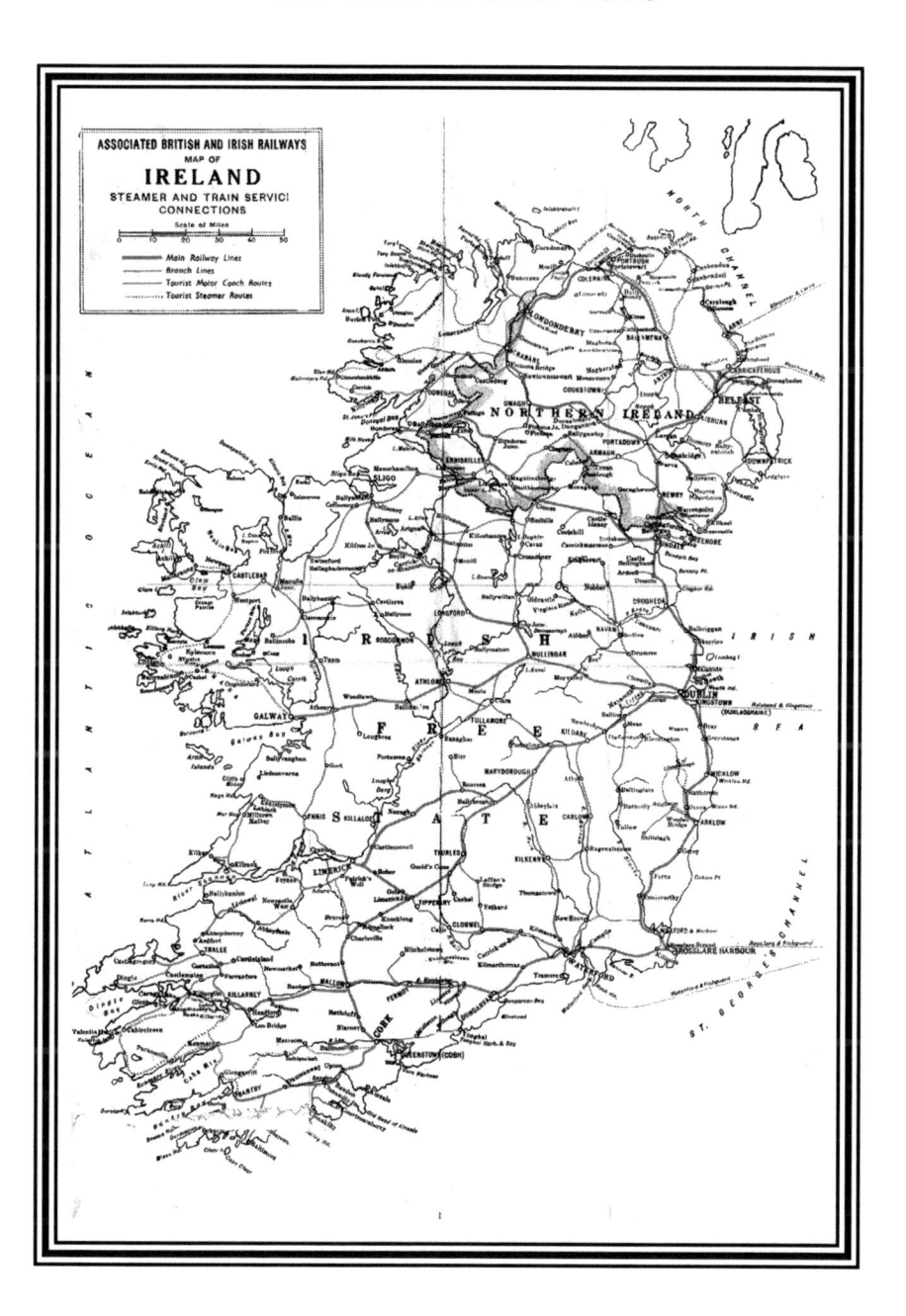

To
Bonnie Scotland

To
America The Beautiful

America the Beautiful

O beautiful for spacious skies,
For amber waves of grain,
For purple mountain majesties
Above the fruited plain!
America! America!
God shed His grace on thee
And crown thy good with brotherhood
From sea to shining sea!

O beautiful for pilgrim feet,
Whose stern impassioned stress
A thoroughfare for freedom beat
Across the wilderness!
America! America!
God mend thine every flaw
Confirm thy soul in self-control,
Thy liberty in law!

Katharine Lee Bates

Introduction

*My daughter Jennifer and son Kevin have frequently asked me to create
a life's history for their children.
So it is that I, James Kenneth Patrick Graham,
now age seventy,
at this writing, begin January 22, 2005.*

Caveat

*As I read the final draft of this autobiography
in August 2010,
I realize—because of the broken and fragmented flow
of writing over months—there are repetitions and redundancies.
Furthermore, as I reread my words written in these past years,
I hope that my endeavor is factual
and that I have not appeared as a braggadocio.
No one has ever liked a braggart, nor have I.*

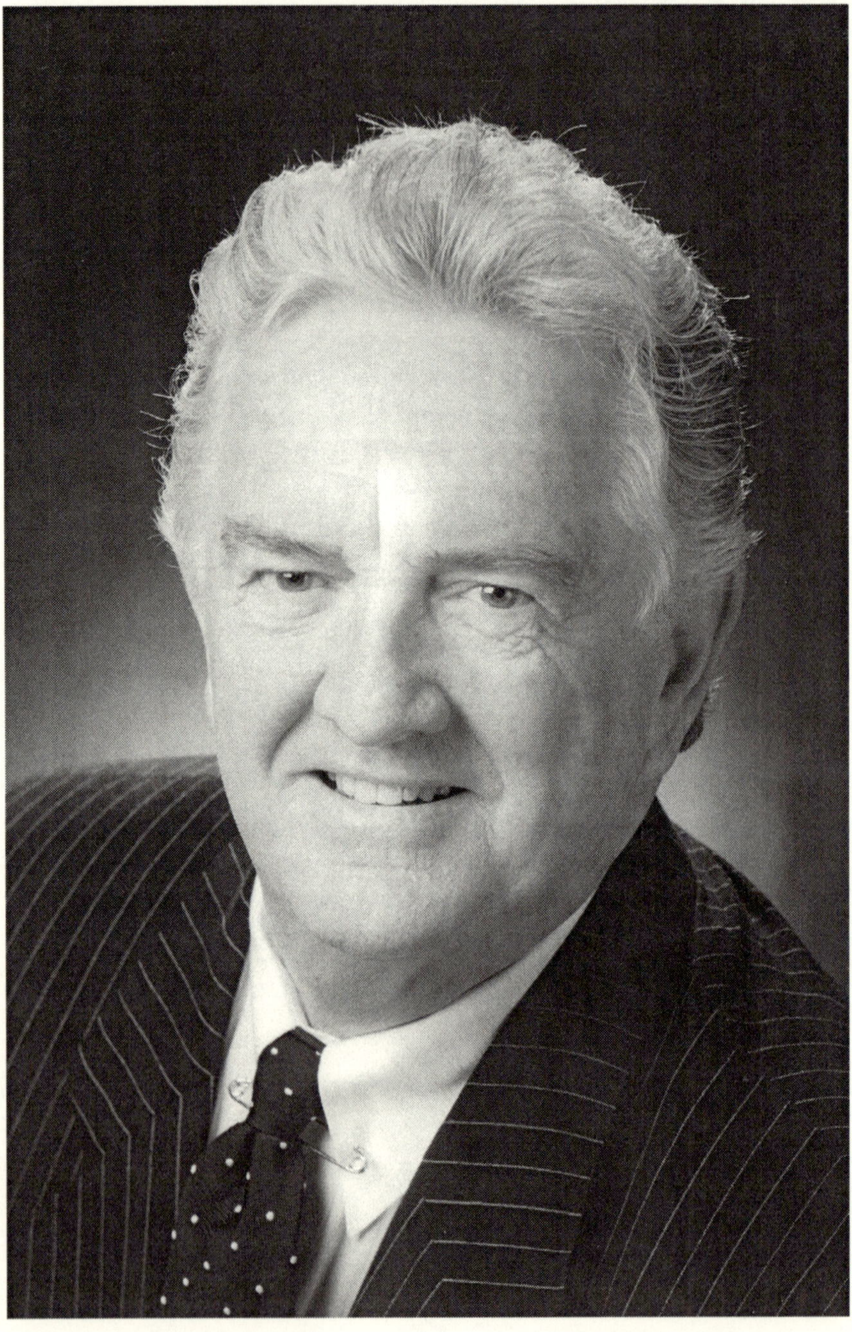

CHAPTER ONE

Heritage and History of the Graham/Boyle Family

As the adage goes, "Each journey begins with the first step." Therefore, going back to our family beginnings, I referenced my eldest brother William Graham's family-tree chart compiled in the 1980s before he died in 1995.

However, a general hereditary caveat is appropriate. As with all family-tree histories, fleeting centuries are replete with lost or missing elements. The Irish-Scottish lineage is subject to these same historical vagaries.

Case in point, some genealogical experts suggest that the *Graham* name (clan) was brought to Ireland in the 1600s by Scottish settlers. To this day, Graham and Boyle are among the one hundred most common names in Ireland—the birthplace of all four of my grandparents.

In fact, Thomas Graham was a large landowner that was listed on properties in County Tyrone, Ireland, in 1819 and 1920. His father preceded Thomas as a prosperous businessman in Ireland, the father dying in 1819.

The Graham family was of the house of Montrose. During the late 1500s-1600s, the First Marquess of Montrose, James Graham—for the record, not me—was Captain General of the king's armies and sons of Scotland. I make this point to illustrate the comings and goings between Scotland and Ireland at that centuries-ago period.

In addition, with the passing of centuries, our historical clan tracking is complicated by the wars and political havoc of the various periods. Most records of the Graham Clan, including those that left Scotland for Ireland, were destroyed in the wars. It is believed that from 1680 to 1685, many Scots left Scotland for Ireland.

It was in this period of the mid-1600s that England was trying to unify Scotland and Ireland under the English Crown, which was a disaster, and resulted in uprisings, particularly over religious differences. It was in the 1600s that England assumed control of the six northern counties of Ireland (including County Tyrone).

King James VI of Scotland and King James I of England controlled the six counties during their respective reigns in the early 1600s. Being Protestants, they expelled the Irish Catholics to the forests and mountains, giving their confiscated land to their Protestant followers.

Subsequent to them, Oliver Cromwell, the so-called Lord Protector, from 1650 to his death in 1660, wreaked brutal havoc on the Irish Catholics. So it was in the context of this tumultuous period that exacerbated the tracing of any remaining historical records of family lineage. It is a fact that it was because of the political and religious turmoil that families emigrated from Scotland to Ireland back to Scotland, and then to America during those unendurable times in past centuries.

However, the Grahams—as did others—soldiered on to preserve the Graham heritage. For example, Richard Graham—viscount of Prestin—was secretary of state of Scotland in 1688. James Graham of Claverhouse—viscount of Dundee—was counselor to King James. He became General Graham after the death of the king and united the Scottish chiefs of the Highland clans. He was remembered by the poet Scott.

In Sir Walter Scott's "The Lady of the Lake." the following verse appears:

> "Fetters and Worden for the Graham
> His chain of gold the king unstrung,
> The links o'er Malcolm's neck he flung,
> Then gently drew the glittering hand
> And laid the clap on Ellen's hand."

The historians relate that the Graham Clan was a large and influential one and at the time of its greatest power, had as its head

James Graham, the Earl of Montrose, who laid down his life for the king.

It is suggested that the Graham family dates back thousands of years. First accounts of Graham to America were about 1720. So it is with this history, we come to present day, still surviving. As a result, I wanted to give this historical background to set the stage for my branch of the Graham Clan. I will now relate the known historical facts of the flow from my Irish ancestors, to my Scottish parents, onto our continuing journey of Grahams in America.

William McGovern
Born in 1839 in Magheraglass, Kildress, Tyrone, Ireland
Died in 1910 in Lisdivin Upper, Donaghedy, Tyrone
My Great-Grandfather . . .

My Grandparents—William Graham and Mary Anne McGovern

William was born about 1856 in Gortaclady, Kildress, Tyrone, Ireland and died on June 17, 1950 in Greenock East, Renfrewshire, Scotland. William married Mary Anne McGovern on January 16, 1883 in Greenock East, Renfrewshire, Scotland. Mary Anne was born about 1859 in Magheraglass, Kildress, Tyrone, Ireland and died on December 11, 1947 in Greenock East, Renfrewshire, Scotland. They had 14 children—pictured are the oldest William and Kate in the late 1880's.

My Father—Robert Graham and his 'older' sister,
Sarah
Photo about 1901 in East Greenock, Scotland

Census—March 31, 1901 Greenock Scotland

Grandfather James Boyle—Bricklayer and his wife, Grandmother Catherine Boyle
Children: John, age 8 (he died in this year); James, age 6; Catherine (Kitty) age 4;
Hannah (Nan), age 3—this was my Mom

My Grandparents—Mary Anne (McGovern) and William Graham in front of their home at 43 Belleville St., Greenock Scotland about 1938

My Graham Family

My paternal grandparents, William and Mary Anne Graham, were born in Gortaclady, Kildress and Magheraglss, Kildress, respectively, County Tyrone, Ireland (now one of the six counties of Ulster in the north). My grandfather, William Graham, was born in 1856 and died on June 17, 1950. He was the son of Michael Graham and Elizabeth Greer Graham. My grandmother, Mary Anne McGovern Graham, was born in 1859 and died December 11, 1947. William and Mary Anne were married on January 16, 1883, in Greenock East, Scotland, having emigrated to Scotland from Ireland for religious freedom and job opportunities. My dad's parents (William and Mary Anne) had fourteen children—a set of twins died in infancy. In order of age, they were William, Catherine (Kate), George, Margaret (Maggie), Matilda (Tillie), Sarah, Robert (Bob—my dad), Rosina (Ena), James, Samuel, Jenny, and May.

My dad, Robert Graham, was born on October 23, 1898, in Greenock, Scotland, and my dad died October 29, 1965, at Highland Park General Hospital in Michigan in the United States.

The Graham family (grandparents) lived at 43 Belleville St. in Greenock. Their home was bombed by the Germans in World War II, and my namesake, Uncle James Graham, was killed by the explosion. After the war, from 1945 until 1950, they lived at 34 Baxter St. in Greenock.

My paternal great-grandparents were (Grandmother's parents) Catherine and William McGovern of Magheraglass, Kildress, County Tyrone, Ireland, and (Grandfather's parents) Elizabeth and Michael Graham, also of County Tyrone, Ireland.

My great grandfather—William McGovern was born in 1839 in Magheraglass, Kildress, Tyrone, Ireland and died in 1910 in Lisdivin Upper, Donaghedy, Tyrone. He married Catherine in 1855 in Strabane, Tyrone, Ireland. She also had been born in 1839 in County Tyrone and died in 1910 in Lisdivin Upper, Donaghedy, Tyrone.

My mother's parents, my maternal grandparents, James and Catherine Boyle, were born in Ireland, near the towns of Boyle and Glenties, in the county of Donegal (the original Gaelic "Na Glenntai"—meaning the Glens). My mom's dad (my grandfather) was James Boyle (born May 19, 1861) in Greenock Middle, Renfrewshire, Scotland, UK.

He died on May 25, 1941 in Detroit, Michigan, USA.

James Boyle's parents (my great-grandparents) were John Boyle and Grace McAuley Boyle. John and Grace had eight children, all born in Greenock Middle, Renfrewshire, Scotland; namely: John (born 1857), Francis "Frank" (born 1859), James (born 1861), Daniel (born 1863), Mary (born 1864), Eder (born 1868), Grace (born 1869), and Rose (born 1870). My great-grandfather John Boyle was born about 1826 in Glenties, Donegal, Ireland and died in 1900 in Greenock Middle, Renfrewshire, Scotland. He married Grace McAuley in 1856 in Greenock Middle, Renfrewshire, Scotland. She (Grace) had been born about 1831 in Dublin, Ireland and died in 1900 in Deal, Kent, England, UK. They had lived in Scotland from the mid 1850's until 1881, when John moved to his residence to Greenock West, Renfrewshire, Scotland until his death, and Grace moved to Penge, Surrey, England (address listed as 35 Palace Square) and later in 1891 to Deal, Kent, England where she belonged to St. Leonard Parish.

My grandfather (James Boyle) married Catherine Boyle Alexander (who had immigrated to Scotland in 1876 from Donegal, Ireland) on July 26, 1891. Catherine's father (James Boyle) died when she was only eight; Catherine's widowed mother married another man with the name of Alexander. Her parents (my great-grandparents) were Hannah Boyle and Charles James Boyle. Hannah Boyle (great-grandmother) was born in 1840 in Glenties, Donegal, Ireland and died in 1910 in Greenock east, Renfrewshire, Scotland. She married Charles James Boyle in 1864 in Glenties, Donegal, Ireland. He was born in 1829 in Glenties, Donegal, Ireland.

The entire Boyle family (grandparents) had immigrated to Scotland in search of jobs. All of their eight children were born in Scotland; the eldest child, John, died at age eight. The other seven children were Jim (a.k.a. Steve), who died July 21, 1968; John (named after the first son who died), died July 26, 1966; Catherine (Kitty), born November 11, 1896, died May 5, 1971; Hannah (Nan) (my mom), born March 30, 1898, in Greenock, Scotland, and died January 28, 1963, in Detroit, Michigan; Frank, born January, 17, 1903, and died September 28, 1964; and Charlie. They are all deceased. James Boyle (my grandfather) died May 25,1941, in Detroit, Michigan. Catherine Boyle (my grandmother) died July 31, 1941, also in Detroit, Michigan. They are laid to rest in Mt. Olivet Cemetery in Detroit.

Ó bAoiġill

O'Boyle Family Crest

	EXTRACT OF AN ENTRY IN kept under the Registration of Births,		A REGISTER OF MARRIAGES Deaths and Marriages (Scotland) Act 1965		1861 - 1921	MC
177	1891 on the Twenty Sixth day of July At St Mary's Greenock. After Banns According to the Forms of the Roman Catholic Church.	(signed) James Boyle Bricklayer (Bachelor) (signed) Catherine Boyle Alexander (Spinster)	28 26	23 Bruce Street, Greenock. 1 Mount Lane, Greenock.	John Boyle Labourer (deceased) Grace Boyle m.s. McAulay (deceased) Hannah Boyle now widow of Charles Alexander (seaman)	Alexander Taylor Robert Jamieson Witness Jane Alexander Witness	1891 July 27th At Greenock. A R Baird Interim

EXTRACTED from the Register of Marriages for the West District of Greenock County of Renfrew this 11th day of July 19 91

Elaine Moman

Registry of Marriage for my Grandparents
James Boyle and Catherine Boyle Alexander
July 26, 1891
St. Mary's Church, Greenock Scotland

Mt Olivet Cemetery
Section Marker

As an aside, my mom's family (parents and children) all immigrated together to America. Of my dad's family, only my dad and his younger brother Sammy immigrated to America. Dad's parents and all the rest of his family remained in Scotland.

Quip: Both grandparents were born in Ireland and both parents were born in Scotland—means my Irish side never refuses a drink, and my Scottish side never pays for one!

Death Certificate for James Boyle
My Mom's Dad—My Grandfather
Died: May 25, 1941 at Frank & Annie Boyle's home
12291 Riad Road, Detroit, Michigan
Funeral at St Jude Catholic Church
Buried in Mt. Olivet Cemetery, Detroit, Michigan

Death Certificate for Catherine (Alexander) Boyle
Died: July 14, 1941 at the home of Aunt Kitty & Pat Gallagher
16190 Mark Twain, Detroit, Michigan
Funeral at Precious Blood Catholic Church, Detroit, Michigan
Buried at Mt. Olivet Cemetery, Detroit, Michigan

James Kenneth Patrick Graham J. D.

A pictorial History of Greenock/Gourock

Greenock Harbour was an important port dating back to the early 1800's. In June 1878, trustees proceeded with the construction of a large wet dock which would handle the increasing steamer traffic and trade ships. Seven years later in 1886, the JAMES WATT DOCK, nearly 200 feet long, 300 feet wide, and 32 foot depth became the only dock on the Clyde where vessels of great tonnage could be kept constantly afloat. Over the next 75 years, major steamship companies docked here and the huge ship yards with dry docks were built.
Many of the world's largest liners and cargo vessels were built here. During WORLD WAR II, this safe harbour was filled from bank to bank with the American troop ships.

DALRYMPLE STREET (East)

Although this view over the East India Harbour is easily located, it shows a number of changes which have taken place along Dalrymple Street and the east end of Cathcart Street since 1959. Most of Brymner Street, running up from the Customhouse has now been demolished, and Dalrymple Street has been rerouted slightly south, cutting out the curve towards the Rue End. Behind the Customhouse were Palmerston Buildings, now the site of a grassed area to the rear of the new Police Station. This building, constructed between 1972 and 1975 at a cost of £900,000 replaced the former cramped headquarters in the municipal buildings where the police had been stationed since 1884.

The foundation stone of the Customhouse was laid on May 2nd, 1817, and the building, arguably one of the finest customhouses in the British Isles, was completed in 1818 at a cost of £33,000. The architect was William Burn of Edinburgh, and the various contractors were D. Mathieson, A. McFarlane and G. Dempster. Inverclyde Sailors' Centre first opened in March 1944 by the Duchess of Kent is now used for homeless persons by the Salvation Army.

In the East India harbour the Clyde Steamers are: on the left "King George V", right "Duchess of Hamilton" and in the dry dock "St Columba".

BELVILLE STREET, 1941
These tenement properties in Belville Street show some of the devastation caused by enemy bombers on the nights of 6th and 7th May 1941. Over the two nights 280 people were killed and over 1200 injured, many seriously. The numbers, however, would have risen considerably had not many people left the town after the first night's bombing to camp out on the moors, in the Kip Valley and at Lunderston Bay. Others to the alarm of the ARP authorities, spent the night in railway tunnels.

Some people who had gone to rest centres after being bombed out of their homes in the first night's bombing were made homeless for a second time when several of the rest centres were hit during the second night's raid. Fortunately none of the hospitals in the area was hit, although the patients at the Royal had to be evacuated for a few days as there was no power or water. The hospital remained open as a casualty clearing station.

No 'all clears' could be sounded as the air raid sirens had been silenced when the power station at Dellingburn had been hit and put out of action. Wardens had to go round their various areas sounding the 'all clear' on whistles.

An emergency one page edition of the "Greenock Telegraph" was printed by hand and pasted on walls all over the town on 9th May.

My Grandparents—William and Catherine Graham— and my Uncle James Graham, lived at 43 Belleville Street. My Uncle James, for whom I was named, was killed in the direct hit by the German bombing. He is listed in the Greenock City Hall Memorial.

TONTINE HOTEL, ARDGOWAN SQUARE
Built in 1808 by Mr George Robertson as a private house the Tontine Hotel stands on the site of the first windmill in the district to be used for grinding corn. At this time it was also the most westerly house in the district.
Mr Robertson, well known in connection with the Shaws Water Scheme, was also reputed to have been the owner of the first private carriage in the town, as well as being the first to own a piano. He also appeared to have taken care of his workers as the men who built the house, apart from being paid a day's wages, were said to have been supplied with three glasses of rum each day.
The house remained as a private home until 1892 when Mrs Buchanan, then proprietor of the Tontine Hotel, Cathcart Street, became the tenant and converted the mansion into an hotel. The Service family took over the hotel in 1907 and continued to run it until 1955. In 1958 the hotel was bought by Lithgows Ltd.
The photograph, taken in 1914, shows the Renfrewshire Hunt leaving the hotel on its way to hunt foxes in a wood at Inverkip. Mr John Service, a member of the Hunt, had persuaded the other members to make the hotel the starting point for this particular hunt.

The history of these twin towns dates to the early 1800's.
This TONTINE HOTEL started as a private home and later became a boarding hotel.
Our family stayed at this hotel under third generation management around 1959.

My parents Robert Graham (October 23, 1898-October 29, 1965) and Hannah (Nan) Boyle (March 30, 1898-January 28, 1963) were both born in Greenock, Scotland. My mom and dad immigrated to Windsor, Ontario, Canada, in 1922. They were married in Walkerville (a suburb of Windsor) Ontario, Canada, on June 2, 1925, with Jean Boyle and Samuel Graham as witnesses and Rev. James B. Neville, Roman Catholic priest, presiding.

1898—Greenock, Scotland—Birth Registry Extract
Hannah Boyle, my Mom and Robert Graham, my Dad

CERTIFICATE OF BAPTISM.

According to the Register of Baptisms kept at St. Lawrence, Greenock, Scotland

Robert, son of William Graham and Mary A. McGovern

formerly .... lawfully Married, Born Oct. 21, 1898

was Baptised at the said Church, by the Rev. Michael Fox on the 27th day of October 1898 and Elizabeth Roe being God-Parents.

I, the undersigned, hereby certify that the above is a true and correct extract from the Register of Baptisms kept at the above Church. As witness my hand, this 7th day of May 19 15

Signature Charles Gallagher

Signature St Lawrences Greenock

Certificate of Baptism for my Dad—Robert Graham
Born on October 23, 1898 and
Baptized on October 27, 1898 at
St. Lawrence Catholic Church in Greenock, Scotland
by Fr. Michael Fox

CODE—5TH EDITION A.B.C.
TELEPHONE:
GREENOCK 1000.
TELEGRAPHIC ADDRESS:
"MAINYARD," GREENOCK.

The Greenock Dockyard Coy. Ltd.

SHIPBUILDERS AND REPAIRERS,

REF. GREENOCK, 17th June, 19 20.

TO WHOM IT MAY CONCERN.

This to certify that the bearer Robt. Graham served with us as an apprentice Angle Iron Smith, for five years between, 24th Feby 1915, and 15th June 1920.

THE GREENOCK DOCKYARD CO., LTD.

John McKie .... SECRETARY

Robert Graham
43 Belville Street
Greenock

June 17, 1920
Dad's 'reference' certification as he left 'The Greenock Dockyard' in Scotland to emigrate to America

1612

Form 2203
U. S. DEPARTMENT OF LABOR
NATURALIZATION SERVICE

TRIPLICATE
(To be given to the person making the Declaration)

No. ....

UNITED STATES OF AMERICA

DECLARATION OF INTENTION

☞ **Invalid for all purposes seven years after the date hereof**

State of Michigan, } ss: In the Circuit Court of Wayne County.
Wayne County,

I, _Robert Graham_, aged _23_ years, occupation _Mechanic_, do declare on oath that my personal description is: Color white, complexion _fair_, height _5_ feet _9½_ inches, weight _142_ pounds, color of hair _Brown_, color of eyes _Blue_, other visible distinctive marks _None_
I was born in _Greenock, Scotland_
on the _23_ day of _Oct._, anno Domini 1_898_; I now reside at _2221 Cortland Ave, High Pk_, Michigan.
I emigrated to the United States of America from _Glasgow, Scotland_
on the vessel _Assyria_; my last foreign residence was _Scotland_; I am _not_ married; the name of my wife is _____; she was born at _____
and now resides at _____
It is my bona fide intention to renounce forever all allegiance and fidelity to any foreign prince, potentate, state, or sovereignty, and particularly to _Geo. King of Great Britain, England_, of whom I am now a subject;
I arrived at the port of _New York_, in the State of _N.Y._, on or about the _6_ day of _Aug._, anno Domini 1_922_; I am not an anarchist; I am not a polygamist nor a believer in the practice of polygamy; and it is my intention in good faith to become a citizen of the United States of America and to permanently reside therein: SO HELP ME GOD.

Robert Graham
(Original signature of declarant)

Subscribed and sworn to before me in the office of the Clerk of said Court at Detroit, Mich., this _16_ day of _Aug_ anno Domini 19_22_

Thos. F. Farrell
Clerk of the Circuit Court.
By _Roy Brown_, Deputy Clerk.

Dad's (Robert Graham) arrival in the United States of America
Port of New York
August 6, 1922
His declaration, having left the port in Glasgow Scotland
traveling on the vessel—Assyria
and disclaiming allegiance to King George I of Great Britain

Certificate of citizenship: Robert Graham
Petition 83532
January 14, 1935

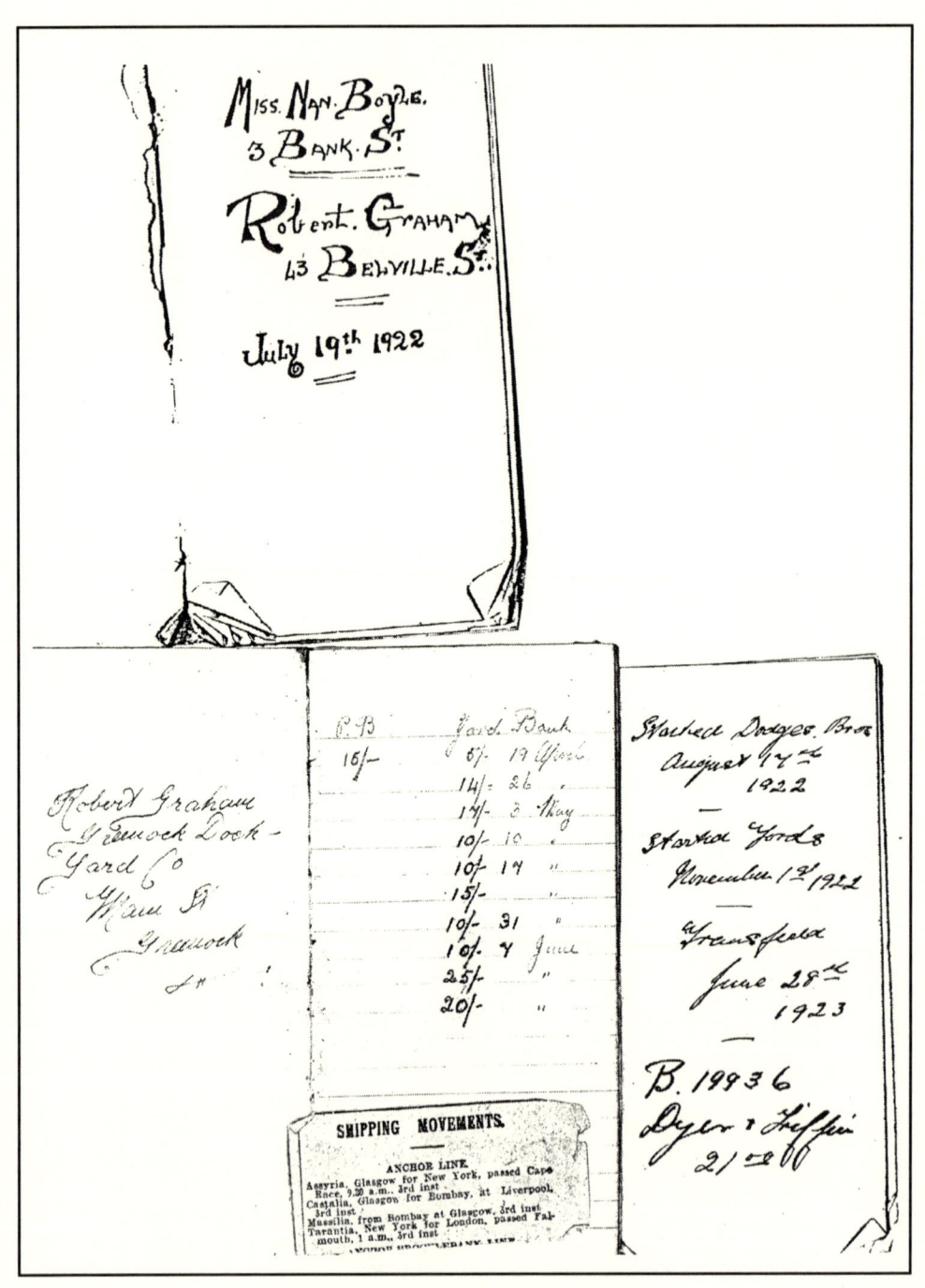

Excerpts from Dad's diary notes

About 1922 . . .
My Mom—Hannah (Nan) Boyle and her sister Catherine (Kitty) Boyle Gallagher

About 1925-1926
Detroit Michigan Family Wedding Celebration
Top Row: Eddie McKnight and his bride—Sarah Graham McKnight, my mom—Nan Boyle Graham and my dad—Robert Graham; Middle Row: James Boyle (grandfather), unknown, Anne (Frank's wife) Boyle, Catherine Boyle (my grandmother on Mom's side), Bill Shanahan (husband of Jean Boyle): Bottom Row: Pat Gallagher, Kitty Boyle Gallagher, unknown, Jean Boyle Shanahan

Hannah (Nan) Boyle Graham on her wedding day
in Walkerville (Windsor) Ontario

Wedding Day—June 2, 1925
Walkerville Ontario
The bride and groom—Robert and Nan Graham

Nan Graham—my Mom—1928

1927
Dad, Mom, and sister Catherine (held by Dad)
(bottom row Center) returning to America from a visit
to Scotland

About 1932 . . .
Detroit Michigan
L to R: Dad (Robert Graham Sr.,
Mom (Hannah (Nan) Graham, and dad's younger
brother Sammy. (Sammy died at a young age in the
late 1930's)

Mom's Social Security Card

Catherine (age 3) and William (Age 1)
1929

Breathless Memories 51

Summer 1929
My brother Billy and Dad
(Bob Graham)

Summer 1929
My Dad and sister Catherine

Winter 1930
My Dad (Robert Graham Sr.)
with daughter Catherine
and son William

52   James Kenneth Patrick Graham J. D.

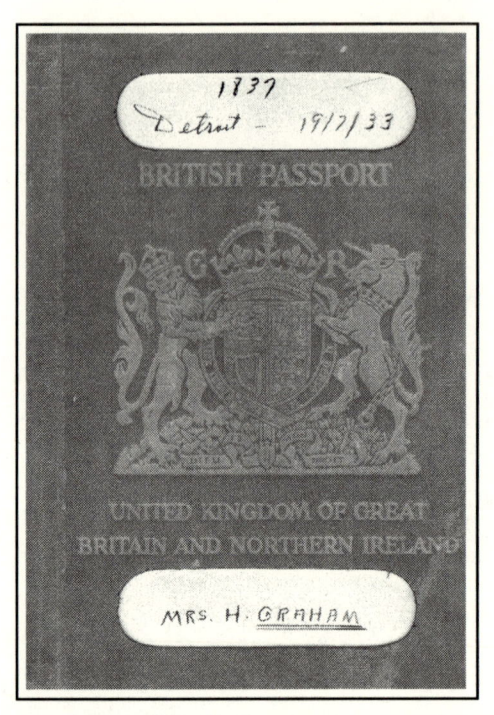

Mom's Passport
United Kingdom of Great Britain and Northern Ireland

Passport used for visit to Scotland in 1933

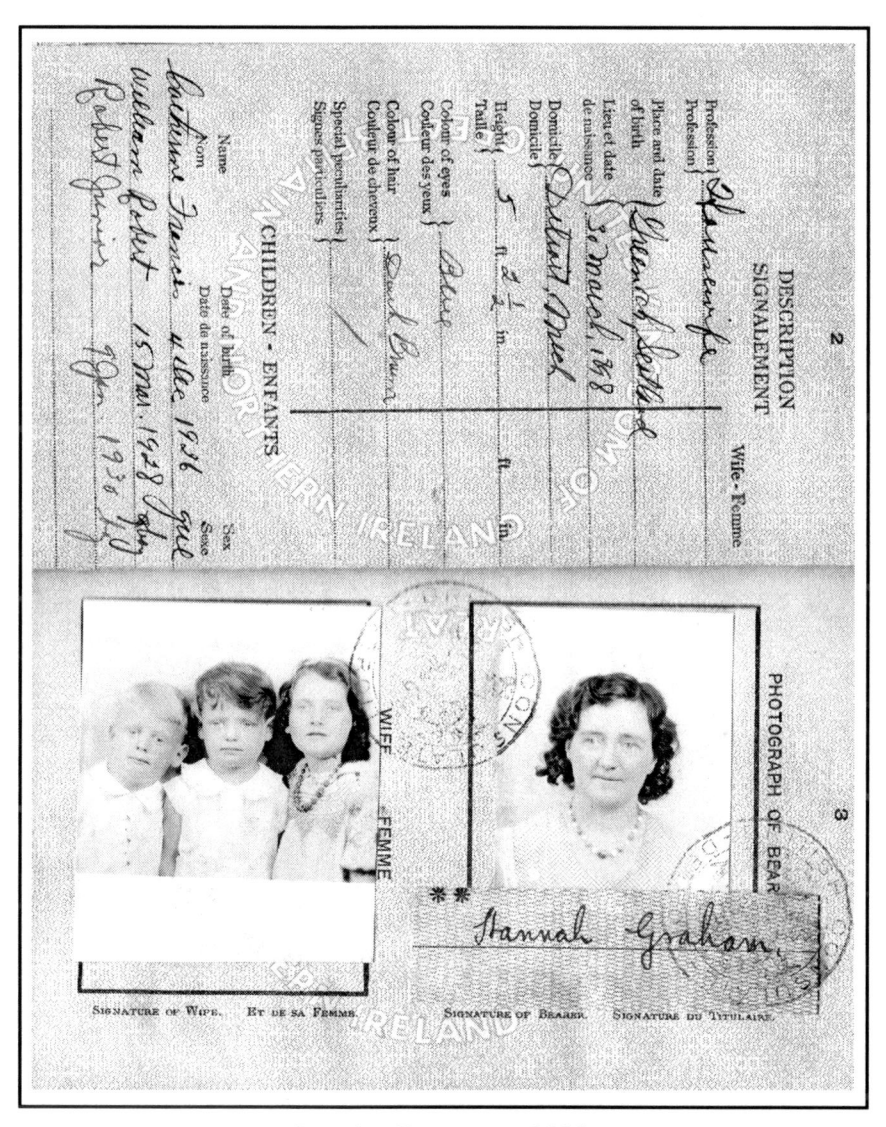

Interior Passport—1933
Mom and my Sister—Catherine, and brothers—
William and Robert Jr.

. . . about 1940
Grandfather James Boyle
at home in Detroit Michigan

. . . about 1950
Mom—Hannah "Nan" Graham, Aunt Kitty (Boyle) Gallagher,
Grandmother O'Neill, Uncle Frank Boyle (husband of Aunt
Annie),
Aunt Annie (O'Neill) Boyle (wife of Frank),
Uncle Pat Gallagher (Aunt Kitty's husband)

My parents (Bob and Nan Graham) had five children: Catherine Francis (married William "Bill" Jordan in 1948, had six children), William Robert Graham (married Pat Wriggle on December 23, 1950 and they had five sons), Robert James Graham (married Lorene Bolanger in 1950 and they had three children).

1953
My Parents' home—193 E. Arizona, Detroit, Michigan
L to R: brother Bob Graham, sister Catherine (Graham) Jordan holding baby daughter Nan Jordan, my Mom "Nan" (Boyle) Graham, my Dad Robert Graham Sr.,
Jim Graham, and Catherine's son Brian J. Jordan

Death Certificate for Hannah "Nan" (Boyle) Graham
Died on January 29, 1963 at North Detroit General Hospital
Funeral was at St. Benedict Church, Highland Park, Michigan
Buried at Mt. Olivet Cemetery, Detroit Michigan
Later moved to the Graham Chapel at Holy Sepulchre Cemetery in 2001

1945
My older brother, Robert (Bobby)
in the middle at his U.S. Army post in Japan

Family Photo—my sister Catherine and Bill Jordan's Wedding
June 1948
Back row: Jim Graham, bride Catherine Graham Jordan,
Bob Graham, Bill Graham
Font: Dad Robert Graham, mom Nan Graham

Death Certificate for Robert Graham
Died on October 29, 1965 at Highland Park General Hospital
Funeral at St. Benedict Church, Highland Park, Michigan
Buried at Mt. Olivet Cemetery, Detroit Michigan
Later moved to the Graham Chapel at Holy Sepulchre Cemetery in 2001

Breathless Memories 59

The 70's . . .
Bob Graham,
Catherine Graham
Jordan, Bill Graham,
Jim Graham

The 80's
Bill Jordan, Bill
Graham, Jim Graham,
and Bob Graham

1988
Jim & Betty (Opalewski) Graham, Bill & Catherine (Graham) Jordan,
Bill & Pat (Wriggle) Graham, Bob and Lorene (Bolanger) Graham

Yours truly, James Kenneth Graham married Elizabeth "Betty" Elaine Opalewski on November 30, 1957, at St. Raymond Catholic Church in Detroit, Michigan.

The officiant was Fr. Hogan, and in the style of the day, the Wedding Mass, luncheon, and dinner reception filled the entire day. We were blessed with two children: Kevin James born on November 6, 1960, and Jennifer Elaine born February 19, 1970. Betty died on April 8, 2000, in Aventura, Florida.

Son Kevin married Virginia Marie Caradonna on October 23, 1993. Their son Christian James Graham was born on July 15, 1994, and was a special favorite of his "Gannie" (Betty Graham).

Jennifer married Steven James Nykerk on October 4, 1997. Elizabeth Anne was born on June 20, 2001, and her sisters—the twins—Keely Noelle and Natalie Elaine were born on May 18, 2004. As I write this, we take great joy in our children and grandchildren. They are the love of our life.

On October 18, 2002, yours truly married Cynthia "Cindy" Elaine Zerbiec Dailey, a friend of Betty and myself from our parish, St. Hugo of the Hills Catholic Church. We were married in St. Ninian's Catholic Church, Gourock, Scotland with Msgr Tom Monaghan officiating.

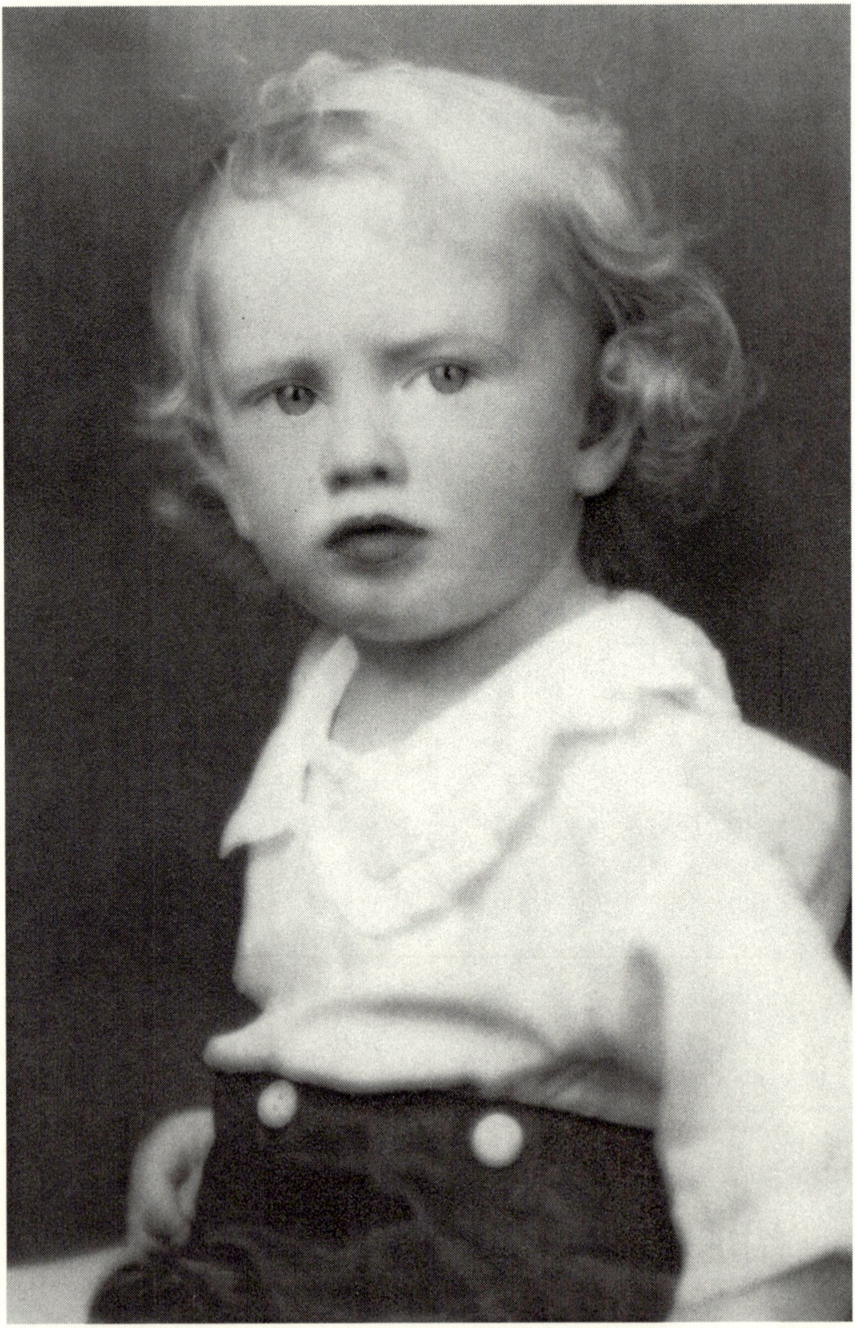

CHAPTER TWO

Childhood

I was blessed with great parents. My mom and dad (Nan and Bob Graham) were individually, and as a paired team, the best of parents.

My mom was a terrific mother and homemaker. She was to her children—to neighbors and all who knew her—a kind, gentle, and fine person. My dad was a strong father. He was a disciplined dad and always a good family man and provider. To my good fortune, my mom and dad were good parents to be proud of.

I was born in Detroit on March 8, 1934, at home. I was the fourth of five children. Catherine (born December 4, 1926), Billy (born March 15, 1928), and Bobby (born January 19, 1930) preceded me. Baby Marianne was, I believe, stillborn or died at birth on February 4, 1939. As I recall—being around four years of age—the delivery was at home, and as recalled vaguely, the Doctor laid the baby Marianne on the table. That is the only scene I remember.

In the 1930s, 1940s, and 1950s, our home was at 193 E. Arizona (near 6 Mile and Woodward) in Detroit, Michigan. Before I was born, the family lived on Minnesota (near the Bill and Bella Abercrombie family). As I was told, they then lived on Brush St., (again same neighborhood) between E. Arizona and Edgevale St., the Sam Guttenberg family was our neighbor.

My parents then bought the 193 E. Arizona home—I think it was previously occupied by the John Donneley family members of our parish St. Benedict.

63

Our family home on Arizona Street
The house is still standing—most of the homes in the neighborhood are gone—this picture was taken in 2009 with the house looking just as it was except for the tree growth.

Our neighbors were the Dan and Bella Ralston family (cousins of the Abercrombie's) at 181, next-door the Archie and Ivy Bateman family at 187, and on the other side at 199 lived the Charlie and Sophie Stefanson family.

My neighborhood friends were many, but as a child, mostly, the next-door twins—Tony and Jim Stefanson—and Kenny Bateman were my pals.

Some summers were spent at Camp Cooke, with the St. Benedict Boy Scout H. P. 14 near Port Sanilac, Michigan, on Lake Huron. Billy was an Ad Altare Dei Medal winner. Dad was assistant scoutmaster. I also served as an altar boy in grade school and sang in the boy's choir with Mr. Rene Becker, who was the choir director and organist.

Two Very Special parents

My Dad
Robert Graham Sr.

My Mom Hannah "Nan" Boyle Graham

1933—the year BEFORE I was born!

1933 two brothers on a pony—
Bobby, age 3 in front, and Billy, age 4
193 E. Arizona
about 6 months before I was born . . .

Jim, the picture-perfect toddler

Certificate of Birth

VITAL STATISTICS DIVISION

MICHIGAN DEPARTMENT OF HEALTH
Division of Vital Statistics
CERTIFICATE OF BIRTH

Aff. Filed 8-16-73
State Office No. 394626

PLACE OF BIRTH — County of WAYNE, City of Detroit

Registered No. 4530
(No. 17221 ____ St., ____ Ward)

FULL NAME OF CHILD: James Kenneth Graham

Sex of child: M
Twin, triplet, or other: 1
Number in order of birth: 1
Legitimate? Yes
Date of Birth: March 8, 1934

FATHER
Full Name: Robert Scott Graham
Residence: Detroit
Color or Race: W
Age at Last Birthday: 35
Birthplace: Scotland
Occupation: Layout Man

MOTHER
Full Maiden Name: Hannah Boyle
Residence: Detroit
Color or Race: W
Age at Last Birthday: 35
Birthplace: Scotland
Occupation: Hsw

Number of child of this mother: 4
Number of children of this mother now living: 4

CERTIFICATE OF ATTENDING PHYSICIAN OR MIDWIFE

I hereby certify that I attended the birth of this child, who was born alive at 5:50 on the date above stated.

(Signature) C. H. Mayou
Dated: March 13, 1934
Address: 17909 John R

I hereby certify that the foregoing is a true copy of the record on file in the Detroit Department of Health; attested by the raised seal of the City of Detroit.

Irene Rendz
IRENE RENDZ
Division Head, Vital Statistics

Dated OCT 8 1974

Certificate of Baptism

**Church of
St. Benedict
60 Church
Highland Park, MI 48203**

This is to Certify

That James Kenneth Graham
Child of Robert Graham
and Hannah Boyle
born in Detroit, (CITY) Michigan (STATE)
on the 8th day of March 19 34
was **Baptized**
on the 8th day of April 19 34
According to the Rite of the Roman Catholic Church
by the Rev. W. L. Shaw
the Sponsors being { Chas Boyle
Anne Boyle

as appears from the Baptismal Register of this Church.

Dated May 22, 2002

Pastor

**Birth Certificate
James Kenneth Graham born March 8, 1934**

Breathless Memories 71

My First Communion
St Benedict Church—May 1942
I am standing in front of our family home at
193 Arizona St., Detroit, Michigan

Jim (age 14) in the summer of 1948
on the step of Dan & Bella Ralston's cottage
in Leamington, Ontario, Canada

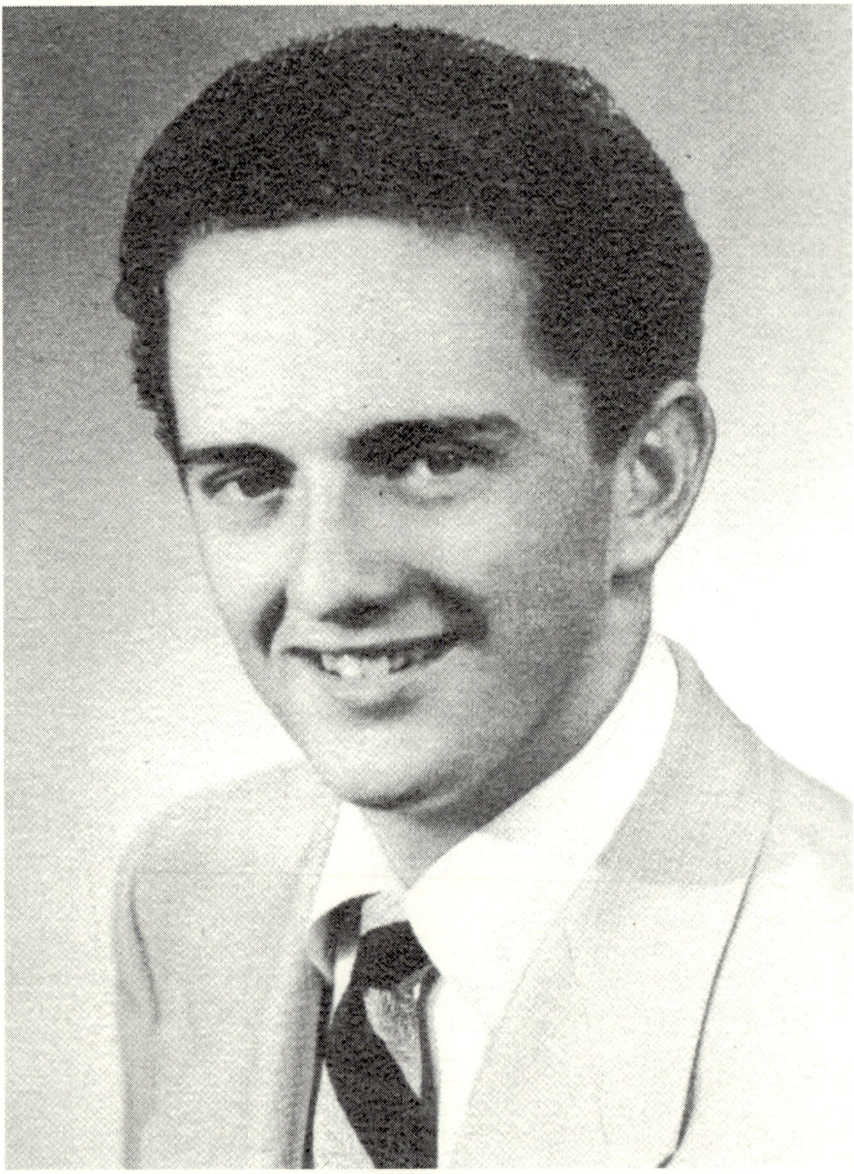

CHAPTER THREE

Schooling

(Grade School)

I attended Greenfield Park Elementary School for kindergarten. At that time, it was the largest elementary school in the city of Detroit. Mrs. Lenahan was a kind and good teacher.

My lifelong friend, Mike Vanderlinder, was my best friend. Also good friends were Andy Krizan and Bobby Fahoome. Sadly, Mike and Andy have passed away.

I began first grade in 1940 at St. Benedict Grade School, and my siblings—Catherine, class of 1945, Bill, class of 1946, and Bobby, class of 1948. I remember my mom sent me to my first day of school with my brother Bill. I vividly recall my brother Bill—a sixth grader himself—walking me to school that first day. Since school started with Mass, I recall Bill taking me into church, introducing me to my teacher Sister Francesca, and then showing me into my pew with my classmates.

My sister and brother had set a good record of academic excellence and behavior. Therefore, I had to live up to their example and was a very good, mostly all-A student. In fact, when Cardinal Mooney was installed as cardinal in 1948 at Blessed Sacrament Cathedral, I was selected to represent the school. I rode the Woodward streetcar up and back to the memorable, high-profile Mass. I was quite honored by the designation.

My kindergarten pal Mike Vanderlinder started at St. Benedict with me. Mike lived on Savannah at Brush about eight blocks north of me. Mike would walk to my street, and we would walk the last several blocks to school together. My other good friends became Tom Kummer (later known as Jay Sebring—was murdered on August 8, 1969 at age thirty-six by the Manson family in California), Jack Campbell, and many other pals, including also Ray Grattan.

Interestingly, Maureen Bailey (part of our seventh—and eight-grade class) always entertained us. She later went to Hollywood and—among other roles—played Wendy in the TV special *Peter Pan*. Joan Leslie (who was in my sister Catherine's class at St. Benedict) became a movie star acting with Jimmy Cagney, Humphrey Bogart, and Cary Grant—good talent from our old school.

In grade school, I played on all school teams—football (quarterback), basketball (forward), and baseball (pitcher and second base).

My teachers—all good—were Sr. Francesca (strict), first and second grade; Sister Marie Frances (kind) third and fourth grade; Sr. Anita (old) fifth grade; Sr. Marie Frances (nice) sixth grade; Mrs. Gauthrat (nice) seventh and eighth grade. The principals were Mother Marie Kathleen and then Mother Amata.

St. Benedict Church
60 Church Avenue
Highland Park, Michigan 48203

St. Benedict Church

Crest and Pennant—St. Benedict Grade School

Signature of Parent

Please sign and return within 3 days

Sept. Oct.	*Robert Graham*
Nov. Dec.	*N. B. Graham*
Jan. Feb.	*N. B. Graham*
Mar. Apr.	*Robert Graham*
May June	

St. Benedict
ELEMENTARY SCHOOL

REPORT
OF
James Graham

Promotion Record

Promoted from grade __2__
to grade __3__
Date _____
Signed _____
Principal

Report Card for the Second Grade
Signed by Mom and Dad

Name James Graham

Grade 2   Year 19 41 19 42

This report is sent home at the end of each two months so that fathers and mothers may know how their children are getting along in school.

A stands for VERY HIGH QUALITY work.

B stands for HIGH QUALITY work.

C stands for ORDINARY work.

D stands for POOR work.

U stands for UNSATISFACTORY work.

The work of the school is so arranged that every pupil at least should do Ordinary work in every subject. If you are not satisfied with the marks that the student has earned, a conference with the Sister will help secure better work next month.

THE DAY'S WORK:	Sept. Oct.	Nov. Dec.	Jan. Feb.	Mar. Apr.	May June
Religion	B	A	A	A	A
Reading	B	A	A	A	A
Spelling	A	A	A	A	A
Arithmetic	A	A	A	A	A
English	B	A	A	A	A
Handwriting	A	A	A	A	A
Social Studies					
Art	A	A	A	A	A
Music	B	A	A	A	A
Health	B	A	A	A	A

GOOD HABITS:

| Study | B | A | A | A | A |
| Courtesy | B | A | A | B | A |

TIME LOST:

Days Absent		1	2	1½	
Times Late					
Tuition	Paid	Pd.	Pd.		

Charlie Longo, Jim Graham, Alvin Risi, and Jack Campbell
Outside St. Benedict School—Winter 1948

Jimmy's signature

James Kenneth Patrick Graham J. D.

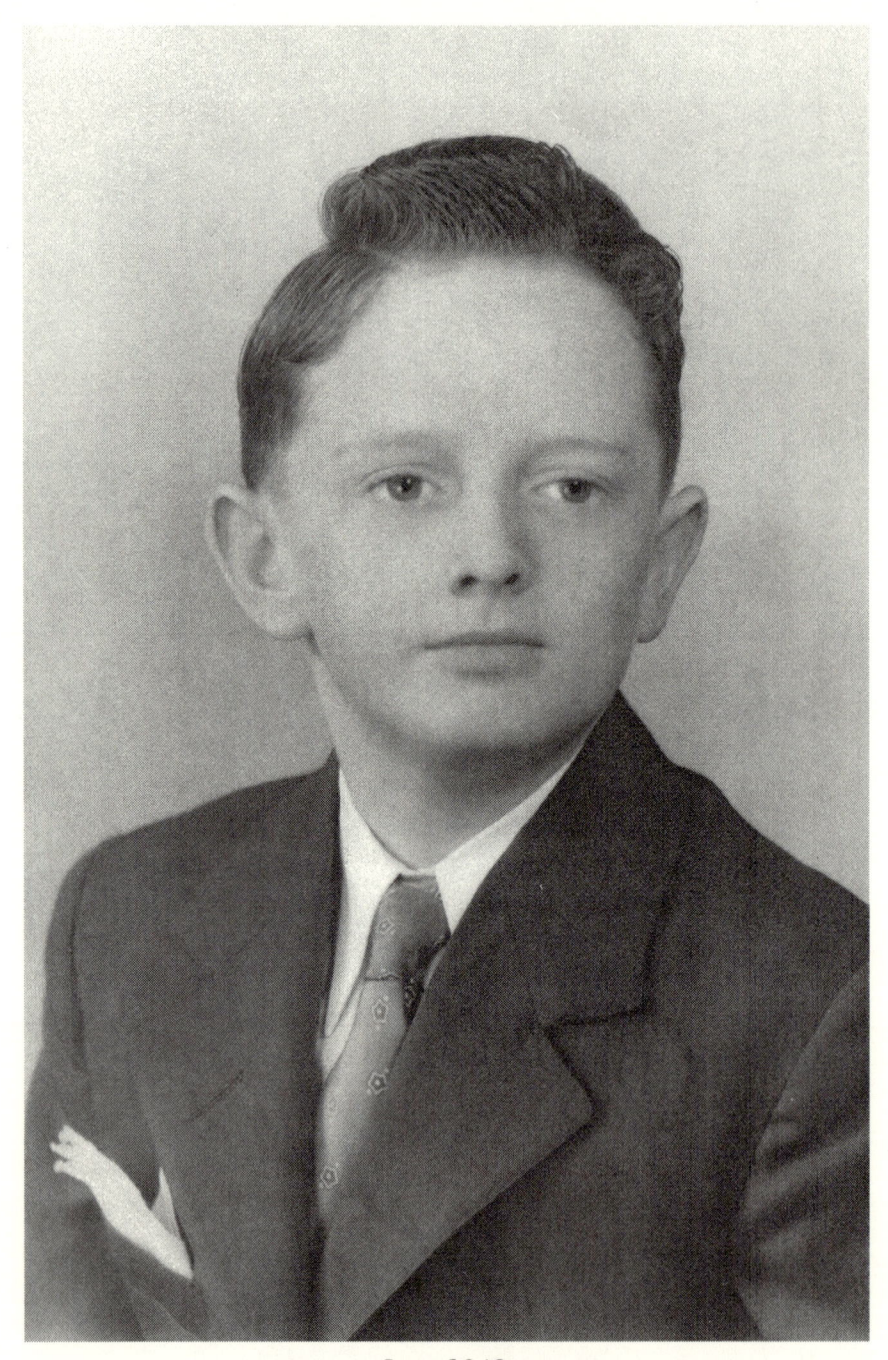

June 1948
Eighth Grade Graduation
St Benedict School, Highland Park

THE CUB

Masthead for the High School Newspaper

(High School)

As I was in the eighth grade, I began thinking of high school. Although my three siblings went to St. Benedict High School, times were good, and I decided to go to University of Detroit High School, now known as U of D Jesuit. My dad was a successful as general foreman at Chrysler Corporation (Plymouth Motor, Mt. Elliot facility) Detroit, Michigan, so my parents were fully supportive.

I took the entrance exams and started U of D High School in the fall of 1948. Tom Kummer, Jack Campbell, and Charlie Longo started with me from St. Benedict, but all dropped out after freshman year.

Freshman forward

80 *James Kenneth Patrick Graham J. D.*

1949 FRESHMEN — UNDEFEATED IN 15 GAMES

Team Picture—U of D Freshman Basketball Team
Bottom right

Coincidentally, Christian was looking at high schools (U of D Jesuit, Catholic Central, Brother Rice, and Notre Dame). All have open houses, mailings, etc. We went to U of D High (Christian, his mom and dad, and me) on Sunday, November 6, 2006. We talked to the president, Fr. Kiser, and toured the facility.

> *NewsFlash—Spring 2008!*
> Good News! Christian has selected U of D Jesuit High School . . . In fact, he said to me, "Papa, do you realize that I will graduate in 2012—sixty years after you graduated from here in 1952." "Thanks, Christian, you really know how to hurt a guy!"

> *News Flash—Spring 2009!*
> Christian achieved First Honors for the Fall '08 and Spring'09 Semesters . . . Yeah!

> *News Flash—Winter 2010!*
> Christian achieved First Honors '09 Fall Semester!

Auction prize Street sign in front of University of Detroit High School and Academy

Jim and Christian on the entrance balcony
outside U of D High

Winter 2010

With all the emphasis on recruiting students at about $10,000 per year (my tuition was $150 per year), the question of how I selected U of D High arises. I can't really pinpoint the reason. There was no recruiting. Catholic Central High School, at that time, was on Belmont near Blessed Sacrament Cathedral and a straight run by the then DSR streetcar on Woodward. Mike Haughey (deceased) was a year ahead of me at St. Benedict's and went to U of D High. Maybe it was providential, but I took the entrance tests, passed, and started at U of D High in September of 1948.

I rode the DSR bus from 6 Mile and Brush to Hamilton and then transferred to the 7-Mile bus to 7 Mile and Cherrylawn. My curriculum was the college prep course (Latin, French, Math, Science, etc.). I played on the football, basketball, and baseball teams. Our school colors were scarlet and white—the school mascot, the Cubs—and many of us, as we played varsity sports, touted our "Letter" sweaters that were scarlet, with a scarlet "letter" edged with white. Throughout the four years, I participated in all three sports with enthusiasm—I was a second baseman in baseball, a forward in basketball, and a quarterback in football. My senior year in the fall of 1951, we played a memorable game: After Western High School took a 6-0 lead into the fourth quarter, I led the team on a drive (including a quarterback sneak, several passes, and a special goal-line play, thirty-one-trap, with a fullback plunge), resulting in a 7-6 win! Great memories!

GRAHAM—Quarterback

1951—Senior Year—Varsity Quarterback
Yearbook Photo

Football Memorabilia

Breathless Memories 85

FOOTBALL HEROES of '51

U of D High School Varsity Football Team—1951
Jim—second from left in front row # 77—quarterback

VARSITY TEAM

TOP ROW: Monahan, Higgis, Ransford, Pfeil, Bichler, Whitlock, McDonald, Pedemonte, Obermeyer, Kostinksi, McGough, Schim, Wermer, Nowak.

MIDDLE ROW: J. Klein, McInerey, Hein, Dyment, Burke, Feighsen, Baths, Liavnia, Pilonski, L. Brown, Roberts, Peacock, Slater, Hogan.

VARSITY TEAM

BOTTOM ROW: Slimak, Graham, Lyons, Redder, Iannetti, Frank, Kenny, Boyer, McGinn, McDonald, McGarry, Vizakkara, Dunowski, ABSENT: Rocke, P. Walker.

JAMES K. GRAHAM

Jim showed his popularity by being elected class president in sopohomore and junior year . . . played intramural and varsity football.

Jim Graham

Senior Class Yearbook Picture and Signature

I enjoyed and gained much from my four high school years. Again, I was a good student. My friends were Joe Machiorlatti, Tom Chisholm, Jim Roche, Jerry Maurer and many other good pals. We created the Top Hat Club and brought in major entertainers for dances.

I was class president in my sophomore and junior years. I only missed being elected again in my senior year because a close pal didn't vote for me, and I lost by one vote—his, I was told, because of envy. It was a good lesson from trusting an untrustworthy person. It reminded me of the old expression, "Keep your friends close, but your enemies closer." Also, our yearbook was titled *Cub 75th Anniversary 1952*.

Coincidentally, one friend, while professing to be my "best friend," broke my friendly trust on two subsequent periods over the years for petty jealousies. Life's disappointing experiences many times are your best teachers.

As I have done with boyhood neighborhood friends, St. Benedict Grade School pals, high school chums, and college buddies I have stayed in touch with, I would recommend this solidarity to all as a lifelong habit. It works!

Upon graduating from University of Detroit Jesuit in 1952, I prepared and did enter the University of Detroit in the fall of 1952. I belonged to the Economic Club and the Air Force ROTC on campus.

88 *James Kenneth Patrick Graham J. D.*

1956—Air Force ROTC Wing
University of Detroit

Breathless Memories

**June 1956
University of Detroit
Graduation Portrait**

Engaged Couple—Jim and Betty
College Graduation Reception
June 1956

Jim in Hollywood, Florida
One of the summers between college years—
to make a little money and get some R & R
I drove a car for Mr. Packer from Packer Pontiac.
The destination was Florida—the Atlantic Coast—
just a few miles north from our present condo in Sunny Isles Beach.
Today's Hollywood coast motels are still much the same,
Whereas most other areas have torn the two-story buildings down
in favor of multi-story high-rise buildings.

I graduated with a bachelor of science degree in 1956. I applied and was accepted at Detroit College of Law in the fall of 1956. During law school, I joined the Fr. Cotter Knights of Columbus Council. I became judge advocate of the council. I also acquired my real estate license and my securities license in my plan to be as fully credentialed as possible in case any diverse opportunity would arise, I would be ready

DCL from the 'sky'
100 Elizabeth Street,
Detroit, Michigan
(now the location of Comerica Park—
the home of the Detroit tigers)

Front entrance of Detroit College of Law

During law school studies, I worked at the Dearborn Beer Distributor in the warehouse at good money, $2.75 per hour. Summers, I worked in factories, many secured by my dad at Plymouth and Dodge Plants. I enjoyed spending time at my parents' summer home on Lake Erie at 11 Conover, Leamington, Ontario, Canada. I also enjoyed boating and golfing with Bill Abercrombie Jr. whose parents lived in our Detroit neighborhood and cottaged in Leamington also.

The Beach at Seacliffe Park on Lake Erie in Leamington, Ontario. Jim's parents bought two lots adjacent to a peach orchard in 1948 at 11 Conover and built a large 3 bedroom home. This was our vacation home for many years—after Mom died in 1963 (age 65) and Dad died in 1965 (age 67), we (Cath, Bill, Bob and Jim) sold the home in 1966.

Graham Family Cottage

As an update, on Sunday, September 2, 2007, Cindy and I (along with her son, Rick, and friend, Jean), traveled to Leamington, Ontario, for a bit of nostalgia. We drove to the site of my parents' cottage—11 Conover Street—finding it in beautiful condition. I went to the door, and Dr. and Mrs. Murray Pearce, the current owners, were home. After introducing myself, I asked them who they purchased the property from, thinking that the property had been through many hands. Dr. Pearce replied, "We purchased this home from the Graham family forty-one years ago." Unbelievable! Murray Pearce grew up in Leamington and brought me up to date on all the local pals that I had known as a teenager around this Lake Erie resort.

I graduated on schedule in June 1959 with a Juris Doctor degree. My parents and wife Betty attended the graduation-diploma award ceremony at the Rackham Building in Detroit. I remember my friend Bill Abercrombie took some photos in my cap and gown in scenic Palmer Park—near our homes. Sadly, Bill died on January 13, 2008. Two good pals from law school—even to this day—were Dave Leach and Gene Sikora.

James K. Graham—Juris Doctor
Detroit College of Law

My graduation from Detroit College of Law with my proud parents Robert and Nan Graham at the Rackham Building for commencement—June 1959.

Jim and Betty at the Graduates Reception
Veterans Memorial Building

My formal educational goals achieved on schedule, I had to put my career on hold to go into the U.S. Army. Following an honorable discharge, I was admitted to the Michigan Bar Association, after—of course—passing the 2 ½-day Bar exam at the University of Michigan.

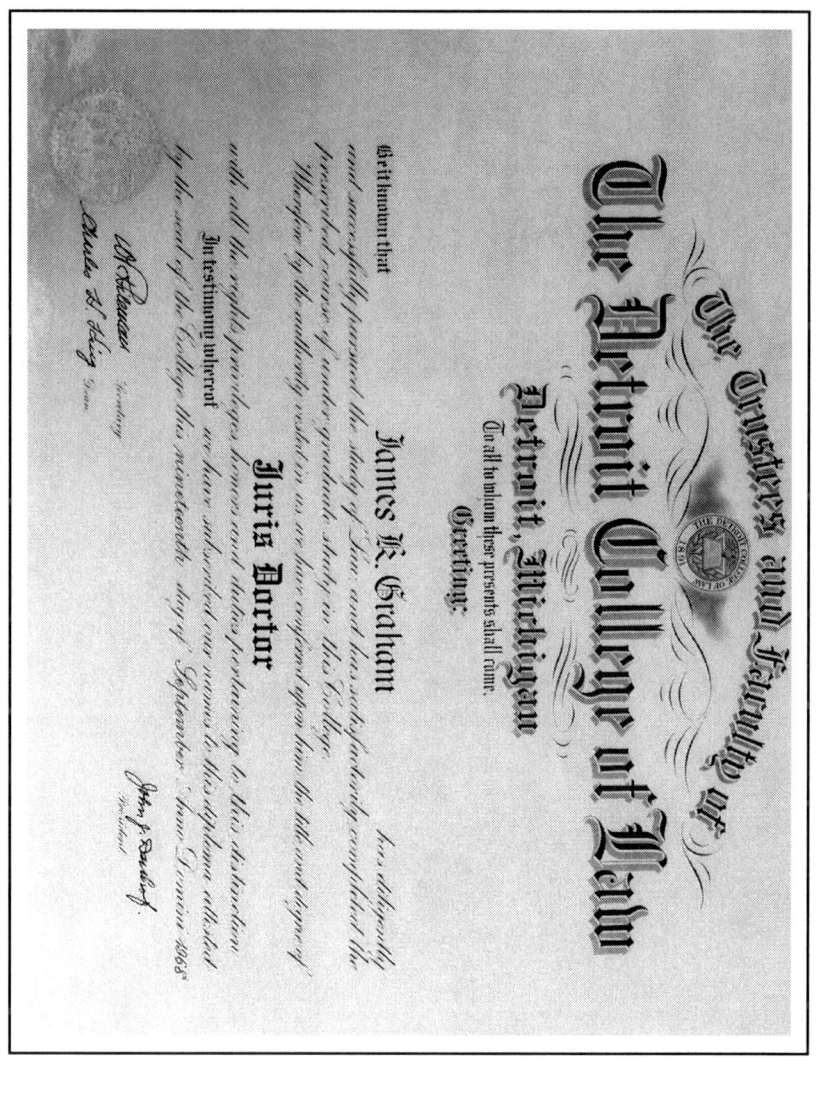

Diploma JD—Detroit College of Law
1959

Admittance to the Supreme Court
Of the United States of America
April 19, 1971

On the recommendation of its Board of Commissioners, the State Bar of Michigan recognizes and honors

James R. Graham

as an attorney who has achieved 50 years of membership.

50-year Golden Celebration

Charles R. Toy
President, State Bar of Michigan
May 2010

State Bar of Michigan Certificate Honoring 50 Years of Service

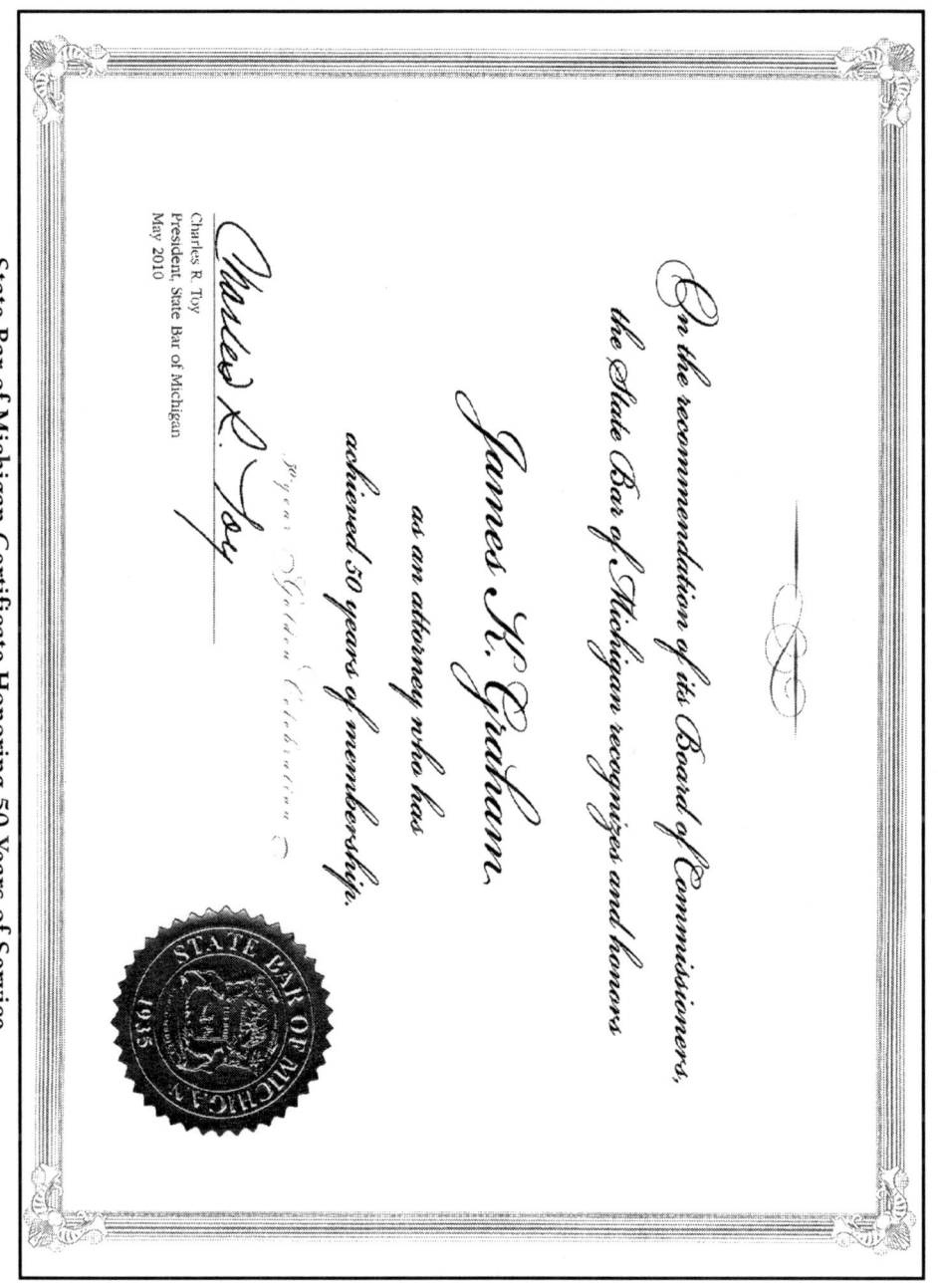

RESOLUTION OF APPRECIATION

The Board of Commissioners of the State Bar of Michigan extends congratulations to our 50-year honorees for proudly serving our profession since 1960. We thank you for your unfailing loyalty and extraordinary contributions to the welfare of the citizens you serve. Your dedication to the rule of law and commitment to supporting the Constitutions of our nation and state, respecting our courts and judges, and practicing law with integrity, civility, and concern for the public are deeply appreciated.

NOW THEREFORE BE IT RESOLVED by the Board of Commissioners of the State Bar of Michigan that honor, recognition, and gratitude are bestowed on our honorees for their 50 years of membership in the State Bar of Michigan.

Adopted by the Board of Commissioners, March 26, 2010.

Charles R. Toy
Charles R. Toy, President

State Bar Resolution of Appreciation 50 years of service

50 Year Honorees
May 2010—St John Conference Center
Plymouth, Michigan
Jim seated 'first' in the front row left

The Newly Married Couple
Jim and Betty
After Mass in the Aisle
St. Raymond Church

CHAPTER FOUR

Marriage and Children

Elizabeth Elaine (Betty) Graham was introduced to me through Mrs. George (Rose) Toner, a good friend of my mom and dad and a nurse at North Detroit General with Betty's mom. The hospital had a bowling league that they bowled in, at the Palmer Park Recreation and Bowling Alley. The P. B. was in my neighborhood at 6 Mile Road and Woodward Avenue, where I worked during law school, keeping the books.

Betty and I hit it off well. She was the head nurse for Dr. Bernard Leiberman, an obesity specialist at Woodward and 7 Mile, Detroit.

**Betty and Jim in the summer of 1957,
at the Graham Cottage in Leamington, Ontario**

After a couple of years, Betty and I were married on November 30, 1957, at St. Raymond Catholic Church between 7 and 8 Mile roads, near Schoenherr Rd., in Detroit. My brother (William Graham) and Betty's sister (Bernardine Clinton) were the witnesses with Fr. William Hunt officiating. We went to Niagara Falls, Ontario, for our honeymoon and stayed at the Falls Way Inn.

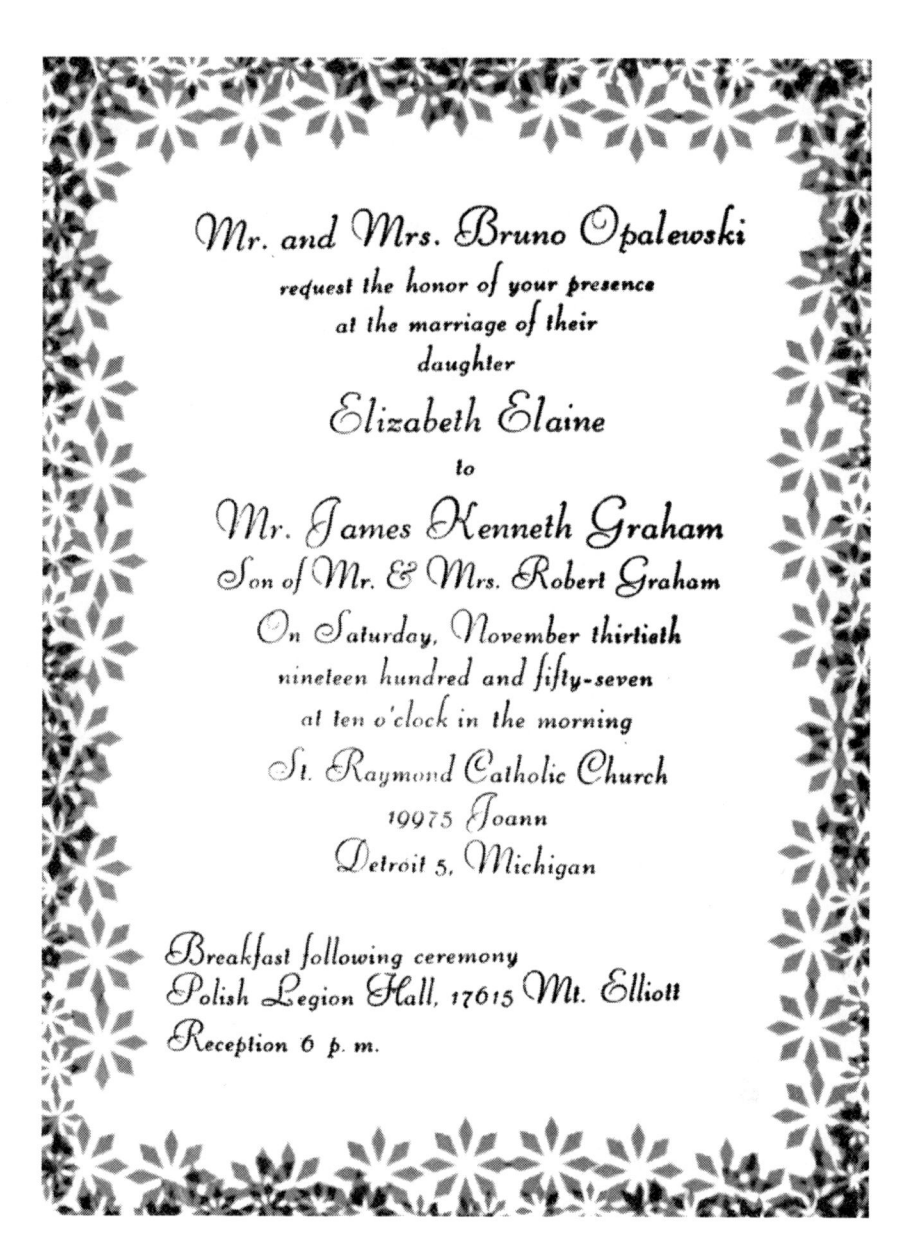

Mr. and Mrs. Bruno Opalewski
request the honor of your presence
at the marriage of their
daughter

Elizabeth Elaine

to

Mr. James Kenneth Graham

Son of Mr. & Mrs. Robert Graham

On Saturday, November thirtieth
nineteen hundred and fifty-seven
at ten o'clock in the morning

St. Raymond Catholic Church
19975 Joann
Detroit 5, Michigan

Breakfast following ceremony
Polish Legion Hall, 17615 Mt. Elliott
Reception 6 p. m.

What a romantic kiss!

Presenting the new couple on the steps of
St. Raymond Catholic Church
November 30, 1957

A Radiant Bride and Handsome Groom
"The new couple—Mr. and Mrs. James K. Graham"
November 30, 1957
Polish Legion Hall on Mt. Elliott

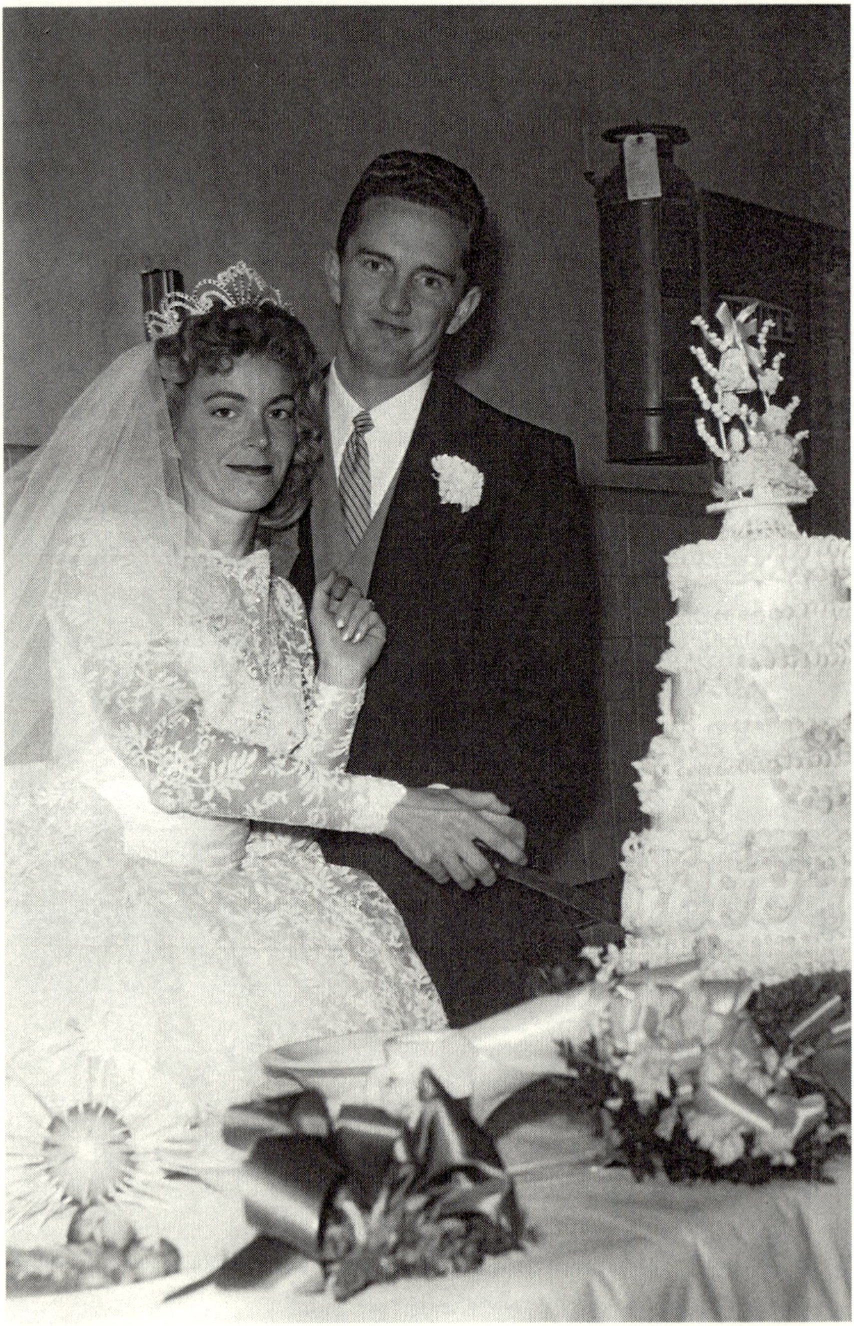

Breathless Memories

November 30, 1957
Jim and Betty's Wedding Reception
L to R: Pat Gallagher—cousin (usher), Jim Graham—groom,
Brian Jordan—nephew (ring bearer),
Bill Graham—brother (best man), and Bob Graham—brother (usher)

Family Picture
Left to right: Lorene and Bob Graham, Pat and Bill Graham,
Jim and Betty,
Jim's parents—Nan and Bob Graham,
Catherine Jordan
Children: Steven Graham, Brian Jordan, Nan Jordan, and Kevin Jordan

"Sweet satisfaction"

Certificate of Marriage

Church of

St. Raymond Catholic Church

20103 Joann - Detroit, MI 48205

This is to Certify

That James Graham

and Betty Opalewski

were lawfully **Married**

on the 30th day of November 19 57

According to the Rite of the Roman Catholic Church and in conformity with the laws of the State of Michigan

Rev. W. Hunt officiating,

in the presence of William Graham

and Bernadine Clinton Witnesses,

as appears from the Marriage Register of this Church.

Dated June 29, 2001

Rev. Andrew T. Tomaszk
Pastor

We lived with Betty's parents on Nunneley Road in Clinton Twp until we built a new home at 13351 Iowa, Warren, Michigan (near 13 Mile Rd., and Schoenherr). It was a great home, and Betty was a terrific homemaker and cook. We had the family over for many holidays as my dad, Betty's dad, and I beautifully finished the basement with a full kitchen. We belonged to St. Edmund Parish. The pastor was Fr. William McGoldrick for whom I had been an altar boy when he was an assistant at St. Benedict in the 1940s.

Summer 1959?
Camping trip to northern Ontario,
Several hundred miles north of Sault Saint Marie
With Billy Abercrombie

We happily welcomed Kevin James Graham at his birth on November 6, 1960—the same day our first Catholic President John F. Kennedy was elected. A great day all around!

Proud new parents, Betty and Jim, with baby Kevin in January 1961 at Betty's Parents' (Bruno and Emily Opalewski) home on Nunnely Road in Clinton Twp, Michigan

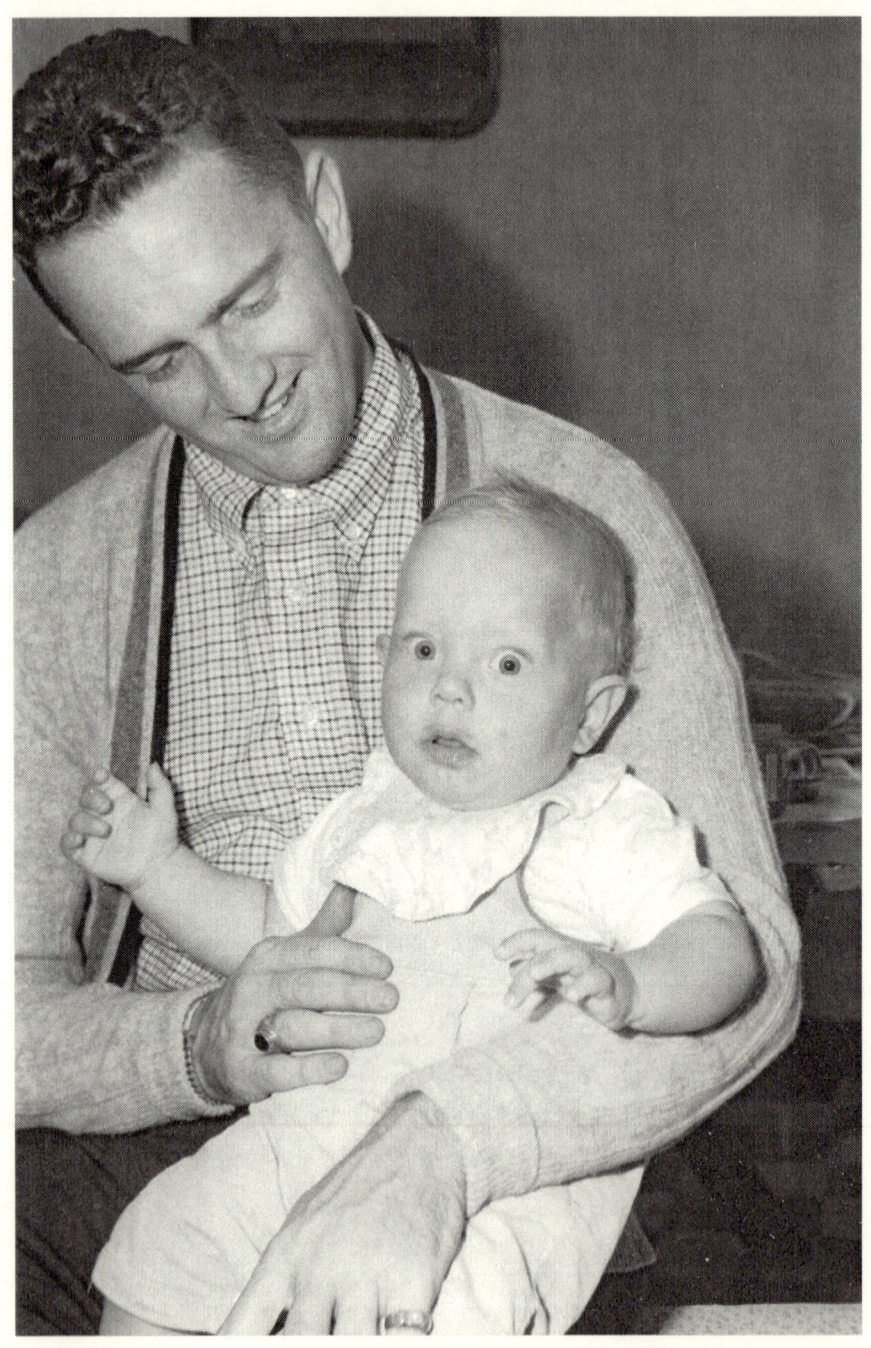

1961 Jim (Dad) and Kevin

Proud grandparents—Bob and Nan Graham—
With their son, Jim and one-year old grandson, Kevin.
November 1961 in their home at 193 E. Arizona, Detroit.

Family Christmas at Jim & Betty's home
13351 Iowa, Warren, Michigan

Kevin attended Brookside School-Cranbrook in Bloomfield Hills. When he was first enrolled, we lived in Warren with a considerable drive to the school. We looked for some home sites in Bloomfield Hills and purchased a lot from Sidney Griffin-Builder. We built a new home at 575 Woodway Ct. in Stillmeadow Subdivision. We moved in July 9, 1969. The in-ground kidney-shaped swimming pool at the house was the neighborhood haven for all the kids in the summers there.

**575 Woodway Ct.,
Stillmeadow Subdivision
Bloomfield Hills
Summer 1970**

"Abercrombie" cottage on Erie Street
Leamington, Ontario, Canada
L to R: Dan Ralston, Kevin Graham,
Billy Abercrombie,
his mom, Isabelle (Dan Ralston's sister)

Betty was a very nurturing mom and a very good teacher/influence for Kevin. Later, I managed Kevin in Little League where he was a good baseball player. I also served on the Birmingham/Bloomfield Hills Little League Board of Directors.

Once again, we were blessed with Jennifer Elaine Graham on February 19, 1970. Betty and I had hoped for more children but were thankful to have Kevin and Jennifer. Again, Betty was the best mother with Jennifer—a great counselor, friend, and influence. We, just as with Kevin, were supportive of her at Marian High School and, in particular, Jennifer's outstanding tennis career. Betty drove her all over the state for tournaments. Betty enjoyed watching her daughter and playing tennis herself. Jennifer ultimately was captain on the Oakland University Tennis Team.

1967—Washington D.C.

1968—Mt. San Jacinto, Palm Springs, California
Kevin and his Dad

1966—In the backyard of our home at 13351 Iowa, Warren, Michigan—Kevin and his Dad

Kevin (age 5) and Dad at home

1973—Jim, Kevin, and Jennifer

Breathless Memories 123

1971—Jim, a proud Dad, with Jennifer
outside the family home 575 Woodway Ct. Bloomfield Hills, MI

Family photo for Election Campaign—Jim ran
successfully for the Bloomfield Board of Education

1971—Miami Beach, Florida
Olympia Motel on Collins Avenue
Our family celebrated many vacations from 1957 until today
At the beach on the Atlantic Ocean.
Adjacent to this property was the Tropicana Motel
Which was torn down in 1982,
And on which property our current
Tropicana Condo was built.
On a "nostalgia" vacation in the summer of 1984,
we noted that the new building was just completed.
Out of curiosity, we decided to walk up from the beach
And were shown the highest available unit (6th floor)
on the southeast corner.
What a "million Dollar" view—The beach, the Atlantic Ocean,
the sky, the Intracoastal waterway,
Bal Harbour Beach hotels, the skyline of Miami, etc.—
Suffice to say, we purchased Unit #605 and have
enjoyed vacations ever since 1984 there.

1972—Winter fun with a 'new friend—Frosty' in the
family backyard on Woodway Ct
Jim, Jennifer, and Kevin

Jim with Kevin (age 11)
Fisherman's Wharf, San Francisco, California
1972

1972—Birmingham Eccentric Newspaper
Family Photo
Jim ran successfully for the Bloomfield Board of Education
575 Woodway Ct.
Jim, Jennifer (age 2), Betty and Kevin (age 12)

June 3, 1973
Little League Team
Team Manager—Dad—Jim Graham—far left
Kevin (age 12) back row—3rd from right

1975—Hilton Head Beach on Vacation
Jim, Kevin, and Jennifer

1975—Relaxing in Florida

1977—Niagara Falls
Kevin, Jennifer (age 7), Dad

May 1978—Jennifer's First Communion—
Overlooking the pond at St. Hugo of the Hills Stone Chapel
Dad (Jim), Jennifer, Mom(Betty), Kevin

April 1978
Guadalupe Island Caribbean Cruise
Jim and daughter, Jennifer

1975—Hilton Head Beach
Kevin and Jennifer, Jim and Betty

1977—Palm Springs, California
Mt. San Jacinto State Park—
Dad and Jennifer at the top of the tram
overlooking Coachella Valley

April 1978
Caribbean Family Vacation

1978—Las Vegas, Nevada
Sand's Hotel Showroom—
Kevin's 18th Birthday
L to R: Jennifer, Kevin, Jim, Betty,
our guests Bill Abercrombie, and Betty's Mom
(Emily Opalewski)

April 28, 1979
Family gathering at our home in Warren
L to R standing:
Cousins, Jim, Frank and Anne Boyle, Cathy and Ed Alexander,
Aunt Ann Boyle, sister Catherine Jordan, wife Betty Graham,
Bill Jordan
Kneeling in front: Barbara Boyle and Jim Graham

1981 Las Vegas, Nevada
Poolside
Jim, Jennifer, Kevin, and Betty

1981
Jim and Kevin Graham relaxing in the Jacuzzi
Next to the swimming pool at our winter home on
Frank Sinatra Drive in Rancho Mirage, California

1981
Jim and Jennifer enjoying the deck
On our home in
Rancho Mirage

Feb 19. 1986
Home in Rancho Mirage, California
Frank Sinatra Drive
Jennifer's 16th Birthday
Jim, Betty Jennifer, and Kevin

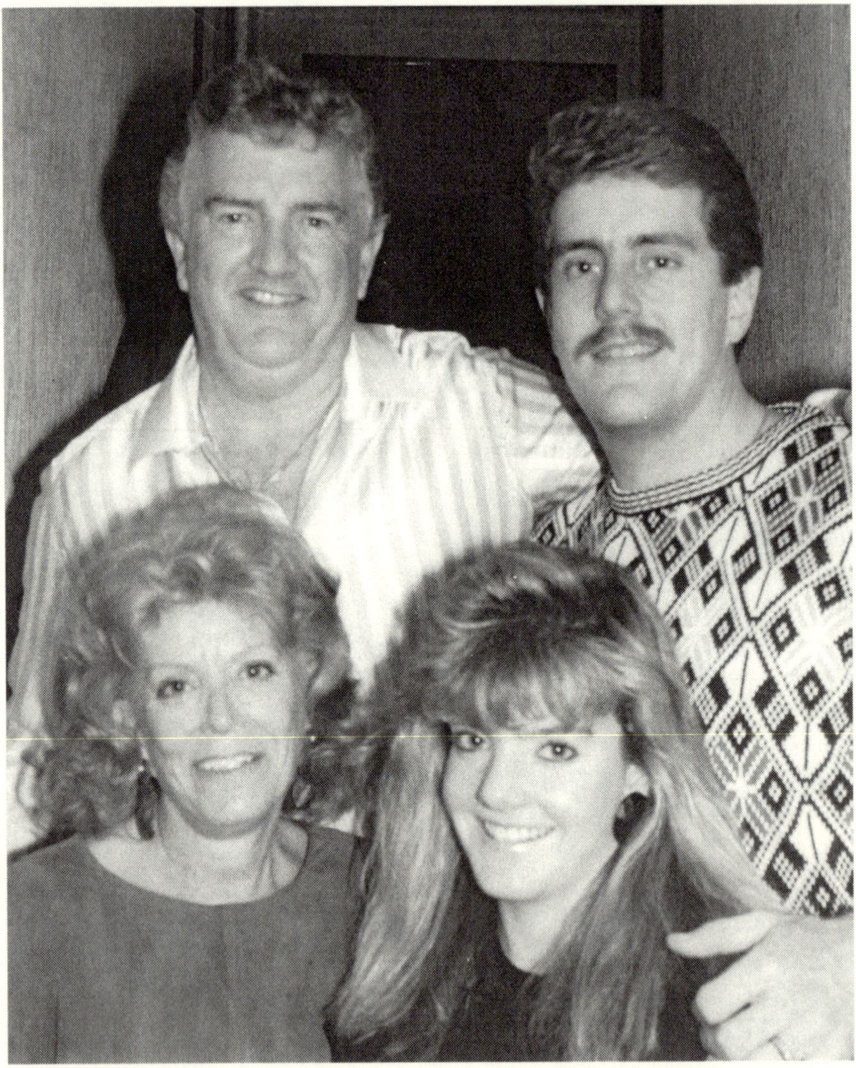

Brothers Bob and Jim Graham—mid 1980's
Tropicana Condo
Miami Beach Florida (now Sunny Isles Beach)

1985—Paris, France
Wonderful dinner at Maxim's restaurant
Jennifer, Jim, Betty and Kevin

1987—Caribbean Cruise
Betty, Jim, Jennifer

1989—Palm Springs Airport
Jennifer and Dad

**1989—Caribbean Cruise
Kevin, Jennifer, Betty, and Jim**

**1991 Miami Beach
Tropicana Condo
Mom and Dad celebrating Jennifer's
21st Birthday**

December 1992
Kevin and Dad enjoying a round of golf
Palm Desert, California

1993—First Christmas in our new home on
Heron Ridge Drive

Breathless Memories 139

1994
Lifeboat Drill on a Caribbean Cruise
Jennifer, Jim, and Betty

After his graduation with an undergraduate degree at St. Mary's of Orchard Lake, Kevin attended and graduated with a Juris Doctor from Detroit College of Law and then passed the Michigan Bar. We were very proud of him.

June 1987
A very special graduation
Kevin receives his Juris Doctor from the
Detroit College of Law
Proud Dad—Jim, Kevin, Jennifer, and beaming Mom—Betty

Thanksgiving 1992
Celebrating at our home on Woodway Ct.
Kevin J. Graham is engaged to Virginia M. Caradonna
L to R: Lorraine and Jack Caradonna (Virginia's parents),
Kevin, Virginia, Betty and Jim Graham

In 1993, Kevin and Virginia Caradonna, MD, were married at St. Hugo of the Hills. They had met at Providence Hospital where Virginia and Kevin worked. On July 15, 1994, the entire family, including Betty and I, were thrilled with the birth of our first grandchild, Christian James Graham.

October 23, 1993—St. Hugo of the Hills Church
Virginia Mary Caradonna and Kevin James Graham Wedding
L to R: Jim, Virginia, Kevin, Betty, Jennifer

**Wedding Bliss—the Morning After!
Virginia and Kevin outside
her parents' home on October 24, 1993**

Best Man Jim with Jennifer and Betty
October 23, 1993

Breathless Memories 145

Baptism of Christian James Graham
St. Hugo Church
November 20, 1994
Proud Grandparents—Jim and Betty Graham, and Jack and Lorraine Caradonna—Surrounding proud parents Virginia and Kevin

July 15, 1995
Christian's 1st Birthday
L to R: Christian, Dad-Kevin, Gannie-Betty, Auntie-Jennifer, Special Guest-Big Bird, Mom-Virginia, and Papa-Jim

Gourock Scotland
September 2, 1995
The Graham Family attends the wedding of
Sharon McDevitt and Eugene Lafferty
L to R: Virginia & Kevin Graham, Jennifer Graham,
Eugene and Sharon Lafferty, Jim & Betty Graham

1995
Tennis break near our Florida condo

February 28, 1996
Papa and Christian (age 18 months) in the surf—
Vacation at our Tropicana Condo in Sunny Isles Beach with
the Newport Pier in the background

September 1996
Regional Office party recognizing
the first employee to celebrate 30 years
as an employee with VALIC—Jim Graham—
L to R: Betty, Jennifer, Jim—Papa, Christian,
Virginia and Kevin

"An awesome trio"

Papa, Gannie, and Christian

August 1999
Enjoying dinner at Papa Vino's =
Bill and Catherine Jordan (Jim's sister), Christian,
and Betty (Gannie) and Jim (Papa)

In 1997, Jennifer married Steve Nykerk, a Michigan Technological University graduate engineer who was raised in Traverse City, Michigan. As in Kevin and Virginia's case, it was a beautiful wedding at St. Hugo of the Hills Church.

October 4, 1997—Wedding Day—Jennifer Elaine Graham and
Steven James Nykerk
L to R: Dad, Jennifer, Steve, and Mom

1999
Steve and Jennifer at a friend's wedding
in Buffalo, New York

Early 2000
. . . on the beach in front of our condo at
Sunny Isles Beach, Florida . . .
The 'Newport Pier' in the distance
(often pictured on CSI Miami TV series)

On June 20, 2001, Elizabeth Anne Nykerk was born. Sadly, her Gannie Graham (Betty) had died April 8, 2000. Happily on May 18, 2004, twins—Keely Noelle and Natalie Elaine—were born. All beautiful babies!

**Papa holds his first granddaughter
Elizabeth Anne Nykerk
One week old . . . June 2001
Surrounded by proud Mom—Jennifer and proud Uncle—Kevin**

**2001
Christian (age 7) with his First Cousin Elizabeth and Papa**

May 19, 2004
Beaumont Hospital
The twins Kelly Noelle and Natalie Elaine (one day old) with their
"big sister" Elizabeth Anne and Papa

SPECIAL NOTE...

On Monday, September 27, 2010
Delaney Renee Nykerk was born at 1:45 PM,
weighing 8lbs. 10oz. at Royal Oak Beaumont Hospital.
Her proud parents, Steve and Jennifer Nykerk
and her big sisters, Elizabeth, Natalie, and Keely
welcomed her with great joy.

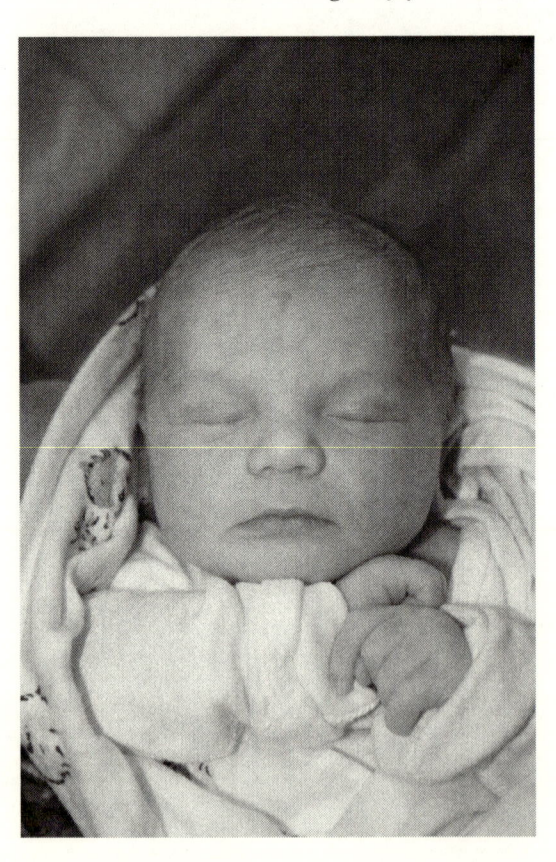

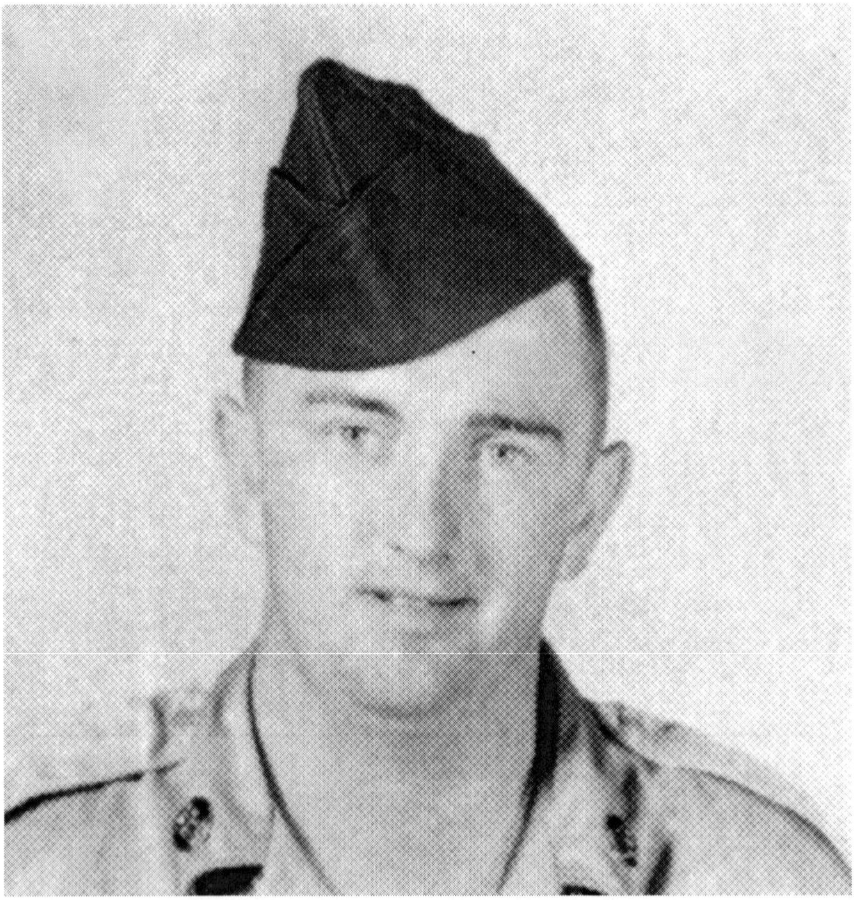

CHAPTER FIVE

Military Service

    Continuing the family tradition, I served in the U.S. Army from September 1959 to April 1960. My brother, Bobby, had served in the U.S. Army from 1945 to 1946 in Japan. Bobby joined with my parents' permission at age fifteen. He was a great speed ice-skater and won the Far East Championship while in Japan.

    Billy served in the U.S. Army in the early 1950s in Korea during the Korean War. My mom was greatly worried for Billy and prayed daily for his safe return. He did return home safely after his tour of duty.

    Fortunately, there was no conflict waging when I served. I did my basic training at Fort Leonard Wood in Missouri. I was appointed training platoon sergeant by the regular army master Sgt. Modey Grey. While fellow law school pals like Charlie Burke and Paul Carrier hated our two- and three-hour-speed marches to the rifle range, etc., I enjoyed the walking—as I do today on the beach at Sunny Isles, Florida.

    I flew home for Christmas, at which time Betty gave me a beautiful diamond ring, which I cherish to this day.

Fort Leonard Wood

FORT LEONARD WOOD

A History

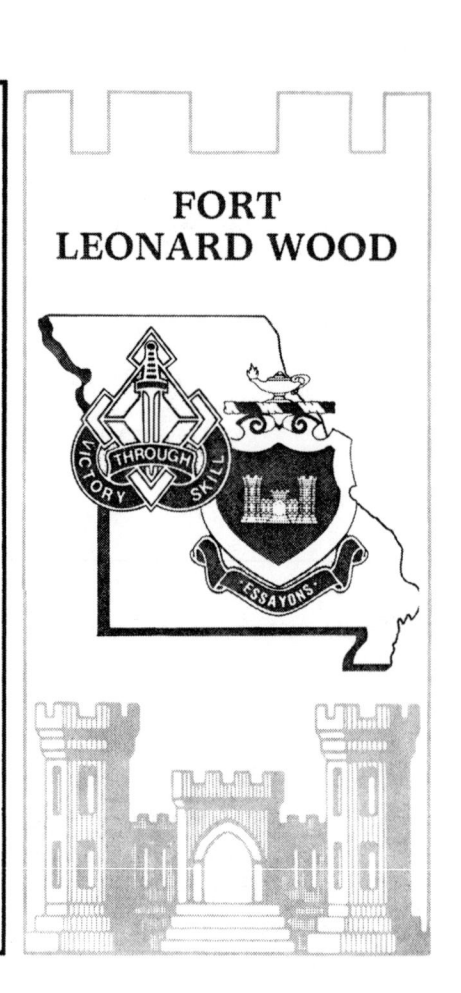

Fort Leonard Wood yearbook photos with Jim, second from right

Jim on command duty in front of Command post
Company C

1959 Ft. Leonard Wood, Missouri

Company C Command Post—1960
Ft. Knox, Kentucky

After basic training, I was assigned to Fort Knox, Kentucky, for advanced training. Flying back after Christmas, I remember the bumpy, five-stop plane ride to Lexington airport.

Ft. Knox was a much better camp. Unlike in Ft. Leonard Wood (jokingly called Ft. Lost in the Woods), we had gas-powered heating (as opposed to coal-heated barracks and showers.). I was selected High Honor Graduate at the conclusion of basic training at Ft. Leonard Wood.

At Ft. Knox, I became a tank commander and was again named training platoon sergeant by the regular army master Sgt Eisermann. Both he and Sgt. Grey were 82nd and 101st Airborne, WWII Battle of the Bulge vets.

Commanding an M-50 tank was something. This huge-tracked vehicle could knock over trees like twigs. Also, firing the 50-caliber machine gun with tracer bullets was interesting. Firing the M-90 artillery gun was also something.

At Ft. Knox, I was selected and awarded the Outstanding Regimental Training Award personally by the post commander, General Butcher. Pictures taken in General Butcher's office, award-certificate ceremony, and letter to my parents are swell memories. As well, I won the Sharpshooter awards at the rifle range.

I was honorably discharged in April 1960, as my tour of duty was fulfilled.

**1960—Ft. Knox, Kentucky—
E-2 James Graham receives the Regimental Outstanding trainee award from Post Commander General Butcher in the General's office**

Sharpshooter Award—1960—Ft. Knox, Kentucky

DEPARTMENTS OF THE ARMY AND THE AIR FORCE
NATIONAL GUARD BUREAU

REPORT OF SEPARATION AND RECORD OF SERVICE IN THE **ARMY** NATIONAL GUARD OF **MICHIGAN**
AND AS A RESERVE OF THE
TYPE OF DISCHARGE **HONORABLE**
(No erasures or alterations in this form if valid)

1. NAME (Last, first, middle initial)	2. SERVICE NO	3. GRADE	4. ARM OR SERVICE	5. TERM OF ENLISTMENT
Grahan James K.	27090301	Pvt E2	Armor	3 yrs.

6. ORGANIZATION HqTrp 1stReconSq 246thArmor	DATE OF DISCHARGE	8. PLACE OF DISCHARGE
HOME STATION Detroit, Michigan	16 Feb 61	Detroit, Michigan

9. PERMANENT ADDRESS FOR MAILING PURPOSES	10. DATE OF BIRTH	11. PLACE OF BIRTH
193 E. Arizona Detroit, Michigan	8 March 1934	Detroit, Michigan

12. CIVILIAN OCCUPATION (Include name and address of present employer, or if unemployed, the last employer)
Lawyer State Farm Mutual Auto Ins. Marshall, Michigan

13. RACE			14. MARITAL STATUS			15. U.S. CITIZEN	
WHITE	NEGRO	OTHER (Specify)	SINGLE	MARRIED	OTHER (Specify)	YES	NO
X				X		X	

16. COLOR EYES	17. COLOR HAIR	18. HEIGHT	19. WEIGHT	20. NO DEPENDENTS
Blue	Brown	5 FT 11 IN	175 LBS	Two

MILITARY HISTORY

21. DATE AND PLACE OF ENLISTMENT	22. MILITARY OCCUPATIONAL SPECIALTY AND NUMBER
22 July 1959 Detroit, Michigan	Personnel Carrier Driver 133.10

23. MILITARY QUALIFICATION AND DATE (i.e. Infantry, Aviation, Marksmanship Badge, etc)

Sharpshooter Rifle M-1 28 Oct 59

24. DECORATIONS, CITATIONS, MEDALS, BADGES, COMMENDATIONS, AND CAMPAIGN RIBBONS AWARDED OR AUTHORIZED
(This period of service)

Sharpshooter Badge

25. PRIOR SERVICE (Branch of service, inclusive dates, and primary duty with MOS)

None

26. LENGTH THIS SERVICE			27. TOTAL SERVICE FOR PAY PURPOSES			28. EDUCATION (Years)			29. HIGHEST GRADE HELD
YEARS	MONTHS	DAYS	YEARS	MONTHS	DAYS	GRAMMAR	HIGH SCHOOL	COLLEGE	
1	6	24	1	6	24	8	4	7	Pvt E2

30. SERVICE SCHOOLS ATTENDED AND DATES

None

31. REASON AND AUTHORITY FOR DISCHARGE

By reason of expiration of maximum time limit for Inactive ARNG membership(par 6b(3). Par 3 SO 34 Michigan Military Estab dtd 17 Feb 61.

32. REMARKS (This space for completion of above items or entry of other items specified in NG directive)

NGB Form 55a mailed to EM at last known address. Reverted to USAR control to complete remaining service obligation of 4 yrs 5 mos 6 days.

33. SIGNATURE OF PERSON BEING DISCHARGED (Full name)	34. SIGNATURE OF OFFICER AUTHORIZED TO SIGN (Type name, grade, and organization)
Not available for signature	JOHN R. ANDERSON Capt Armor Hq Trp 1st Recon Sq 246th Armor

NGB FORM 22
15 JAN 58
1. Insert either Army or Air
2. Insert either Army or Air Force
REPLACES NGB FORM 22 DATED 15 NOV 49, WHICH IS OBSOLETE
GPO : 1958 O - 455859

My Honorable Discharge paper from the
U.S. Army National Guard
February 16, 1961

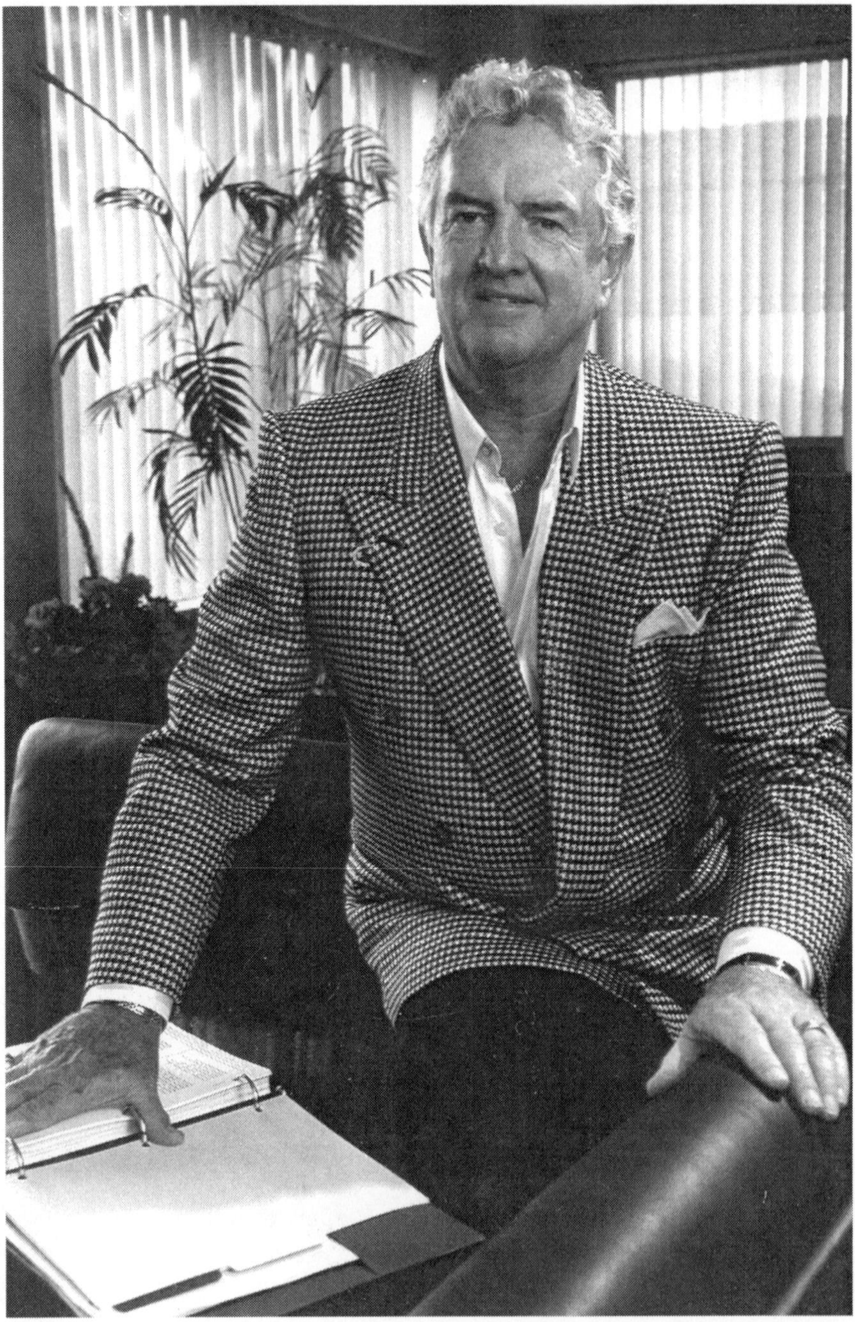

CHAPTER SIX

Working Career Summary

(Grade School—eleven to fourteen years of age)

I worked at Oriental Provision Company, cutting crates of celery for the chop suey, etc., at the rate of $.75 per crate. In addition, I sold the evening edition of the *Detroit Free Press* on my Palmer Park Apartment route (Merton St. west of Woodward on the north side of 6 Mile Road) for $.02 daily and $.03 ¾ cents on Sunday. Any leftover papers were sold at the Dakota Inn Rathskeller – which is still in business today –on the way home, or they were sold to traffic that stopped at lights at 6 Mile and Woodward.

One of my fun jobs as a kid was in 1948-1949. It was during my transition from 8th grade at St. Benedict's to 9th grade at U of D High. I was a Page—not for royalty—at the main Detroit Public Library on Woodward Avenue (across from the Detroit Institute of Arts). My pay, as I recall, was $.65/hour—I'm still living on the residuals!

I would ride the Woodward streetcar (DSR) round-trip from Six Mile Road to Warren.

Not only did the job give me a working knowledge of the inside of a major library, but also instilled some people skills, and a work ethic requiring shirt and tie!

I also caddied weekends at the Detroit Golf Club on Ponchartrain Drive in Detroit.

(High School)

I worked summers at small tool shops. One summer, my brother Bill—the marketing director at Ross Operating Valve on Golden Gate Street—got me a shop job. Another summer, I worked in the shop at Air Tech Screen on 7 Mile and Oakland, both in Detroit. After my last year of high school and graduation in 1952, my dad got me summer jobs at Plymouth Motor Factory and Dodge Forge Plant, again both in Detroit.

(College and Law School)

A variety of jobs . . .

Summers, as I said, were in the factory. During the school year, I kept the books and worked the cash register for bowlers at the Palmer Park Bowling Alleys (fifty-two of them) on 6 Mile and Woodward. The owner, Joe Wisper, and I remained close friends until he died in his late nineties. Betty and I flew to California for his funeral—we had had lunch with him many times while visiting Miami Beach, Florida.

At Christmas, I also delivered mail out of the Highland Park Post Office. My route was near 7 Mile between Oakland and Dequindre. Funeral Director Al Desmond's parents were on my route.

I also secured a warehouse job at the Carling Beer Distributor at $2.75 per hour (Wow!). A number of my pals (Joe Sullivan, etc.) from U of D also worked there.

Another job was for an independent contractor—Jack Snyder—who had a grandfathered franchise with the *Detroit News*. I would load the truck at the downtown *Detroit News* printing shop and then drive out Grand River to Schoolcraft west—dropping off bundles of newspapers at the corners. The end of my deliveries was near Madonna College (now University) in Livonia.

In retrospect, I believe that the many jobs I had as a youth, prepared me and motivated me to subscribe to a good work ethic. Particularly jobs at Air-Tech screens where grinding metal finishes and putting the screens into the chemical degreaser tank were demanding.

Likewise, the summer jobs at Chrysler Corporation—Plymouth plant and Dodge Forge plant were good disciplines. In particular, the afternoon shift (4PM to Midnight) on the motor block production line, was very noisy and physically demanding. I still remember the experience of leaving the noisy shop and having the outside, midnight silence ring in my ears. However, a good work experience with good pay for the 1950's.

(After College)

After completing law school, passing the Michigan Bar after completing military service, I came home to begin my full-time work career.

Jobs were rather tight in 1960. However, I heard from friends that State Farm Insurance Company was hiring attorneys to be Bodily Injury (B. I.) Claims Specialists. I promptly applied. I had to drive to their Regional Office in Marshall, Michigan. I was driving a blue 1951 Pontiac Coupe that my brother Bill had given me. I was in a suit and tie on this early, warm, summer day in 1960. I did the interview, got hired, and was happily driving home on I-94. I got a flat tire, near Jackson, Michigan, and had to change the tire. Thank goodness, it happened after my interview.

My base salary was, I seem to recall, $5,400 plus about $4,000 cost of living plus a fully insured company car (white 1960 Ford) with expense account, plus fringes—a good deal in 1960. I did well and was photo featured in a national State Farm personnel-recruiting booklet.

I enjoyed negotiating settlements with claimants and attorneys, authorized to write settlement checks on the spot. I cultivated many friendships among fellow attorneys.

One in particular, Bob Loesch, was house counsel for Citizens Mutual Insurance. In his capacity, he was also allowed to practice law. On one occasion, Bob came to my State Farm Insurance office at 10 Mile near Kelley in then East Detroit (now the city of Eastpointe) to settle one of his personal cases. We amicably settled the matter, and I began asking him questions about his seemingly attractive job situation.

Even though I enjoyed my work experience at State Farm Insurance, I knew it was not my choice of a career, so I was keeping my eyes and ears open. A University of Detroit friend in 1961 told me there was an attorney position open at Chrysler Defense Engineering in Centerline, Michigan. I applied, was interviewed by attorneys, Bob Nichols and Jack Wooten, and was hired. As an attorney, I negotiated defense contracts for military tanks and tank parts with the Department of Defense. It was interesting and good experience.

Simultaneously, in 1961, a Department Director at Macomb County Community College—Marie Zimmerman (a friend of Betty's), asked me to teach a Business Law class, which I did for two semesters.

As an aside, I viewed my State Farm and Chrysler jobs as a career starter for me. In any event, to my delight, Bob Loesch called and said he was leaving Citizens Mutual Insurance to go into private law practice.

He recommended me to his boss, Attorney Angus McIsaac, and the branch manager—Attorney Bud Goetsch. I set up an appointment and drove to their office at 7 Mile and Greenfield in Detroit. All went well with Angus and Bud, and I was hired in September 1962 as house counsel for Citizens Mutual Insurance. My pay was $18,500 per year plus a car of my choice (new red 1962 Ford hardtop), expense account, nice office plus the right to practice law and accept fees on my private practice—a great deal!

Further, I had considerable authority. I tried cases I chose to handle myself. Bigger cases, I referred to the firm of Conklin (Tom) and Maloney (Joe). The largest cases, I referred to Davidson, Gotschall, et al., also in the First National Building in Detroit. I supervised and authorized settlements when appropriate. Otherwise, I oversaw the case through trial. I really enjoyed this, but I was ambitious, and with the latitude of the job, I pursued additional credentials.

1968
Law office in the Guardian Building Suite 1200
Detroit, Michigan

I had previously acquired my securities license with the firm of Armstrong (Ted), Jones, Lawson, and White offices in the Penobscot Building in Detroit. One friend who worked at a variety of sales venues (securities, insurance, financial planning,) was Al Beeckman. I acted at the attorney in a number of legal matters for Al and customers, namely, wills and trusts, etc. All were pleased with my work.

As a result, in August 1966, Al approached me about a new company coming into the national scene and into Michigan with a pioneering product. He said it was the Variable Annuity Life Insurance Company of America or VALIC. This new pioneering effort would also have a brand new product—i.e., the Variable Annuity. Al said a new director of sales (Bob Phillips) was moving from San Francisco, California, to start the new operation. Al said that Bob was looking for a regional manager and Al had recommended me.

I met with Bob, and he praised the future of opportunities with VALIC as a new venture. The company would only pay $12,500 with a $5,000 raise within a year, plus car and expense account. Bob sold hard and was impressive, and I sensed long-term opportunity. I discussed the job with Betty, and we bet on my potential. Bob Phillips turned out to be an excellent mentor, a good partner, and a fast friend for life.

VALIC DIGEST—FEBRUARY 1968

Mr. and Mrs. James K. Graham of Detroit, left, engaged in conversation with Mr. and Mrs. Donald A. Kammer of Saginaw, Michigan, during the reception given by the Phillips'.

1968
Betty & Jim Graham with Mr. & Mrs. Don Kammer
at a reception given by the Phillips
two years after Jim officially began his career with VALIC.

1968
VALIC Convention
Left side L to R: Jim & Betty Graham, Mr. & Mrs. John Bresler,
Right side L to R: Bob and Maureen Phillips, ?

Below: Surf experts James K. Graham in the rear and Michael H. Sheridan frolic in Atlantic waters off the shores of the Sheraton.

1968
Jim Graham and Mike Sheridan
enjoying the surf in the Atlantic Ocean
San Juan Puerto Rico

VALIC DIGEST
Published monthly by the Variable Annuity Life Insurance Company of America / VOL. 2 NO. 2, FEBRUARY 1968

The scene at the Salon Carnival dinner-dance in the Puerto Rico Sheraton as the VALIC group pauses for the photographer.

VALIC Convention—1968
San Juan Puerto Rico Sheraton Hotel
Back L to R: Glen & Gloria Holden, Mr. & Mrs. Joe Malosch,
Gwen & Tom McKenna;
Front L to R: Bob Phillips, Mr. and Mrs. Joe Leary,
Jim and Betty Graham

The 70's

James K. Graham Receives Management Honor for 1976

Highlighting the Conference was the announcement of the President's Trohy Winner — Detroit, and Manager of the Year — Jim Graham!

The award was a closely guarded secret until presented by Mr. Jack Plumb. Prior to the final announcement, Mr. Plumb kept an air of suspense as he gave "clues" describing the leading manager, becoming more specific as his presentation continued. Once it was disclosed that Jim Graham and his Detroit group had won top honors for 1976, the reps joined together to celebrate their triumph by carrying their manager to the head table. Jim was very obviously proud and pleased, and he generously extended individual recognition and special thanks to his group and wife, Betty. Jim made quite a victory in 1976 as his office won the Market Ratio Contest, led the company on an annual basis and had two members on the President's Cabinet. The appraisal was made by an evaluation of numerous factors — competition revealed great strength ... but Detroit earned the superior honors. Once again, we extend our appreciation and congratulations to Jim, his remarkable reps and devoted office staff.

Breathless Memories 173

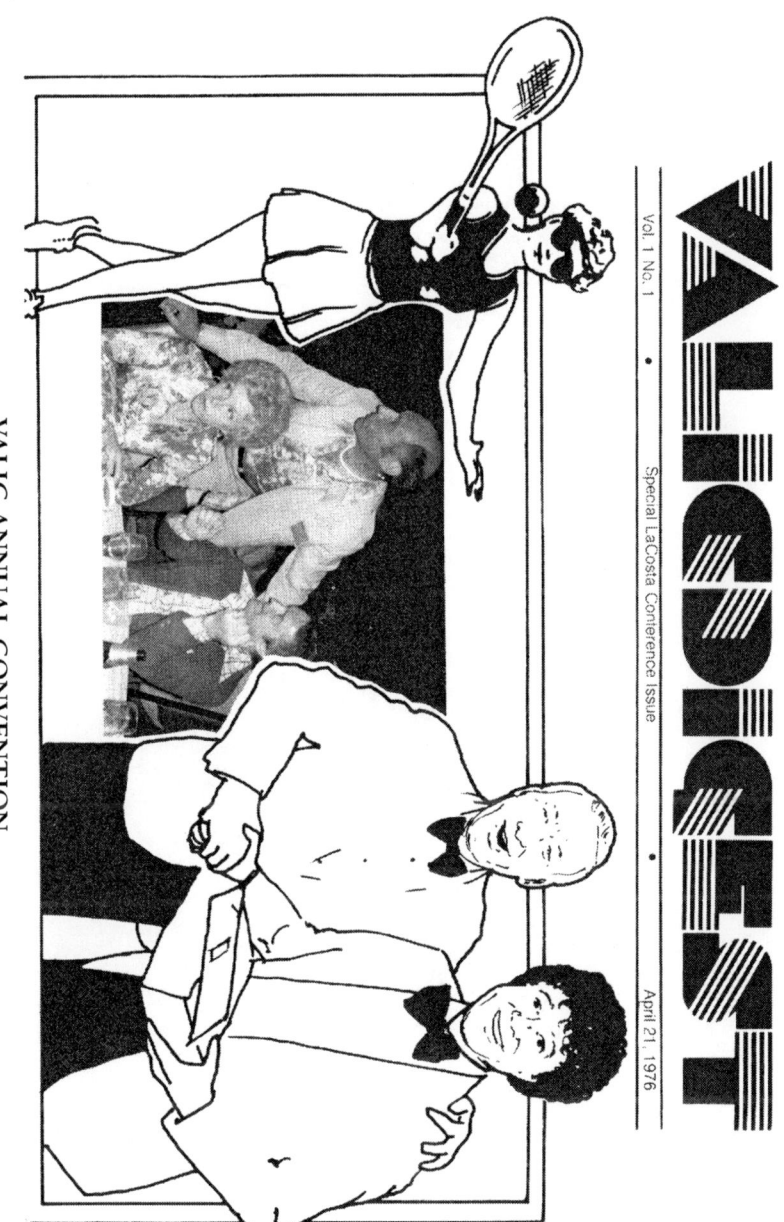

VALIDIGEST

Vol. 1 No. 1 • Special LaCosta Conference Issue • April 21, 1976

VALIC ANNUAL CONVENTION
La Costa, California
Manager of the Year

1977 Miami Beach Convention

Jim Graham
Manager of the Year

Jack Plumb _CEO VALIC presents Jim Graham
as Manager of the Year

Jim's acceptance speech at the Miami Convention

MANAGER OF THE YEAR

JAMES K. GRAHAM- for the second consecutive year - received the great honor of being awarded VALIC's Manager of the Year. The Michigan Office has now won the coveted award five times and Jim said, "... each time is just as sweet".

Excerpts from Jim's comments on his grand victory, "...This is first and foremost a team victory. All of us in the Michigan operation must share in this recognition. The administrative staff back home played an integral part in our success. Furthermore, an indispensible ingredient were my colleagues and our spouses here tonight.

We are extremely proud of our benchmarks achieved in 1977. To mention just a few of them:
1) We set a new production record of 8½ million dollars in new business.
2) We set a new cash flow record of over 21 million dollars.
3) We maintained good cost control by staying within our budget.
4) We placed three on the President's Cabinet and several finishers in the top 25 for the year.

All in all, we are very pleased with the achievement of our pre-determined goals. In accepting this great award, I must remind myself and my colleagues that we have placed a greater charge on ourselvess for *now*, the present - 1978. So to my Michigan associates the refrain is clear, "We've got to take it to the limit one more time..."

Don Burchi, Jim Graham, George Wagman, and Bill Corder

This photo was taken following a sales meeting presentation at the Michigan Office. VAMCO Vice President Jim Graham presented personally inscribed pieces of metal sculpture to each of the three Michigan Representatives who qualified for the President's Cabinet. Graham designed the awards, which were done by Canadian artist, Paul Wellington.

May 1977
Jim Graham, Manager of the Year
presented his 3 leading account reps—
Dante Burchi, George Wagman, and Bill Corder
with a special Canadian sculpture ...
Jim and his 3 reps finished in the Top 5 President's Club

1978—BalHarbour Florida Convention

VALICDIGEST

HOUSTON, TEXAS   MAY, 1977

```
   000••••••••••85959;0••••••••.•
VALIC DET TRMI

WU INFOMASTER   1-028093M363006  12/29/78
TLX VALICTEXAS HOU
ZCZC 6 PD HOUSTON TEX
TLX 235825 VALIC DET TRMI
   REGIONAL MANAGER  THE VARIABLE ANNUITY LIFE INS CO
BT

UNAUDITED PRODUCTION WEEK ENDING 12/29           CUMULATIVE

 1  DET       280,252          1  DET       10,662,348  ← A Company "First"
 2  FLA       239,269          2  MID AM     9,799,318
 3  CLE       233,962          3  CLE        9,168,798
 4  PTL       225,233          4  ATL        7,761,873
 5  N J       217,390          5  DEN        6,498,539
 6  ATL       192,461          6  BLT        6,307,766
 7  FLT       127,199          7  FLA        5,377,345
 8  MID AM    118,303          8  N J        5,235,134
 9  SN MTO    108,451          9  SN MTO     5,201,804
10  DEN        88,705         10  PTL        4,433,014
11  N E        49,680         11  PHIL       4,331,786
12  HOU        37,361         12  HOU        4,205,868
13  PHIL       37,054         13  DAL        3,858,886
14  DAL        29,291         14  PHX        2,921,751
15  L A        22,053         15  N E        2,316,937
16  PHX        10,199         16  L A        1,062,635
17  SLC         6,156         17  MINN         923,405
18  MINN        6,120         18  SLC          658,188

TOTAL       2,017,170         TOTAL        90,719,267
```

A VALIC First - $10,000,000!

With December not yet over, the Michigan office had broken the *Ten Million* sales mark for 1978. This is the first time in VALIC's history that any regional office has achieved double digit business in the millions.

This Michigan office is no stranger to Company records. Almost every year sees the leading office set a new record. In breaking their 1977 Company sales record, this office was 14.5% ahead of its record-breaking pace of 1977.

We all echo Mr. Plumb's congratulations to the Detroit office.

VAMCO Vice-President of our Michigan office shown handing VALIC President, Mr. Jack Plumb, the record-breaking application.

December 1978

VALIC CEO Jack Plumb congratulates Regional VP Jim Graham whose office was the first national office to break $10,000,000 sales record. The article points out that Jim's office exceeded his previous 1977 national record by 14.5% in sales.

JIM GRAHAM
Manager of the Year

Jim Graham accepts the "Manager of the Year" plaque from VALIC CEO Jack Plumb

1979 Oahu Hawaiian Islands

Jim Graham
Manager of the Year

March 8, 1979 marked the beginning of the annual VALIC Sales Convention, which was held in Hawaii. This date also signifies an unforgettable day for the VALIC — Michigan, Vice-President, James K. Graham. While celebrating his birthday, Jim also had cause to celebrate being selected, for the 3rd consecutive year, as the recipient of the coveted "Manager of the Year Award".

As the highlight of that evening's program, President John J. Plumb followed tradition by creating an exciting atmosphere before announcing the winner. After eluding to the winner's essential social and community achievements, Mr. Plumb noted the many recent accomplishments of the winner's Regional Office that led to his unprecedented third consecutive win of Manager of the Year.

In his remarks Jim acknowledged gratitude to the contribution of his regional office administrative staff back home, his sales associates and their spouses, as well as the Home Office personnel.

Jim closed by thanking the other regional offices for their outstanding competition that was a significant factor in pushing the Michigan office to a new record performance. All in all, this opening evening award set the tempo that carried throughout the entire Hawaiian meeting.

Left to right—Jack Plumb, Betty and Jim Graham, Oscar Newton, Lois and Howard Meyer, Justine and Don Burchi.

1980 San Diego California

National VALIC Convention at the Del Coronado Hotel

Betty & Jim Graham at the national Convention

Breathless Memories 181

The Detroit Office achieved positioQ #3, Jim Graham accepts the award.

Jim Graham, Jack Plumb CEO, and Woody Woodson, Chairman of VALIC and American General

SPECIAL RECOGNITION AND TROPHIES AWARDED...

Detroit Office achieved "PLACE" position in the Summer Sweepstakes Contest, Jim Graham proudly accepts.

Jim Graham receives the 'Achievement Trophy' from Jack Plumb, then VALIC CEO

James Kenneth Patrick Graham J. D.

1996 Jim Celebrates 30 years with VALIC

STATE OF MICHIGAN

Special Tribute

James K. Graham
30th VALIC Anniversary

LET IT BE KNOWN, That it is a distinct pleasure to pay tribute to James K. Graham as he celebrates his 30th anniversary with the VALIC Company on September 21, 1996. James has certainly earned the respect of all those around him as he has continually set standards in his consistent dedication and excellence in his job performance.

James K. Graham was first hired into VALIC as a Regional Manager in 1966. Since that time he has received numerous awards and has stood out from his co-workers as a leader in his profession. James was Manger of the Year for four consecutive years between 1974-1978. He has also served as President of the VALIC Manager Association and a twelve time Gold Circle Winner. In addition to all these honors James has become the first VALIC employee to exceed ten million in annual sales and will now become the first employee to reach thirty years of service with the company.

James K. Graham has established a work ethic by which all his colleagues should follow. At a time when job turnover is rampant and loyalty is weakening, James stands out in the business world. When the employees of VALIC need to look for inspiration in their job performance they need to look no further than James K. Graham. We salute you on this day for all your tireless efforts and the examples for which you have set.

IN SPECIAL TRIBUTE, Therefore, This document is signed and dedicated to James K. Graham on the celebration of his 30th anniversary with VALIC. May he know of our deepest admiration and best wishes for his continued success.

Michael J. Bouchard, State Senator
The Thirteenth District
The Eighty-Eighth Legislature
At Lansing
September 21, 1996

Jim Graham at the podium with an acceptance speech
after receiving the State of Michigan plaque top

September 1996
. . . remembering 30 years earlier . . .
Jim on his 30th Anniversary with VALIC
next to a picture of himself in his previous office
in the Guardian Building Suite 1200
as an attorney in Detroit, Michigan

Warm Wishes and Congratulations

AMERICAN GENERAL CORPORATION

HOUSTON, TEXAS

ROBERT M. DEVLIN
PRESIDENT

September 21, 1996

Mr. Jim Graham
Regional Manager
VALIC

Dear Jim:

My heartiest and sincere congratulations to you on your 30th anniversary with VALIC. This is certainly a significant achievement, not just in the fact that you are celebrating 30 years, but more importantly for the numerous and significant contributions that you have made to VALIC and in turn, American General.

I look forward to our continued association and wish you and your family God speed.

All the best,

Bob

2929 ALLEN PARKWAY · HOUSTON, TEXAS 77019-2155 · (713) 831-2000

American General's CEO—Robert Devlin recognizes Jim's 30 year career

HARRY C. COPELAND, JR.
SUITE 274
200 EAST 62ND STREET
NEW YORK, NEW YORK 10021-8209
212-752-0291

September 20, 1996

Dear Jim:

    The occasion of your 30th anniversary as the first and only VALIC employee to attain that lengthy service brings me the opportunity to express to you my great pride in your many business and personal achievements.

    As I'm sure you know, my greatest career satisfactions not only come from observing the success of VALIC as a company, but also, most particularly the individual personal successes of that great early group of VALIC builders - a group whose talents, drives, beliefs and dedication you so finely represent.

    The importance of the Detroit Board of Education case was, and still is, the most signal landmark in the VALIC history and your personal leadership in the ongoing development of that case is a landmark financial services marketing and administrative feat.

    Congratulations to you as you continue your exemplary professional excellence. Hope to see you soon if you come New York way and every good wish for you and your family's health and prosperity.

Most Sincerely,

Harry C. Copeland, Jr.

Original Founder and Chairman and CEO of VALIC Harry Copeland sends regards

AMERICAN GENERAL CORPORATION

HOUSTON, TEXAS

HAROLD S. HOOK
CHAIRMAN
CHIEF EXECUTIVE OFFICER

September 10, 1996

Mr. James K. Graham
Regional Manager
VALIC
1301 West Long Lake Road, Suite 340
Troy, Michigan 48098-6349

Dear Jim:

Congratulations on your 30th anniversary with VALIC. In a world filled with "summer soldiers and sunshine patriots" it's a great pleasure to salute your commitment and dedication to building VALIC over thirty tumultuous years.

I remember well the leadership you exercised with the regional managers during my first few years in Houston. The reason I mention this particularly period is because I think VALIC's destiny was at risk at that time. It wouldn't have taken much to tip the balance in directions that would have forestalled the great progress that has been achieved.

Although, as the old saying goes, success has many fathers ..., you can rightfully claim - and I will support your claim - to a healthy portion of the parentage credit for VALIC.

On a personal note, Jim, it has been fun and I look forward to our association in the future and to as much golf as we can work in.

Sincerely,

Harold S. Hook

HSH/vh

2929 ALLEN PARKWAY · HOUSTON, TEXAS 77019 · (713) 831-1001

American General President Harold hook send good wishes

VALIC

★ An American General Company

Thomas L. West, Jr.
President

September 20, 1996

Mr. James K. Graham
Regional Manager
VALIC
1301 W. Long Lake Rd.
Suite 340
Troy, MI 48098-6349

Dear Jim:

Let me add my congratulations to those you have already received on this momentous occasion of your 30th anniversary with VALIC. I want to present you a B.E.S.T. Award in recognition of all that you have done representing our fine company for so many years.

Please accept this recognition as a small token of my appreciation for all you have contributed to VALIC's success.

I wish you even greater success in your next 30 years -- many of which will be spent representing VALIC just as you have done so well for so many years.

Best Personal Regards,

Tom

Thomas L. West, Jr.

The Variable Annuity
Life Insurance Company

2929 Allen Parkway
Houston, Texas 77019
P.O. Box 3206
Houston, Texas 77253-3206
(713) 831-6000
Fax (713) 831-4940

30th Anniversary congratulatory letter from company President Tom West

Honorable Glen Holden

September 20, 1996

Mr. James K. Graham
Regional Manager
VALIC
1301 West Long Lake Road, Suite 340
Troy, Michigan 48098-6349

Dear Jim:

After more than a decade of efforts on the part of John Marsh, the Variable Annuity Life Insurance Company overcame many "objections" and seemed ready to present its new concept to the public. VALIC opened its Detroit office in April of 1965 and soon became the hallmark and model for the explosion of the Variable Annuity in America.

Fortunately for VALIC, and all of us, you were put in charge of operating the Detroit office by Bob Phillips, an energetic, innovative marketing man who ran that office. I was then President of VALIC and I needed a manager in other parts of the country so we approached you about taking one of these promotions. You, however, preferred to stay in the Detroit office and to fine tune it to a more efficient and successful model for the continuing growth of the company. Your calm, careful and superlative refinement of operations in Detroit was good for all of us. A few short years later, Bob Phillips was transferred from Detroit and the entire operation, of course, came under your direction.

For 30 years you have maintained the excellence that was so important to us in the success of VALIC. It has been truly a great opportunity and compliment to be associated with the beginning of an industry like the variable annuity. There is no question that we all participated in setting the standard nationwide for this great concept for our clients' retirement stability and peace of mind. The variable annuity is probably the finest product ever devised as a source of investment income and you are one of those that for 30 years have accelerated its growth and acceptability to the public. Few people have the opportunity to experience 30 years contributing to the unqualified success of a new industry and I, as much as anyone, have been able to appreciate the value of your contributions.

Most sincerely,

Glen Holden

2121 Avenue of the Stars • 34th Floor Fox Plaza • Los Angeles, California 90067
(310) 557-9248 · (310) 788-5599 FAX

Ambassador Glen Holden (former Ambassador to Jamaica And former VALIC CEO in the 1960's) cites Jim's accomplishments and friendship

VALIC

★ An American General Company

Stephen D. Bickel
Chairman and
Chief Executive Officer

September 3, 1996

Mr. James K. Graham
Regional Manager
VALIC
1301 W. Long Lake Rd., Suite 340
Troy, MI 48098-6349

Dear Jim:

I would like to extend my congratulations to you on the occasion of your 30th anniversary of service with VALIC.

When you joined VALIC in 1966, VALIC had $25 million of assets and had collected $10 million of premium income. The Detroit Region alone collects 10 times as much premium and has 60 times as much assets as the entire company did in 1966.

In 1966, the name of the Company was Variable Annuity Life Insurance Company of America, with its home office in Washington, D.C. 1966 was an exciting year for VALIC. 1966 premium income was triple the amount of 1965 premiums. The value of a share of VALIC stock in 1996 ranged from a high of $48 to a low of $14.

Six months after you joined the Company, American General became the principal stockholder of VALIC. One year later the Company was reincorporated as The Variable Annuity Life Insurance Company, and the home office was moved to Houston. You have served under two of the five presidents of the D.C. company and all of the ten presidents of the Houston-based Company. I don't think anyone else has or ever will have that distinction.

Mr. James K. Graham
September 3, 1996
Page 2

You and I have shared many experiences over the last three decades. We have been through booms, busts, recession, inflation, wars, rebellions, hurricanes, and blizzards. Together, with our associates, we have helped the price of American General stock grow from less than $4 per share in 1966 to almost $40 per share today.

Since becoming manager of the Detroit Region in 1974, the region has grown to more than $100 million of annual premium income and $1.5 billion of participant account values. During your tenure, you earned the Manager of the Year Award four times, in 1974, 1976, 1977, and 1978. You have played a major role in the VALIC's development, and you have been a valued advisor to every VALIC President. Your greatest achievement, however, is the organization of 58 representatives, 20 employees, and 47,000 participants that comprise the Detroit Regional Office. VALIC is proud of every one of you.

I hope that you will take great pride in the accomplishments of the Detroit Regional Office and yourself. Please accept my warmest congratulations.

Sincerely,

Steve

Stephen D. Bickel

Congratulatory letter from VALIC CEO Steve Bickell to Jim noting not only his distinguished 30 year career, but also his standing as the longest serving VALIC employee.

1997

James K. Graham
Executive "Extraordinaire" towards the end of an illustrious career
VALIC office in Troy, Michigan

To:	Jim Graham
cc:	Tom West, Joe Osborne, Ron Kopke, Sandra Ritchie, Gwen Hughes
From:	Jeff Johnson
Date:	03/06/97 04:45:03 PM
Subject:	ONE IN A MILLION

I'm pleased to tell you that VALIC has just signed its one millionth customer, and he is in your region! His name is Keith Todd, a new customer at Daughters of Charity - Providence Hospital in Southfield The Retirement Plan Specialist is Mary Centers.

As part of the One in a Million celebration, we would like to fly Mr. Todd and Ms. Centers down to Houston for one night and one day to ceremonialize the event. We'll put them up in a hotel, take them out to dinner, and have a small ceremony at the Home Office with VALIC's executive Committee.

In order to proceed, I need your approval to contact Mary and, once contacted, to also contact the Mr. Todd.

We'll, of course, keep you fully informed. But we need to "check out" the relationship before we commit to promoting it.

Can we proceed??

March 6, 1997
"One in a Million" Memo
VALIC had just signed its one millionth customer
from Jim's Region

THIRTY Incredible years with VALIC

1999 soon to say Good-Bye

I spent thirty-three years with VALIC, retiring on December 31, 1999, with a five-year consultant contract ending December 31, 2004. My bet paid off handsomely as I had a great career and helped pioneer VALIC the company and the product—the variable annuity. Some of this is repeated in the section on Financial Accomplishments. But in terms of my professional career and the undreamed-of financial achievements that my VALIC experience afforded me, it bears repetition. The lifestyle, enjoyment of family, travel, assisting friends, and good career were blessings.

AMERICA'S RETIREMENT PLAN SPECIALISTS℠.

James K. Graham
Regional Vice President

VALIC®
★ An American General Company

Business (248) 641-0022
Toll Free 1-800-44-VALIC (DET)
Fax (248) 641-0282

The Variable Annuity Life Insurance Company
1301 W. Long Lake Rd., Suite 340 • Troy, MI 48098-6349

An ending to an illustrious career with VALIC

JAMES K. GRAHAM
ATTORNEY AT LAW

1744 HERON RIDGE DRIVE
BLOOMFIELD HILLS, MI 48302-0723

(248) 338-7332

"The Retired Corporate Executive—Always an Attorney"
Integrity, Honesty, Loyalty, and Service

The 'Retired' Executive at his home
in Bloomfield Hills, Michigan

A further blessing was the mentorship, support, and friendship—most of all—during my business career and all those years after retirement. I have commended Bob Phillips, but I am also indebted to other corporate leaders who aided and enhanced my career success. They are as follows: Woody Woodson, chairman and CEO of American General Corporation in Houston; Harold Hook, successor to Mr. Woodson; Mike Poulos—especially—successor to Harold and supporter during the "1984 Pearl Harbor;" John Graf, CEO of AIG VALIC and a class guy, especially at my retirement; lastly, for decades—Jim Costello—a genuine friend. If America had more executives like these men as CEOs today, the corporate meltdowns would *not* have occurred.

As a personal career postscript, Bob Phillips asked me to invest and act as attorney for a new venture, The Polo Store in La Jolla, California. But first, we had to go to New York City and make a deal with Ralph Lauren.

1975—At one of our meetings with Ralph Lauren, movie star Cary Grant sat in on part of the session. He was on the board of Faberge. I was impressed with his friendliness and same-as-screen looking appearance.

1980—In Las Vegas, I became friends with Gianni Russo who owned a restaurant in Las Vegas and appeared in movies, particularly in *The Godfather I*. At that time, he was married to singer Dionne Warwick. He invited me to her birthday party at the Beverly Hills Hotel in Beverly Hills, California.

We had many personal introductions, pictures, and conversations with many celebrities, including the then LA mayor, Ed Bradley.

1990—The Beverly Hills Hotel, California—
Dionne Warwick with 'friends' John O'Sullivan,
John O'Reilly, and Jim Graham at her birthday party

1990—John O'Sullivan, John O'Reilly, and Jim Graham with
Danny Thomas at the Party for Dionne Warwick

1993—The St. Hugo travel group was in Rome and was invited to a personal audience with Pope John Paul II. As Pope John Paul shook my hand, I smiled and addressed him, "Jak sie masz (How are you?), Your Holiness." He started to move toward Betty, but stopped, smiled broadly, and said, "Molte bene!" In such incredible surroundings, this was a light-hearted moment. After all had greeted the pope, we celebrated his feast day with a birthday cake—it was the feast of St. Carl, his namesake, Karol—and sang "Happy Feast Day." Quite a moving experience!

**Wow! A private audience with the Pope!
In the receiving line . . . Pope John Paul II,
Cindy and Tom Dailey, Jim and Betty Graham**

Breathless Memories 201

October 1993 at the Vatican in Rome
In the Pope's private chambers . . .
Enjoying the pope's Feast Day with Father Tony and Friends . . .
Jim, center back, Cindy, leaning front, and Betty, two from right

1993
Betty and Jim tossing coins into the Trevi Fountain,
Rome, Italy
Remember the song by the Four Aces "Three Coins in the Fountain"

1993—Trevi Fountain—Rome, Italy
Our entire tour group in front of the newly
restored historical fountain . . .
Betty and Jim—second from left
Tom Dailey—sixth from left back
Cindy—fourth from left front

1993
Jim and Betty walking through the Vatican Garden
Behind the Dome of St. Peter's . . .
Cardinal Szoka was then President of the Vatican . . .
and lived in the presidential palace with these gardens!

2005—Once again, on the Seventy-fifth Anniversary St. Hugo pilgrimage to Rome, our St. Hugo group enjoyed an audience on the dais in St. Peter's Square with Pope Benedict XVI. Our seats were only a few feet away from the cardinals, dignitaries, and the pope himself. Light rain didn't dampen our excitement as the St. Hugo group's name was announced . . . another incredible moment.

2006—Cindy and I attended a charitable fundraiser for the Sisters of the Holy Eucharist at the "Max" (The Detroit Symphony Orchestra Hall). We reminisced about the founding days of Legatus (a Catholic organization for successful Catholic business executives)—as charter members—with Thomas Monaghan (the Domino Pizza founder and owner). After the concert, at a private afterglow, we enjoyed a pleasant meeting with the performer Jose Feliciano.

James K. Graham, Trustee
Sacred Heart Major Seminary Board of Trustees

CHAPTER SEVEN

Charitable Endeavors and Political Associations

My parents and family always observed charitable giving as part of our Catholic Christian commitment. My parents' example set the tone for my life's charitable/community endeavors. I remember neighbor Dr. Butch Glass asking me in the 1970s, "Where do you find the time for a successful marriage and family, career achievement and charitable/community contribution of time, talent, and money?"

The obvious reply was, "You become more efficient in your use of time and just make the time to contribute." In the interest of time, I will enumerate a sampling of my extracurricular work, including two elected terms to the Bloomfield Hills Board of Education.

(1) University of Detroit Economic Club
(2) Knights of Columbus—Judge Advocate Fr. Cotter Council
(3) U.S. Army
(4) Birmingham/Bloomfield Little League—Board of Directors and Team Manager
(5) Bloomfield Hills Board of Education (elected twice) held all offices including Presidency (1972-1980)
(6) University of Detroit Jesuit High School—Alumni Board of Directors (contributed $5,000 plus annual gifts, etc.)
(7) Detroit College of Law—Alumni Board of Directors

(8) Detroit College of Law—Presidents' Club (contributed $10,000 as Charter Member plus annually)
(9) Legatus—Charter Member
(10) St. Patrick Senior Center, Detroit (contribute $3,000—broken kitchen equipment at Christmas)
(11. Marian High School Dad's Club fundraiser Auction ($3,000)—a wonderful day in Sparky Anderson's Box at Tiger Stadium
(12) St. Benedict (Highland Park) Foundation—Chairman (contributed $10,000)
(13) St. Hugo of the Hills—(Part of five-person New Church Building and Design Committee) oversaw new church construction in 1988-89)
(14) St. Hugo of the Hills Church—contributed $104,000 (stained-glass window in tabernacle area of new Church) Some years later, noting an architectural defect that blocked the congregation's view from the church proper—contributed $18,400 to raise the ceiling opening over the tabernacle area.
(15) St. Hugo of the Hills Church—contributed $50,000 (created Christian's Place—a children's room in memory of Betty)
(16) Congressman Joseph Knollenberg—Finance Committee and annual contributions
(17) Sacred Heart Major Seminary—Board of Trustees and Finance Committee (annual Support contributed) ($5,000—Cardinals Memorial Garden)
(18) Stillmeadow Homeowners Association—Board Member and Officer
(19) Williamburg Estates—Board Member
(20) Created $250,000 Mausoleum at Holy Sepulchre Cemetery for family. I moved my parents and Betty's parents from Mt. Olivet Cemetery. Large Cross at the Cemetery Entrance—Major Donor.
(21) St. Hugo of the Hills Parish Seventy-fifth Anniversary (2005), Cindy and I were the chairpersons for the yearlong celebration
(22) As the co-chairperson of my U of D Jesuit High School Fifty-fifth Reunion on June 15, 2007, I donated $1,100.00 in support of the school

(23) Heron Bay Homeowner's Association Board of Directors
(24) Dues paying member for the American Legion
(25) Madonna University—$5,000 major donor in Cardinal's Square Garden and Lecture Hall—Science building
(26) University of Detroit annual support
(27) Sacred Heart Major Seminary Desert Experience
(28) $2,500—Seminarians to the Holy Land

In addition to these more intensive activities, I have always financially supported many, many charities as generously as possible (Fr. Flanagan's Boys and Girls Town, Catholic Services Appeal, Cathedral Renovation, St. Lawrence Seminary, Holy Sepulchre Cemetery (large monument cross at entrance), etc.

As they say, you get more from giving than you do from receiving.

June 9, 1975
Bloomfield Hills Lahser High School Commencement at Meadowbrook
James K. Graham, President of the Board of
Education presented the diplomas and delivered the
commencement address to the graduates and attendees

Bloomfield Hills Board of Education
1972
Jim Graham, far right back row

St Hugo of the Hills Church, Bloomfield Hills, Michigan
Jim standing in front of "tree of life" stained glass window
Behind the Tabernacle in the Reservation area.
Jim and Betty commissioned artist Margaret Cavanaugh
when the church was being built—
on the day of Betty's funeral, the family placed
a plaque dedicating the window to Betty.

Christian's Room

Nursery opens

Parents of young children at St. Hugo of the Hills Parish, Bloomfield Hills, now have a nursery where toddlers can play and listen to Bible stories while their parents attend Mass. Christian's Room opened last month following a special blessing ceremony by Msgr. Anthony Tocco (above). The nursery was dedicated to the memory of the late Elizabeth "Betty" Graham, wife, mother and grandmother in an offering by her family. Christian Graham (right) stands in the playroom, which has a Noah's Ark theme with a handcrafted wooden ark. Volunteers supervise the children's activities.

January, 2001
Christian's Room was blessed and formally dedicated
St. Hugo of the Hills Church

Jim and Cindy Graham
Chairpersons for the Seventy-Fifth Anniversary Year
St. Hugo of the Hills Parish
2006-2007

In support of the beautification of Holy Sepulchre Cemetery,
the large cross and main entrance sign were erected
with the help of donors, including Jim Graham and Family

Detail of the bronze 'Graham' crest
on the floor of the Graham Chapel

Graham Chapel—Holy Sepulchre Mausoleum
Marble floor reflecting the stained glass window
created by Margaret Cavanaugh of Mary, Queen of the Universe
"Rejoice and be Glad, Yours is the Kingdom of God"

Beautiful glass and brass entrance gate with crystal etched Graham crest, Pink and black marble named altar, Family chapel dedicated in 2001

2008
Sacred Heart Major Seminary
Dedication ceremony for the new
Cardinal's Memorial Garden

May 4, 2007   The Michigan Catholic | **19**

76 receive Sacred Heart degrees

Jim Graham – Bd. of Trustees
PHOTO BY GREG SHAMUS

Sacred Heart Major Seminary conferred degrees upon 76 graduates last Saturday, April 28, during the 83rd Baccalaureate Mass and commencement. "Regardless of the degree you have attained, you each are invited to give credible and convincing witness to our Lord's presence, to instill spiritual values in a society wishing to transcend the fleeting promises of a material world," Msgr. Jeffrey Monforton, rector, wrote in his program message. "May you communicate an unquenchable thirst for God, providing others concrete ways in which to love our Church and her faith we proclaim." Deacon Anthony Camilleri, who will be ordained a priest later this month, received his Master of Divinity, along with three others. Among other degrees received included pastoral studies, theology, diaconal studies and music. Bishop Earl Boyea, front center, celebrated the Mass.

Sacred Heart Major Seminary
Post Graduation Mass Ceremonies
Trustees, Faculty, Clergy, and Graduates
May 2005

April 2010
Sacred Heart Trustees
Jim Graham, Bob Baker, Kathleen McCann, Chris Rutkowski

Trustee Jim Graham and Cindy in the vesting room before Vespers

Graduation Ceremonies April 2010—Sacred Heart Major Seminary Trustee Jim Graham (3rd from the left)

University of Detroit Academy and High School
Pavers in front of entrance:
Jim is at the top left of large Class of 1952 square,
"Jim Graham, Class President twice and athletics"

1992
University of Detroit High School Class of 1952
Jim Graham presents a check to Fr. Malcolm Carron, President
L to R: Frank Prebenda, Jim Graham, Stan Bartnicki,
Jesuit Priest, Larry Nahrgang, Bill Cosgrove,
Tom Chisholm, President Fr. Carron, Bob Baker

... appearing in "THE DETROIT NEWS"

The Tigers made it one awful weekend

Bob Talbert's column ending with auction prize description.

> as well I missed it.
> Sunday I slipped into Sparky's box seats next to the Tiger dugout and talked awhile with Jim Graham and his family. Jim won six seats, autographed balls and caps with a $3,000 bid at a Marian High School Father's Club education fund auction Sparky and I helped with earlier this summer.
> When I think how bad I felt, think about Graham: He paid $3,000 to sit in the rain and pain Sunday afternoon. That's about what Willie Hernandez gets paid a pitch. Hernandez felt worse than anybody in the park.
>
> *Your Rained-on Tiger Fan,*
> **Bob Talbert**

Highlights in the article . . .

Fall 2009
Madonna University
Cindy and Jim attend the dedication of the new
Lecture Hall and Science Building
Architectural drawings for the Cardinal's Square were unveiled

Breathless Memories 221

June 2010
Madonna University—Livonia, Michigan
Adam Cardinal Maida and Edmund Cardinal Szoka
enjoying a quiet moment before the formal dedication
of the new Cardinals Square Garden

June 2010
Jim in front of dedication wall and plaque
in the Cardinals Square—Madonna University
Presidential Donors—
James and Cindy Graham

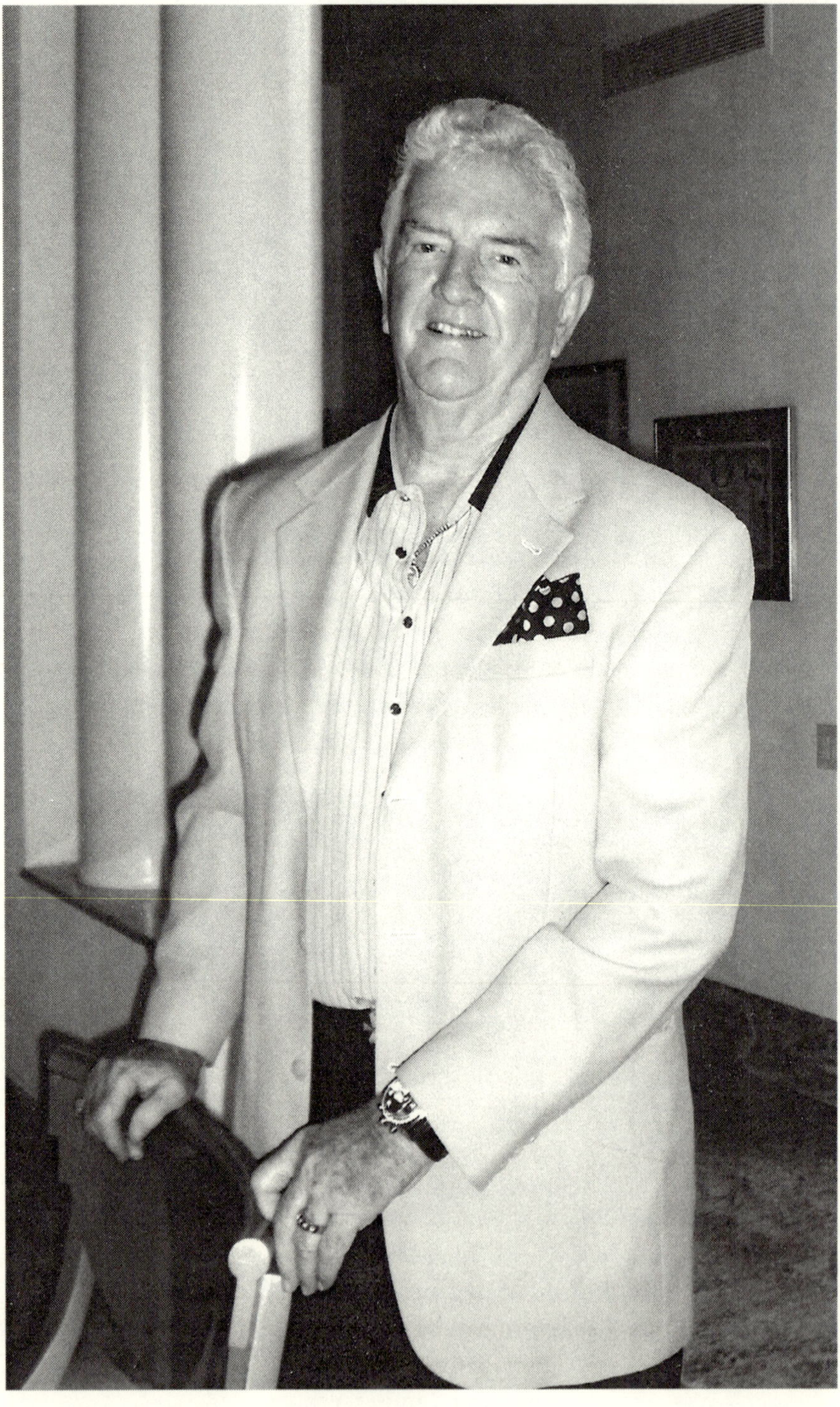

CHAPTER EIGHT

Friends

They say, "You can pick your friends, but not your relatives." In the same way, it is said you are lucky in your life to have the number of fingers on one hand as trusted friends you can count on—for anti-American liberal friends, that means five—Ho! Ho!

I have been blessed in many ways. I had a great mom and dad, sister, Catherine, brothers, Bill and Bob, as good friends—a harmonious family!

Then special blessings—wife Betty for forty-three years, a best friend—along with son Kevin and daughter Jennifer, and upon remarriage, wife Cindy, a parish friend, became a best friend.

Many cousins, the Boyles (including Scotland), the McDevitts, the Hanleys, and nieces and nephews—especially thoughtful nephew Brian James Jordan—have been good pals.

In terms of space, I will recall friends and business associates from different periods of my life:

(1) Childhood: Jim and Tony Stefanson
(2) Grade School: Mike Vanderlinder, Tom Kummer a.k.a. Jay Sebring (killed in July 1969 by the Manson family), Jack Campbell (whereabouts unknown), Ray Grattan, Virginia Philion Rozman, Jerry Millen, Kay Van Poppolen Reilly
(3) Teachers (Friends): Sr. Marie Frances, (St. Benedict), Fr. Murphy, Mr. Pellino (U of D High School)

(4) U of D Jesuit High School Friends: My good friends—especially on teams—Joe Machiorlatti, Tom Chisholm, Jim Roche, Bob Roskopp, Frank Prebenda, Jerry Maurer, and Jim Lacey

(5) University of Detroit—I was a friend with some of the above who went from high school to college and also some others including Jerry Coyne, Bill Markle, and Charlie Rutherford while in college.

(6) I was so busy with college and working I did not have as much time to socialize.

(7) Detroit College of Law: Again with work and studies, I had my hands full. However, Dave Leach, Gene Sikora, Herman Campbell, and Paul Carrier became good buddies.

(8) Work career opened up doors to new friends nationally. Of course, Jim Costello from Philadelphia is a best pal; also, Dr. Tom Brobyn, Mike Poulos, Bob Devlin, and John Graf. Larry Barnett who died twelve years ago was among this group, mostly from my VALIC career. At my prior career with Citizens Mutual Insurance, there was Bob Loesch, Larry Cremen, and Bob Ortolan. Also, John Reilly and Tim Sullivan—both deceased—and John O'Sullivan and Bill Reedy were, and are, good friends.

(9) Neighborhood (6 Mile and Woodward) included many and some from the above childhood and St. Ben's group. Danny Lorigan, Bill Abercrombie, John Ralston, and the Stefanson twins—Jim and Tony—were a few of the most prominent from the neighborhood.

(10) On a national scale, a business associate in Texas called me for assistance. He represented entertainer Willie Nelson, who, because of bad management, was having IRS problems. In October 1992, I met with Willie Nelson in Branson, Missouri. Subsequent to this meeting, Willie invited me to attend his concert that evening insisting that I sit on the stage near his sister Bobbie, his pianist. Thankful for my assistance and advice, he also gave me a copy of his autobiography with the inscription, "To Jim, Thanks . . . Willie Nelson 1992."

(11) A business trip to Las Vegas in January 2000 resulted in another enjoyable experience. After golf, Betty and I dined in the company of Joe Torre and Dow Finsterwald. Joe Torre gave me an autographed copy of his new book. Dow

Finsterwald also wrote, *"All the best to the Graham's."* Joe Torre also presented us with an autographed baseball for Christian dated January 23, 2000.

Friends come in many varieties.

Some like Betty, Kevin, Jennifer, Cindy, brothers (Bill and Bob), sister (Catherine), nieces, and nephews—Nan and Brian Jordan and Brian Graham, Bruce and Alan Graham—my cousins, the Boyles—in Scotland, the McDevitt's, the Hanley's, and their families; and friends like Bob Phillips, Jim Costello, Mike Poulos, John Graf, Msgr. Tony Tocco, Archbishop Allen Vigneron, Msgr. Jeff Monforton, Msgr. Tom Monaghan, and Fr. Eoin Murphy (and many more) can be trusted—thank God.

Some lose your trust because they sell out for selfish gain. Having your faith in someone broken is a sad commentary on the flawed person.

But, it is always best to view a disloyal friend's dishonor as a cheap way to really see what they are, particularly for future trust.

So, pick your best friends wisely.

Best Friends Forever
Brother Bobby, Jim, Sister Catherine, and brother Billy

1995
Handsome Jim and Bedazzling Betty

Breathless Memories 227

The Jordan Family
Nephew-Brian, Niece-Nan, Nephew-Jimmy,
Brother-in-Law-Bill Sr., Nephew-Bill Jr., Niece-Marianne

September 2003—
Surprise pre 70th Birthday Party at Fox & Hounds Restaurant
Nephews Bob & Alan Graham, Son Kevin, Jim,
and Nephews Bruce Graham and Brian Jordan

Jim with first cousins, Catherine (Boyle) Alexander, Jimmy Boyle

Wedding Reception for one of the "Neighborhood Gang" at the local hall on John R.
Standing L to R: Dick Marshall, Jack DePotti, Pat Carr, Ted Jackson, Tony Wasakowski, Charlie Ott, Leonard Barbito, Unknown.
Kneeling L to R; Eddie Ashor, Mike Vanderlinder, Sam Boyian, Jim Graham, Bob Jardine, Rick Galenas

St. Benedict Friends
Jim, Marty Halloran, Ray Grattan, Diane Halloran,
Kay Reilly
on the steps of St. Benedict Church, Highland Park, Michigan

Summer 2005
Enjoying a 'story or two' at Gus O'Connor's Irish
pub in Rochester, Michigan
L to R:
Jim Graham, cousin Ed Alexander, cousin Frank Boyle,
Kevin Graham, cousin Jim Boyle

April 2006
Sacred Heart Major Seminary
Spring Baccalaureate Vespers
In the sacristy with
Cindy, SHMS Rector—Rev. Steven Boguslawski, and Trustee Jim

April 2009
Rev. Msgr. Jeff Montforton—SHMS Rector-President and Jim

June 2008 Oakland, California
Bishop Alan Vigneron shows off his nearly finished
"Christ the Light" Cathedral
(the dedication took place in September 2008)
set on a promontory point overlooking a lake outlet to the San Francisco Bay Waters Cindy and I were houseguests of our friend, the Bishop, for several days as he produced itineraries for us to sightsee Missions and Vineyards, while enjoying culinary treats with him in the evening!

June 2008—Golden Gate Bridge, Sausalito, California
Dave Leach and Jim . . .
Dave and I graduated from the Detroit College of Law in 1959
Wow! Still good friends!

Bob Ortolan, Jim Graham, Lee Halsey
Larco's Restaurant—
Troy, 2008

2002
Fiftieth U of D High School reunion
Tom Chisholm and Jim Graham

2002
Fiftieth U of D High School reunion
Class of 1952
L to R: Classmates: John Klein,
Cousin Frank Boyle, Jim Graham, and Jerry Maurer

234 *James Kenneth Patrick Graham J. D.*

**Autumn 2005
New York City offices of Curragh Inc.
Overlooking Central Park
Jim with good friend Bob Devlin
(former Chairman of American General Corporation)**

December 31, 1986
At the home of Jim & Betty Graham on
Frank Sinatra Drive in Rancho Mirage California
Jim Costello, Bob Phillips and Jim Graham
celebrate the dawn of the New Year

Breathless Memories

**The 1970's
Jim & Betty—two very good friends!**

**July 1999
Jim's retirement Party
At the Detroit Westin Hotel on the Detroit River
Jim greeting his friend and mentor since 1966
Bob Phillips from Palm Springs, California**

1988
Jim Graham, with his Eminence Cardinal Edmund Szoka,
Msgr. Anthony M. Tocco, and John O'Sullivan

American Irish Historical Society

More than 700 attended the $1,000 per person fundraiser at New York's Waldorf-Astoria. The event was the 104th annual dinner for the American Irish Historical Society.

8. Michigan representative Jim Graham(left) of Bloomfield pictured with actor Liam Neeson.

Birmingham/Bloomfield Eccentric Newspaper
December 2001
Jim Graham attended the 104th Irish American Historical Gala
with friends at the Waldorf Astoria Hotel
in Manhattan NYC—
The guest of honor was Actor Liam Neeson

Breathless Memories 237

December 2001
Christmas Party
at Heron Ridge Drive home
L to R: Joe and Rose Genovesi, Msgr Tony Tocco,
Cindy and Jim

June 2004
Celebrating the baptism of
Natalie and Keely Nykerk
Phil Nowakowski, Tom Radascy,
Nieces—Deborah Nowakowski, and Patty Radascy,
and "Uncle" Jim

Good Friends on a pier in Nantucket
Jim Costello, Tom Brobyn, Jim Graham
September 2005

His Eminence Adam Cardinal Maida with his friends
Jim & Cindy Graham
(Chairpersons)
Celebrating the 75th Anniversary Mass
St. Hugo of the Hills Church
September 2007

On the Streets of Gourock, Scotland
October 2002
Andy Hanley and Jim

1985—Gourock Scotland
Jim
with
Aunt May Graham and Cousin Margaret Ward Mc Devitt

Fox & Hounds Restaurant—Bloomfield Hills, Michigan
'69 ½ (surprise—70) Birthday Party
Jim Costello, Bob Phillips Jim Graham, Bob Bendall,
Tom Brobyn

Jim with one of his favorite nephews—Brian Jordan
Celebrating his '36th anniversary of his 39th birthday'
March 8, 2009

June 2008
Hyatt Century City, California Hotel
Niece—Deborah Nowakowski, Jim and Cindy, Phil Nowakowski

Dad with his beautiful daughter Jennifer

Christmas Morning 2005
Joys of the Season!

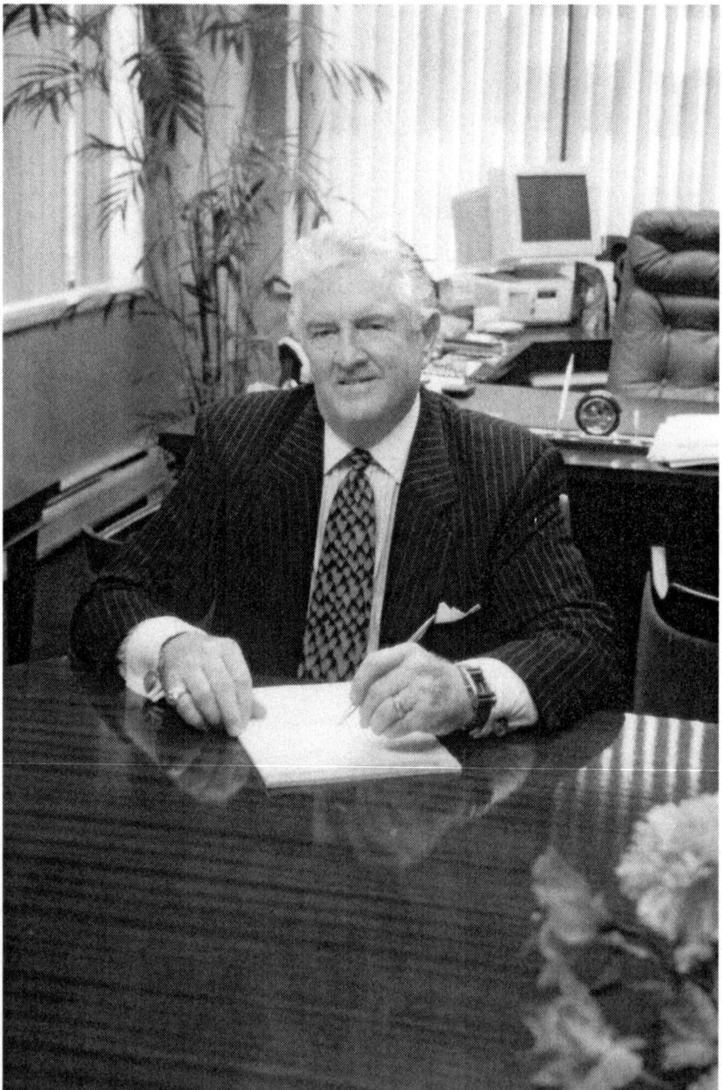

CHAPTER NINE

Deaths (Eulogies)

*T*he loss of a loved one—while an inevitability in life—is always heartrending. I vaguely recall, as a young child, the sorrow evidenced by my mom when her parents died in Detroit and were buried at Mt. Olivet Cemetery. Likewise, my dad was sorrowful about the loss of his parents in Greenock, Scotland. I am pleased I had the opportunity to visit all the gravesites in the United States and Scotland.

The birth/death of baby Marianne in the late 1930s was hard on my parents. My mom (Nan Graham) had surgery for diverticulitis in l963. The surgery was a success, but Dr. Siero prescribed chloromycetin—a newer, strong antibiotic. No check was made for Mom's tolerance. Many cases, years later, confirmed that this RX affected blood cells and caused aplastic anemia in a number of patients. Tragically, it precipitated this in Mom and she died six weeks after successful surgery in 1963 with cause of death as aplasic anemia at North Detroit General Hospital. Mom was a model mother. She was gentle and very kind.

My dad (Robert Graham) was by then retired and liked to work around the house at 193 E. Arizona, Detroit, and the cottage at 11 Conover, Leamington, Ontario.

After Mom (who was born March 30, 1898) died on January 28, 1963, Dad threw himself into household projects. He retiled the entire cottage floors using the adhesives of the time. Unfortunately, the cements were toxic. Working long hours in the late autumn in a closed environment, Dad inhaled too much of the fumes of the adhesive.

In any event, after a few months, he experienced neck pain. He went to the doctor and had tests done. He was admitted to Highland Park General Hospital (now closed). He was diagnosed with multiple myeloma and died within several months on October 29, 1965—another painful loss of a great father. (He had been born on October 23, 1898, in Greenock, Scotland—as was Mom)

On January 1, 1995, my brother Bobby took his dog for a walk on the acreage he and his wife Lorene owned in Leonard, Michigan. When he returned to the house, he collapsed on the living room floor with a cerebral stroke. Bobby was taken to Rochester General Hospital (Crittendon Hospital) and lived in a coma for about ten days. He died on January 18, 1995, at age sixty-five, and he is buried next to his wife Lorene, at White Chapel Cemetery in Troy. They had three children.

My brother Bill was the Boy Scout. His high school yearbook editor referred to his "Van Johnson looks," a reference to a movie star of that era.

In April 1995, Billy was showering to go to work. His wife Pat heard him call, and she found he was having a cerebral stroke. He was rushed to Beaumont Hospital where he lingered for about five days in a coma and then died on April 5, 1995. His organs were donated.

Billy was sixty-seven and another terrific brother to me, the youngest. Bill was a very involved dad with his five sons and was active at the shrine of the Little Flower Parish.

Catherine (born December 4, 1926) was seventy-three when she died on January 2, 2001. She was not feeling well, and she was diagnosed some months earlier with amyliodosis (a dysfunction of proteins).

Catherine was a super sister—also a fine student and pianist as a younger person. Catherine and Bill Jordan had seven children—one died a crib death at six weeks, their son Kevin died at age eighteen in an auto accident, and sadly, Jim Jordan died in December 2007. Catherine was a better sister, daughter, and mom, than one could not ask for.

Betty and I were married forty-three years. She and Jennifer traveled to our condo in Miami Beach to attend a tennis tournament. I was scheduled to come a few days later. When I arrived, Jennifer had said her mom (Betty) wasn't feeling just right, so they had decided to go to a doctor. The doctor said she had a slight case of pneumonia and admitted Betty to Aventura General Hospital in Florida. The doctor predicted that after a few days of antibiotics and rest, Betty would be sent home. Her first night in the hospital, she shared a room with an elderly woman terminally ill with lung cancer. The woman died that night.In retrospect, I personally feel the contaminated room contributed to Betty's demise. We see many situations where a healthy patient is infected by a viral hospital environment. Betty celebrated her sixty-eighth birthday on April 2, 2000, in the hospital.

After several days of talking to the doctors, I insisted that Betty wasn't improving, but getting more ill. They said, "Be patient, it takes time for the antibiotics to kick in."

On Saturday morning, April 8, 2000, the hospital called us at the condo to say that Betty had died. Jennifer and I were flabbergasted by this unexpected news. We rushed to the hospital, and to our shock, Betty was indeed gone.

In questioning the doctors, they claimed she buzzed the nurse saying she had trouble breathing. They said, "A blood clot formed in the leg and traveled to her healthy heart, killing her." In discussing this with doctors in Michigan, it was a clear case of medical malpractice—just as was the case with my mom. As the old saying tragically goes, "You go to the hospital well, and come out dead."

The sudden shock of Betty's passing was painful for all, particularly since she had been such a fine woman, excellent wife, and devoted mother. Msgr. Anthony M. Tocco (Fr. Tony, our pastor) celebrated the funeral Mass with four other priests (Fr. Bob McGrath, Fr. Eoin Murphy, Fr. Charles Kosanke, and Fr. Bob Schuster) concelebrating. Cindy, as director of music at St. Hugo, prepared and played the music at St. Hugo of the Hills Church, our family parish. The prayers, music, eulogies, and attendees in church all added to the spirit of Betty's memory. Fr. Eoin Murphy sang "Danny Boy" at the cemetery mausoleum. It was very moving! Friends came from around the USA: Jim Boyle from Florida, Bob Phillips from California, Jim Costello and Tom Brobyn from Pennsylvania, John Graf from Houston, Mike Poulos and Bob Condon from Texas, Bob Bendall from Ohio, and Paige Davis from Maryland.

Elizabeth (Betty) Graham was temporarily laid to rest at Holy Sepulchre Cemetery mausoleum. At this time, I commissioned a special chapel to be designed within the mausoleum, with a stained-glass window (designed and crafted by Margaret Kavanaugh—a well-known glass sculptor) depicting Mary, the mother of God, and featuring pink Italian marble and a black granite altar with the Graham crest and initialing. Upon completion of this Graham family room, Betty was transferred to this beautiful site. Both sets of parents—Robert and Nan Graham and Emily and Bruno "Brownie" Opalewski—as well as Betty's young twelve-year-old brother (Erwin) also were moved there.

Death confronts us with the great mystery of life. One must go on, celebrating the life accomplishments and memories of that life passed into eternal glory. "Faith cushions despair!"

A Sampling of Eulogies for Dear Ones . . .

Eulogy for William R. Graham
Shrine of the Little Flower Church
Royal Oak, MI
April 8, 1995

The entire family, in particular Bill's wife Pat and their sons Steve, Bruce, Alan, Kurt and Bob, thank you for coming and paying your respects today to Bill's memory. Jack Salter and I are proud to be asked to give testament to the life of a fine human being, Bill Graham. Although the task is impossible, we will do our best.

We grieve today because we have all lost a part of ourselves. Suffering the painful loss of two loved ones suddenly in just three months is devastating. Never was the profound biblical admonition, "God's way is not our way" more true than in the case of my brother Bill. From our perspective it is impossible to comprehend this loss. However, we have no alternative but to look beyond this valley to a brighter horizon.

Bill's life was a testament to quality living. The history of his life demonstrated that he was the kind of person who makes a society successful. Even in dying, he was giving, as his kidneys, liver and cornea were donated to some grateful recipients through the Michigan Gift of Life Program.

As the eldest son of Nan and Bob Graham, he was terrific brother to Catherine and our brother Bob, who we just sadly lost in January, as well as myself.

Bill was married to his wife Pat for forty-four wonderful years. They have five sons, three daughter-in-laws and are grandparents to five grandchildren.

Bill served honorably in combat in the Korean War with the U.S. Army. I remember to this day how my mother prayed daily and worried about his safe return, which came to pass.

Bill graduated from St. Benedict High School and Lawrence Tech. I fondly recall under Bill's graduation picture in his class year book, where the class prophecies are made. It said, "Bill's, Van Johnson appeal, will take him far". (Van Johnson was a movie star of the 1940's.) In school, he played football, basketball, and baseball. Throughout my life I respected

Bill as a doer; whether in academics, athletics, his family, little league coach, his business career and as a good citizen.

Bill was a role model in many ways. An intrinsically good person, a fine husband, a loving father and a great brother. While we mourn this deep loss, we must acknowledge and celebrate a beautiful life.

Bill and Pat have been outstanding parents. As members of this Shrine Parish for 40 years, they graduated all five sons from Shrine High School and currently have grandchildren attending and maintaining the Bill & Pat Graham tradition here at Shrine. As an usher and active community volunteer, he always did his share and then some.

Bill and Pat's record of family success is underscored by the fact that they motivated their five sons to become successful with careers in Marketing, Advertising, an Attorney, Medical Doctor and Educator.

This achievement by itself is impressive and as any parent with kids in college today knows, the sacrifice and cost that accompanies the successful raising and educating of a family is a life-long labor of love.

That was Bill—a long with Pat. He always stayed the good course throughout his multi-faceted life. It is said that each generation stands on the shoulders of the previous generation. Just as our parents emigrated to America in the 1920's for a better life, Bill laid a greater foundation for the next generation.

While a loved ones' voice is stilled, the good memories live on forever. Our memories of Bill are all good, quality memories.

From my earliest days, my older brother Bill and sister Catherine were leaders for Bob and me. Bill was a good student, an active scout leader in old Highland Park 14. He was a senior altar boy and won the exceptional Ad Altar Dei Medal as a youth for excellence in scouting and altar service. I remember the photo in the newspaper to this day. Bill was an achiever to be looked up to; a model older brother who was accomplishing things even as a boy. As a result, he was truly valued by his parents and family. I remember as if it were yesterday, that my mother entrusted me to Bill on my first day of the first grade at St. Benedict's in Highland Park, five and a half decades ago. I am reminded again back through the years how my parents—even then—valued Bill's judgment.

In the 1940's, all St. Ben's students began the day at 8:00 AM with Mass. I remember Billy taking his six year old brother into church and making sure I was in the correct pew and that the nun knew I was there. That is "big time" treatment, when you are a kid starting first grade.

It also occurs to me that while Billy was always steady, Bobby—God rest them both—was more adventuresome.

In a light-hearted sense I wonder if Bobby had been my chaperone that autumn day in 1940, rather than entering a church, I might have ended up at the pool room on John R, shooting "8" ball and drinking beer (only kidding Bobby!)

Further, I remember Bill as the boy entrepreneur. He had a shopping news route and used to pull me on the sled loaded with papers over the snow to cover each house on his route. When Bobby took over the route, he also pulled me on the sled, to the nearest manhole cover and delivered the papers at one stop (down the manhole). But, in fairness, he did replace the manhole cover. In the interest of accuracy, I should point out clearly that while I warmly recall this one incident—one kid's prank was just that. I would not want Bob to be judged by one occurrence. We all did foolish things as kids but I still laugh at this incident. So it takes these examples to lighten our load. But, it underscores the great and loving memories of two great brothers—different in personality, but both always there when you had a need. I know Bob's family realize I mean no disrespect, as I loved Bob and Billy dearly. But Bob also was one of a kind. So much for the welcome contrast in my two fine brothers.

Lastly for myself, I have only the fondest memories of Bill, including the summer Boy Scout camps with Highland Park 14 near Port Sanilac on Lake Huron. My Dad was an Assistant Scoutmaster and Billy was a Scout Group Leader. Those were the good days of summer as a kid, thanks to Bill, Bob and my Dad. I know my sister Catherine feels exactly the same. Our family was reminiscing and all felt extremely positive about Bill's impact on our lives. Kevin, particularly, since Bill was Kevin's Godfather at his Baptism.

Insofar as Bill's marriage of over four decades to Pat Wriggle, they shared a special love. They cared and supported each other with great affection. In fact they lived for each other.

They especially enjoyed the travel with the children as youngsters. In adult years, they frequently traveled to the boys' homes in North and South Carolina, Chicago, and points elsewhere. In fact, a great trip we shared to Scotland was resurrected when we called relatives Scotland concerning Bill's passing. Andy Hanley mentioned that he and my cousin Myra were on a trip to the Scottish Highlands just last weekend and they commented as they passed a country restaurant that they had last been there with Pat and Bill. Again, always together.

As with all of us, Bill was raised in a household which practiced good discipline, respect, decency and a good work ethic that gave your family a reputation you could be proud of. Again, Bill carried on this tradition as an involved, concerned father. I recall anything that boys were in—school projects, athletics, careers—Bill was interested, helpful and always a "hands-on" helper. He continually kept in touch with his sons and was most proud of them. When we are youthful, we at times question this care and interest but it is in the long-run the wise way.

I like to say, "Life is not a hundred yard dash, but a marathon." So too with Bill, his life was a winning marathon. His wife, sons, grandchildren are living testament to Bill's sacrifice for all of us. In fact, as his sons commented, Bill continually made the effort to call and stay in touch with them, advise and give encouragement on a regular weekly basis. In fact, as a dedicated finisher of all he started—in a poetic sense—it is as if he had completed his earthly duties, ran his race, and went to his rest.

My wife often says that to properly raise your children you must unselfishly put your life on hold for twenty years for that child. Bill and Pat unselfishly devoted their lives to the raising of their family. There is no greater love than this. This personifies Bill's life of commitment. In fact, it is not melodramatic nor an exaggeration to say that within the sum total of the Bill Grahams of America is the catalyst that builds and grows this great nation.

While the family held Bill in the highest esteem, I was impressed with a gentleman who introduced himself to me at the funeral home the previous evening. This disinterested witness, if you will, stated unequivocally that Bill was on of the finest men he had ever known.

He indicated that Bill and hired him twenty-eight years ago. This gentleman stated he was at that time a hard drinker and had a pretty rough and ready lifestyle. He emphasized how Bill helped him in his career and he chose to adopt my brother as his mentor.

But most importantly Bill's pleasant manner, his high ethical standards and his dedication to family so impressed this individual that he changed and up-graded his lifestyle. He emphatically gave Bill full credit and asked me to repeat this as a memorial to a good friend.

Finally, this friend of Bill's said that he often sought Bill's advice as they would meet for lunch every couple of weeks in the intervening years after Bill left for another management position at SMC Inc.

One other incident in our reminiscing at the funeral home jogged our memory back. As in word association—our brother-in-law Bill Jordan—a classmate of Bill's said he always thought of Bill as a terrific swimmer with fluid strokes, which he was. Also, for his great handwriting and calligraphy. In the late 1940's, his swimming expertise reminded Catherine and me of a family outing with several families. Two of the sons of Mr. an Mrs. Boyle went swimming and encountered a drop-off. They could not swim and panic set in. Ever the scout, Bill was first in the water—saved one boy and nearly saved the other, who did drown. Point is, Bill was a doer.

In his business career, he was also long on commitment. He was in management of over a quarter of a century with Ross Operating Valve Co. Again, he assisted me with employment in that shop during my summers while in college. He was in a similar capacity at Finite Filter until they merged and Bill's last seven years were as Manager at SMC Inc. I can say Bill enjoyed his business associates immensely and took pride in being productive. He often said he would prefer to never retire completely—so much for his strong work ethic.

I once read an analogy that I feel applies to Bill. We all know of the beauty of the great Redwood trees of the Pacific Northwest. The living Giant Sequoias cast a large shadow on the earth while they stand tall as a living monument. However, when they are cut and felled, the great shadow of their existence is no more visible with our earthly perception.

Likewise, Bill left a living legacy that cast a giant shadow of accomplishment, including love and an example of quality living we all cherish. He touched all of our lives profoundly and deeply; and the ripples will reside and be perpetuated in each of us for the rest of our lives.

Finally, my last conversation with Bill was last Friday, a week ago. I called him to say I was passing the White Chapel Cemetery and had stopped to pay my respects to our brother Bob. We reminisced about him and tentatively agreed to meet for lunch in two weeks, a meeting I regret that was not to be.

In any event, as an effort to put our lives in perspective, I shared a true anecdote that Monsignor Champlin told at a retreat the night before at St. Hugo's.,

When Pope John XXIII was near the end of his life and eighty-three years of age, he nightly went to the Vatican Chapel to pray before retiring As he told the story the Monsignor said, "I suppose you think I am going to tell you that this saintly person then prayed for two or three hours." In point of fact, Pope John knelt down, looked up at the crucifix and said, "Dear Lord, it's your church and I'm going to bed." The moral of the story is obviously that while we mourn our loss of Bill, we also celebrate the over *six decades of Bill's beautiful being and his legacy to us. Bill's life was not as long as we would have wanted, but the quality of his life was superlative. As with the story of the Pope, we must now trust in faith that Bill has earned a higher level of existence with peace and tranquility in God's hands.*

Therefore, Bill will always live in our hearts and memories as a fine human being whom we all respected and will always love dearly.

God Bless his immortal soul.

Eulogy for Elizabeth E. Graham
Friday, April 14, 2000
St. Hugo of the Hills Church

Good Morning.

I say "good" because you are here to honor Betty with her family. You know it's been said that the weather determines the number of people that turn out at your funeral, well Betty's is determined by her love and your reciprocation.

You know Betty taught her family well and out of deep respect, her thoughts expressed over the years to us will guide us through this funeral service. Betty's maxim was, "To those who are given much, much is expected."

We have tried to plan Betty's funeral as she would plan it. Therefore, a few caveats are in order:

Traditional clothing for funerals is always black but Betty's sentiment was that clothing at a funeral should be colorful because it is a celebration of life. Next, if we utilize a whimsical sense of humor during the eulogy by myself, my son Kevin or daughter Jennifer, anecdotes are given with love and respect for Betty.

First, I owe recognition for the St. Hugo Parish support for my family and, in particular, Monsignor Tony and Father Bob. Thanks to all for the many expressions of sympathy, flowers, prayers, food, etc. Betty loved to have Masses offered for her deceased loved ones and we are having many Masses offered for her by us and friends at the Capuchin Monastery.

My special appreciation goes to our family, and in particular our son Kevin and our daughter Jennifer and their spouses, Virginia and Steve; and to our main man, our grandson Christian. Also thanks to all of you—particularly friends of Kevin Jennifer, Betty and myself who went far beyond the call of duty.

In particular, thanks to Debbie Atty who styled Betty's hair and George Mansfield who did her makeup and nails; her niece Debbie and her husband Phil Nowakowski who did the flowers. Thanks also to Betty's niece Pat Radacsy who has been an all around support at all times

I express on behalf of my family, awesome gratitude to those who traveled from all across America. I want to thank our six concelebrating priest friends who are sending Betty on her way to heaven in the highest spiritual fashion.

You know our Pastor Monsignor Tony expresses a lot of wisdom. He has indicated in the past that a eulogy is like a plane ride that should last eight minutes between takeoff and landing—to go much beyond that will cause the plan to crash and burn. Well Monsignor, with all due respect in order to honor Betty as we must, I am going to have to circle the field a few times.

You may be surprised, but I did not sleep well last night. So please be advised that this is not Billy Graham who is delivering this eulogy, but Jimmy Graham, and it comes directly from my heart.

The dilemma in honoring Betty is that I do not wear out my welcome with you. While a difficult task, I will get it done.

Now for the main event—celebrating the great life of Elizabeth E. Graham. Beautiful Betty preferred "Elizabeth", but childhood names do stick. So Betty is the day-to-day name we love her by. Betty is an impossible act to follow. Betty was sixty-eight years of age on April 2, however, she looked and acted years younger. Her chronological years were sixty-eight, but she was a hundred years old in life's achievements.

We had a wonderful marriage for forty-three years. She was continually energetic and vivacious with a lovely disposition. Betty participated in life with great enthusiasm and was not only a terrific wife, but a super Mom as well.

You know that I am not the most patient person in the world, so she had to be a saint to put up with me for all those decades.

Betty and I met, and fell in love in 1955. Betty's great passion was our family. And as Father Rich said last evening, "Her family was her life." Betty is the heart of our family and also the head of our household, although she used to let me think at times I was. Betty was justifiably proud of her centuries of Polish heritage on both parents' sides. One of our greatest experiences was on one of the many trips with Monsignor Tony, where through his good offices, we received a private audience with Pope John Paul II. The Pope was Betty's hero, and Betty is our hero.

In order to demonstrate her great sense of humor, I would like to tell you a brief story of our private papal audience. We were ushered into a great hall. Soon the Pope entered in his white robe and it was a most emotional moment. The Pope came to each of us in line and as he approached me I thought I would score some points with Betty and impress the Pope and her with my Polish fluency. As the Holy Father approached and handed me a Rosary, we began to shake hands and I said "Jak Sie' Mas', your Holiness." The Pope stepped back a little, gave a huge mischievous grin and was 'obviously' impressed with my polish linguistics! I know this because he answered me in Italian. The Pope replied "Molti Bene".

The pope continued on to Betty, they exchanged some words in Polish, and after he had moved a respectable distance, I turned to smile at Betty and get my reward. Betty smiled graciously and leaned over to whisper in my ear, "You would make a lousy Polack."

So you see, she had a beautiful sense of humor.

Some further insights into the gifts that Betty shared with us during her life on earth. She was a gourmet cook. Betty was a master of human behavior—she knew us better than we knew ourselves. Many people have expressed the gift of intuition that Betty had. Betty loved to travel and we were scheduled and ticketed to travel to Spain in June and cruise the Mediterranean to Monte Carlo and France. This now comes under the category of "We plan and God laughs."

Betty exemplified the maxim "Good things come in small packages." She was in her acts of charity and community services truly a giant in accomplishments. Many mourners have used the same common response to our family: "What will I do without Betty" Because of the many charitable giving of herself and her resources, I have received many testimonials.

In thinking of testimonials for Betty, I thought of the bracelet you often see "WWJD". Or in other words, "What would Jesus do." I thought, "What would Betty do" in the following situations? So I asked myself what would I do and I ask that you silently and in the quiet of your own hearts think what you would do in terms of some of the very small random sampling of things that Betty did in her life for other people.

1. COULD I?
   Pray with a loved one as they were dying and then cleanse the corpse out of respect before the funeral home was allowed to come?
   BETTY DID!
2. COULD I?
   Anonymously pay $5,000 to bring current a mortgage foreclosure, so a terminally ill friend could pass away in their own home, with no repayment expected or asked for.
   BETTY DID!
3. COULD I?
   Over 18 months, care for and run the household as a volunteer for three elderly, terminally ill people in their eighties until they died?
   BETTY DID!

These are just a sampling of the random good works that Betty accomplished in her life. It shows how she touched so many lives. Betty played life big and gave her maximum effort to each and everyone of her endeavors.

I have received many, many testimonials as to Betty's goodness. I would like to share a couple of the most poignant ones:

First, I received a card with some beautiful notes in it from a nun that Betty was very friendly with. I will only quote a part of it. "Dear Family, from the largest to the very smallest of God's creatures they knew they were cared about and loved by Betty, when she spread out a banquet for them in her backyard daily, and they all feasted in peace and unity! Our life and world is a colder place without her living presence among us, we see it in the snow and we feel it in the air. I want to express in poetry the feelings that I have . . .

"Life itself can't give you joy
Unless you really will it
Life just gives you time and space
It's up to you to fill it"

"And that Betty did, there were never enough hours in a day to do for those she loved. May she rest in peace."

The next note handed to me at the funeral home was from another life that she touched of the many legions that owe something to Betty. I will just read an exerpt from it.

"I will tell you my best memory I have of Mom", and I might interject he was only a friend, but he referred to her as "mom" and many, many young people did. "On Ash Wednesday she came into the store and she knew I could not get off work; Betty leaned over the counter and gave me ashes, that will always be tucked away in my heart." "Mr. Graham, take care of yourself, I never met you, but through Mrs. Graham and your kids, I feel I have known you a lifetime."

The last letter is from the wife of our surgeon friend in Philadelphia, his medical specialist wife—Laura Brobyn. She writes, "Dear Jimmy, you and your family are in my daily thoughts and prayers. I've thought so much of how grateful I am to have gotten to know Betty during our Nantucket weekend. I'll cherish the memory of our Saturday night dinner when we shared so many accounts of our spiritual beliefs. Add this to our collection. Mary Beth Costello called me last Saturday to tell me the sad news. I thought of Betty continuously throughout the day. Knowing that Betty would approve of this, I walked outside Saturday night and looked up to the heavens at a particularly bright star I hadn't noticed before. I said aloud, "Betty, I know you're a believer. Remember when we talked about signs?" Send me a sign that you're on the other side—make it something that I'd associate with Detroit—you know, a Motown song or Ford truck or something so I'll know it's from you." On Saturday morning, I woke up to a freak snowstorm with four inches of snow. When I opened my front door at five a.m. to let my dog out, I found a perfectly formed snowball on my front step. The snow on the ground was loose. The snowball had not been tossed; there were no "roll marks on the surrounding ground. I smiled and picked up the snowball and gently put it in my freezer. It will remain there until Tom, Mary Beth, Jim, you and myself will take it out and toast the love of our life and know that Betty is all around. Believe. Love, Laura Brobyn."

This gives you some slight indication of the beauty of Betty's presence in so many lives and the love that she touched us with.

Continuing on with the personal sense of Betty, she was a great believer in tradition. She was always the organizer at family functions. She would stay up all night cooking for Christmas and Easter and loved to decorate our home for all the seasons. She and her family maintained her grandmother's cake bread recipe throughout the decades. The 1999 Christmas Party was in the words of many of the 200 or so who attended, "The best ever."

Betty had a great work ethic that she inherited from her Mom and Dad. She always viewed the problems in life as a challenge to be solved rather than something to complain about. The quote attributed to Robert Kennedy suits Betty perfectly. "Some people see things as they are and say, why? Other people dream of things as they should be and say, why not?" This quote personifies Betty's life of caring.

From a personal standpoint, Betty was an awesome soul mate and partner for life. I must honestly say that any success achieved in our life was due directly to Betty's help and good counsel. She was a very low maintenance spouse in the best sense of the word. She left a legacy of love, as a helpmate, as a supportive wife, mother and grandmother to all she touched in her life.

Sometimes metaphors help ease the pain that we experience in life. I think of Betty in relation to the great stately redwood trees in Northern California. Those trees cast a large shady sense of relief on hot summer days. When they are cut down the beautiful shade is gone forever from our presence. Such is the case with Betty.

However, we have an obligation to ensure that her legacy of love and caring goes on. As a result, her family is establishing the "Elizabeth E.

Graham Nursery" in the St. Hugo School and Church complex. The nursery will be named "Christian's Place" in honor of her very special grandson, Christian. We will draw up plans with the architect and create a room that will be beautiful for children, because that was a special consideration in her life and we will so designate on the memorial plaque.

Betty was a patron of the arts and together we donated the beautiful stained glass that you see in the tabernacle area of this church. It is named the "Tree of Life" and nothing could be more appropriate for Betty—we will think of her always when we look at it.

Betty and I were blessed in our marriage with two beautiful, loyal, dedicated children, Kevin and Jennifer, as well as their spouses, Virginia and Steve. Betty's imprint gives me a great source of pleasure because I see her in them.

However, Gannie's pride and joy was our grandson, Christian. To Betty's credit she was always unselfish and always caring and giving. This gave her an inner as well as an exterior beauty. From our youth to this moment, in my mind, Betty is forever young. Whenever I think of Betty I will always think of the old ballad, "Sweet Sixteen." Betty may have been petite in stature but she was a giant in achievement. In sports lexicon, she played life and its problems with a full court press. Betty was in my viewpoint the Mark McGuire or Michael Jordan of superior performance in her life's achievements.

To paraphrase a poem for loved ones that are lost, I would simply like to say, that we will always see our darling Betty in the soft spring rain, in the warm summer breeze, and the majestic autumn colors and in the love and spirit of Christmas. Betty was truly a "Woman for all seasons."

Most importantly, Betty was a role model, teacher and caregiver of the highest order. She often expressed to me that I had a saintly Mother. My response was that my greatest accolade to Betty, which I often expressed to her in life, I used to say to Betty, "Honey, the greatest compliment I can pay to you is, that you are a complete image and likeness of my wonderful Mother."

I have a unique request to compliment Betty's life and her job well done as the highest standard. Would you please stand? Would you kindly honor Betty's wonderful life with a standing ovation. Thank you.

Your tremendous outpouring of love and support is the most magnificent tribute to Betty's legacy of love. Betty has left this earthly presence, but I truly believe, as she did, that she lives on in a better place.

Let us pledge to emulate Betty's life of unselfish, caring and kindly love for all living things. I close with Betty's own wise words, "It is not the years you live, but the life you put into those years."

May God keep you always, Darling Betty.

Eulogy for Catherine F. Jordan
January 4, 2001 St. Hugo of the Hills Church

Good Morning,

On behalf of Bill Jordan, my brother-in-law, their children and our entire family, thank you for paying your respects to Catherine Jordan.

With our limited grasp of the mystery of life and death, it seems a funeral presents a contradiction in terms. On one hand, we grieve for a devastating loss. While on the other hand, we celebrate the beautiful, productive life of Catherine Jordan.

The leveler of this apparent contradiction is a faith in our resurrection. Catherine—as did our Mother—had a sustaining commitment to this religious belief.

A verse I recently came across epitomized Catherine's belief credo. The verse reads as follows:

When you are born you cry and world rejoices,

Live your life with meaning so when you die

The world cries and you rejoice.

Catherine's great husband of over 50 years, Bill Jordan, wrote a poignant obituary. No eulogy of a wonderful life of 74 years would do justice to Catherine without an elaboration of the facts of her obituary. A brief biographical sketch will interest you.

Catherine Frances Graham was born to our parents Nan and Bob Graham on December 4, 1926. The first of five children, Catherine was always the pace-setter. She excelled at scholastic accomplishments at St. Benedict in Highland Park, and at the University of Detroit, as well.

Catherine was accomplished in music, both singing and piano. To my parents' delight, she always played the piano and lead family sing-a-longs at get-togethers, as was the custom in the 1940's.

Catherine was very attractive and was chosen Queen, for the May crowning, during high school. The May Day procession was very important in those days.

Athletically, Catherine was a good ice skater, fine swimmer and an outstanding tennis player. In fact, I was reminiscing with Cath just two weeks ago about how impressed I was by the tennis tournament she won in her senior year of high school at Highland Park's Ford Field. I kidded Cath at that time that Jennifer got her tennis winning tennis genes from her.

Catherine and Bill had seven children. Tragically, two died young. Their fine children: Brian, Nan, Bill Jr., Marianne and Jimmy, plus eight grandchildren are their pride and joy. They all gave great support during Cath's final days.

Their parents have been great role models. They say, that, "the apple never falls far from the tree." Catherine and Bill's sons, daughters and grandchildren are successful in law, nursing, and business. This is no small legacy in today's world.

Catherine made her statement in life by her high moral standard, her charitable faith and her legacy of good woks.

As for myself, Catherine immeasurably molded my life. She was from my earliest days, an influence on my formation. Because I have known Catherine longer than anyone on this earth, her positive influence has been enduring. Thanks to her, we never had a harsh word.

I could share many fond memories, but one of my most cherished is her giving love. When I was twelve years old, Catherine worked in Downtown Detroit as the old Manufacturers National Bank. She had our Mother send me downtown on the Woodward streetcar where Catherine met me at Grand Circus Park. She took me to Hudson's for a meal, and the to clothier Harry Suffrin, at State and Shelby, and bought me a new Easter suit. What a great sister!

More importantly, Catherine left a monumental mark on this world as a sister, wife, mother, grandmother, and friend. In many respects she defined the word "Mother". She demonstrated unquestioned love and an unselfish and caring nature. She lived a devout Christian life.

We judge a person's quality by how they lived their life. Catherine is not found wanting in this regard. Equally important in assessing life's quality is how one faces death.

Catherine knew she was terminally ill. On our visits and talks on the phone, we were strengthened by her courage in her final days. The strong faith that sustained Catherine in life also sustained her in her final days.

Her courage, dignity, and self-respect was maintained to the end. Within an hour of her passing, Bill, Nan, Jimmy and Tom were tidying up for Catherine, as ill as she was, she joked with them about the job they were doing. That's fortitude!

There is a lesson for all of us in this beautifully lived life. We must draw strength from the example and staying power Catherine exhibited in the life that she lived to the end. We would dishonor her if we did anything less.

Ralph Waldo Emerson wrote: "The ornament of a home is the family who frequents that home." Catherine was the bright ornament that should adorn our own personal home.

Finally, irrespective of how long we live, the Book of Life is brief. Therefore, when our time comes we hope to hear the biblical words that Catherine has heard, "Well done, O good and faithful servant."

Regretfully
I have been unable to locate the eulogy written and delivered for my brother Robert Graham who died in January, 1995 . . .

Eulogy for Lorene J. Graham
James K. Graham
May 21, 2004

Good day!

Thanks for coming this morning to celebrate the life of Lorene Graham. She lived 77 years, which is never enough.

Kathleen and Brian and the family appreciate your presence and support. We all are saddened by this huge loss—but we celebrate her passage to eternal life.

An Irish expression says it best:

> "A lifetime is not measured by the number of *breaths* you take, but rather, by the moments that leave you *breathless*."

Lorene had many blessings in her life that took her *breath* away. They are too numerous to mention, but I will highlight a few:

(1) She came from a fine family
(2) Lorene and Bobby had a great marriage for over 40 years—
I was honored on February 22, 1951 to be their best man (as our oldest brother, Bill, was serving with the military in Korea—just as Bobby had previously served in Japan just after WW II).
What a great day! They were both radiant—a real *breath-taking* couple on a *breath-taking* day.
(3) Lorene was always *breathless* because she was blessed with children:
Robby, Kathleen, and Brian, her granddaughter Paige, and son-in-law, Steve.
(4) Lorene always took our collective family's *breath* away, as she was a lovely warm person to our entire family—what an epitaph—"Lorene was universally loved by everyone."

It is for all of these *breathless* moments of her life that we celebrate a great person and a wonderful life, today.

Because it was a beautiful life, it makes this passing so painful.

However, we are reconciled by the fact that her illness is behind her and she enjoys eternal beauty.

An ancient Chinese proverb prudently states: "What a caterpillar views as death, wise men see a transformation into a beautiful butterfly." This is Lorene's transformation.

Finally, while I know by certain faith, she has passed into eternal happiness, I have further proof by an event that happened last evening . . .

As we were driving home after paying our respects to Lorene, on the spur of the moment, we decided to stop at the new Village Mall. (You know I can't pass up a mall!)

As we were strolling around and discussing what a great person Lorene was, and, how said it was to lose her, we walked by an outdoor gazebo with a trio playing live music.

I, surprised, said to Cindy, "Do you hear what they are playing?" We stopped in our tracks to listen. And to our amazement, they were playing Lorene and Bobby's favorite song: "Sweet Lorraine."

With millions of songs over the centuries, it was no coincidence that, at that moment, in that place, that particular song—their song—came upon us.

The message was loud and clear—Lorene and Bob are together again. Now, I know she rests in peace.

Thank You

Eulogy for Robert S. Phillips
September 12, 2009
Lisle Funeral Home—Fresno, California

Good Afternoon,

To begin Maureen was most gracious when she asked me to say a "few words".

Thank you, Maureen,

However, as you know an attorney can never just say a few words, but I will be brief—hopefully without shortchanging Bob's memory.

First of all, let me express our condolences to you Maureen, Bobby, Linda, Michael and your families.

You know it has been said,

"It is not the breaths you take in life that count, but the moments that leave you breathless that really matter."

Bob created many memorable and breathless moments.

I first met Bob in September, 1966 (43 years ago to the month) in Detroit, Michigan. Bob and Maureen had moved to Detroit to pioneer a new product from a new company—the Variable Annuity Life Insurance Company and its product—the Variable Annuity.

I was a thirty-two year old attorney, and a client of mine had told Bob about my experience in wills, trust, and financials. Long story short—Bob hired me and the two of us hit it off immediately.

Bob accepted a promotion in 1974 and moved to Houston. He recommended that I be promoted and succeed him. In 1975, Bob and Maureen moved to La Jolla, California to pursue new opportunities.

I must say Bob was gifted, and one of those few people that was highly intellectual as well as verbally able to articulate his creative ideas. As a team, Bob the idea man, and yours truly, the lawyer made a good business duo.

Bob would feel I was remiss if I did not acknowledge Ambassador Glen Holden and his wife Gloria seated next to Cindy and me. Glen was our CEO and another of the few former associates who were gifted intellectually and creatively.

As I think back, Bob conceptualized some of these businesses:

(1) The Umpqua River Ranch in Oregon

(2) The Polo Stores with our meetings in Manhattan with Ralph Lauren, CEO—Peter Strom, and even Cary Grant (who was on the Board of Faberge)
(3) Garageman—a garage organizing business
(4) Real Estate Broker in Palm Springs with Maureen. They were good enough to sell us not only one home—near them in Rancho Mirage, but also an incredible home on Southridge Mountain in Palm Springs—still my favorite!

While time does not permit mentioning other major accomplishments, the record shows that Bob had a creative and productive career, all the while being a great person.

He also had a sense of humor that leaves us with breathless memories.

For example,

While reminiscing about Bob's life with my son Kevin, he reminded me of the time in the 1980's when we were driving on the freeway back to Palm Springs from the recently opened Polo Store in Costa Mesa . . .

Kevin was in the back seat and said,

"Mr. Phillips, your new Mercedes 600 is very smooth riding for our speed."

Bob laughed, put his hand over the speedometer on the dashboard and said, "How fast do you think we are going, Kevin?"

I was in the passenger seat and could see we were traveling at well over 100 hundred miles per hour . . .

From the back seat, Kevin truthfully replied,

"I don't know, Mr. Phillips, but we just passed a California Highway Patrol car parked on the shoulder of the entrance ramp . . ."

I rarely saw Bob react in such a non-plussed way, but he retained our speed—the cop probably didn't feel he could catch us and no chase ensued.

With great relief, we had a great laugh once we realized we weren't being pursued.

A second "breathless moment took place at the Tamarisk Villas in Rancho Mirage, at the first home Bob sold us near his own home in the development. There were some fabulous grapefruit trees.

Well, on Saturday morning—Bob and our mutual late pal, John Parsons—could not wait for the regular landscaper to come on Monday morning. So, armed with ladders and chain saws—these two (certainly no gardeners)—took on the trees. One in particular was huge.

. . . like the Three Stooges giving a haircut—Curley shaves one sideburn up higher to match the other too short sideburn, continuing until Moe is bald!

. . . so too, with the tree cutting . . . the large tree became a stump . . .

I still have a belated good laugh at the memory. Bob had a good sense of humor.

So here today, we recount the eighty-three years of Bob's life along with all its bounty. His memory will always live on.

Within that context, I am reminded of the lady who has cut my hair for the last thirty-four years . . . each time I leave the shop, she admonishes me as follows:

> "Remember, yesterday is history
> Tomorrow is a mystery
> And today, is the PRESENT . . .
> A PRESENT to be lived to the fullest."

Bob lived his life to the fullest and what better legacy could he leave us. God Bless, Bob!

October 18, 2002
Lyle Hill overlooking the River Clyde
Gourock Scotland

CHAPTER TEN

Retirement and Remarriage

My thirty-three-year career with VALIC ended in retirement on December 31, 1999. I began a generous five-year consultant contract with VALIC—AIG that concluded December 31, 2004.

What a fabulous retirement party the company threw me! July 17, 1999! It was a beautiful, sunny day. Three hundred guests (employees, family, and friends) were invited. Some came from around the country (Texas, California, Pennsylvania, etc.) to attend my retirement party.

It was a lavish reception and dinner at the Riverfront Banquet Room at the Detroit (now Marriott) Renaissance Center Hotel in a beautiful place with a view of the Detroit River and Windsor, Ontario, as we enjoyed music and entertainment. Ending this part of the celebration, a minor roast with Jim Costello, Tom Brobyn, and me in tuxedos, including a sung parody by the three of us to the tune of "Thanks for the Memory," was indeed a "memory!" The words were written by Laura Brobyn.

July 17, 1999
Detroit Renaissance Hotel
Riverfront Room

The GRAHAM Family
Virginia, Jim—the Honoree, Betty,
Jennifer and Kevin

Jim with a favorite classy friend, Mike Papista

Traveling friends from Pennsylvania—Dr. Tom & Laura Brobyn with the 'Guest of Honor' Jim

Nephew Alan Graham, Niece Debbie Nowakowski, Daughter Jennifer, and Margaret Graham— Alan's wife

Jim and daughter Jennifer

Jim with Mike and Bob Phillips

Brother-in-law, Bill Jordan—Jim—sister, Catherine Jordan

Jim sharing story with guests
Cindy Dailey and Fr. Bob Schuster

Mike Poulos, Jim, John Graf, Kevin, Jim Costello

Jim and Betty smile as the 'toasters' and 'roasters'
share their thoughts!

Pat Laughlin presents a citation from the State of Michigan to Jim honoring his many business accomplishments

Mike Poulos (Chairman-VALIC) and Jim

John Graf (President/CEO—VALIC) with Jim

> Dear Jim,
>
> Congratulations on your many productive years of service to VALIC and, most importantly, your customers. The legacy you have built will be remembered for many years and is inexorably woven into the fabric not just of the Detroit Region, but all of VALIC. To be successful is a wonderful thing, but to do it with style, integrity, and humanity is truly inspiring to those of us who will follow. Best wishes to you and yours, and you will be missed.
>
> Sincerely,

June 1999
Retirement congratulatory letter from
VALIC CEO John Graf

> As one of VALIC's sales pioneers, **Jim Graham** enjoys several unique distinctions. His entire 33-year career with VALIC has been as Detroit regional manager. He has won the coveted Manager of the Year award five times and helped the Detroit region become VALIC's leader in the K-12 market. Jim will spend more time with his wife and family, and is looking forward to traveling more and returning to his interest in the piano, oil painting, and writing.

Feature article on Jim's 33-year career with VALIC

AMERICAN GENERAL
HOUSTON, TEXAS

ROBERT M. DEVLIN
CHAIRMAN, PRESIDENT AND
CHIEF EXECUTIVE OFFICER

July 10, 1999

Mr. James K. Graham
Vice President
American General Retirement Services
1301 W. Long Lake Road, Suite 340
Troy, MI 48098-6349

Dear Jim,

Congratulations on your outstanding achievements. Your many contributions, insights and support over the last 35 years have made a significant difference to American General - I personally appreciate your outstanding performance.

Jim, it is individuals like you who possess a high degree of integrity, a solid work ethic and a high energy to succeed that sets you apart - you are a true professional in every sense of the word.

You are to be commended highly for all you have achieved and I look forward to keeping in touch with you.

God Bless and all the best to you and your family.

Best regards,

[signature]

Robert M. Devlin

2929 ALLEN PARKWAY • HOUSTON, TEXAS 77019 • 713.831.1177

**Congratulatory letter from Robert Devlin
Chairman, President, & CEO—American General Corporation
July 1999**

"Grand Retirement party!"
The 'VALIC Three Tenors' (Tom Brobyn, Jim Graham, &
Jim Costello) singing a parody about Jim's 33 year career . . .
July 17, 1999
Grand Ballroom—Westin Renaissance Hotel
"Thanks For the Memories"

Autographed picture from our neighbor—Bob Hope—
His home was just above ours on Southridge
Mountain, Palm Springs, CA

We then bussed the three hundred attendees to the old Tiger Stadium for the original Three Tenors' last concert together. I might add we had fabulously situated seats in what was the last major event at the old Tiger Stadium. Luciano Pavrotti, Placido Domingo, and Jose Carrera were outstanding. A fabulous, memorable day and evening!

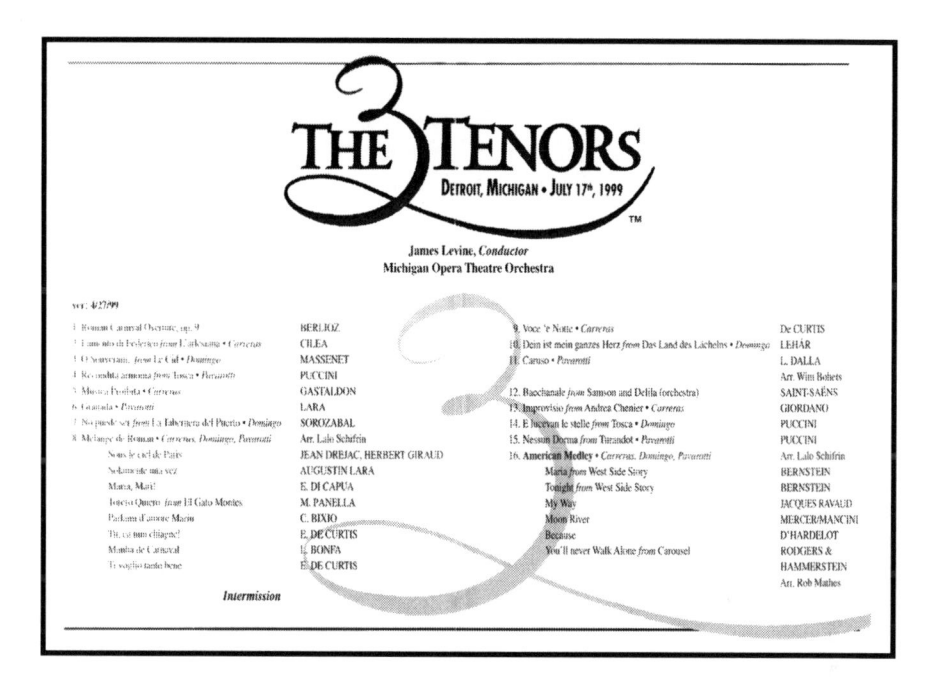

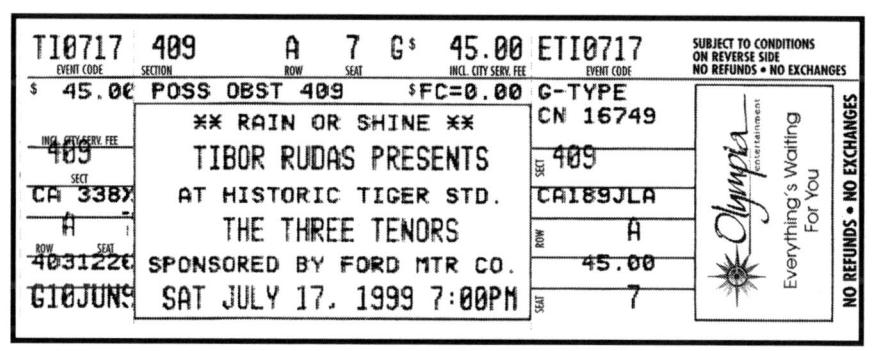

Concert Ticket
Three Italian Tenors
300 guests invited to attend after Jim's retirement dinner
This event was the 'Trios' last appearance together on the concert stage and the last event to be held at Tiger Stadium!

07/13/1998 16:39   408-6557839

Rudas Organization

FAX

page 1/2

DATE: July 13, 1998
TO: Frank Stella — 313-342-8398
FROM: Roger A. Sandau — 408-649-5458
RE: The Three Tenors

Dear Mr. Stella:

Your facsimile to Mr. Tibor Rudas, dated July 10, 1998, has been forwarded to my attention for reply as to the general contractual points for a possible concert featuring The Three Tenors in Detroit, Michigan. In this regard, I have set forth below the relevant financial terms and a short list of the respective obligations of the presenting company and our company:

1. **Fee:** The fee is US$10M and is payable as follows: 25% upon the signing of the agreement (not later than August 28, 1998); 25% on or before November 27, 1998; 25% on or before February 26, 1999; and 25% on or before May 28, 1999.

2. **Obligations:** The presenting company shall be responsible for providing (at its expense) the venue, stage, seating, venue staff, local labor, advertising and publicity.

    Rudas Theatrical Organization shall be responsible for providing (at its expense) the artists, conductor, orchestra and the complete production for the concert, including, sound and lighting equipment, transportation and technical production personnel.

I know that you have invited Mr. Rudas to travel to Detroit, however kindly be advised that he is presently in London mixing the audio and video tapes from the Paris concert under very tight deadlines. Nevertheless, in the event that you are able to proceed forward with discussions under the above-referenced terms, Mr. Rudas will endeavor to find a time to travel to Detroit to engage in more detailed negotiations for this concert.

RUDAS THEATRICAL ORGANIZATION

A Company 'Insider' letter explaining the terms of Performance for the "Three Tenors" concert

Placido Domingo on the big screen

THE THREE MONEYMAKERS

PHOTO FROM FORD MOTOR CO

Jose Carreras (left), Luciano Pavarotti and Placido Domingo greet the press in Detroit. Local restaurants were booked up for the big event.

The Three Tenors
Jose Carerra, Luciano Pavrotti, Placido Domingo

Magnificent view and staging from our seats . . .
The transformation of the stadium to Roman forum was incredible!

Super seats and super people . . .
Jim & Betty Graham, Jim Costello, Tom Brobyn

[DISCOVER DETROIT]

Last Call at the Corner

FOR 86 SEASONS, TIGER STADIUM HAS PROUDLY SERVED AS THE HOME OF THE DETROIT TIGERS. ONE OF THE CITY'S MOST RECOGNIZED LANDMARKS, THE CORNER OF MICHIGAN AND TRUMBULL HAS BEEN SYNONYMOUS WITH BASEBALL IN THE MINDS OF DETROITERS FOR 100 YEARS.

That will all change after this year.

Next season, the Tigers will take up residence in the new Comerica Park on Woodward, making this the final time fans can experience a game in one of the original ballparks.

Even before there was a Tiger Stadium, the location at Michigan and Trumbull had served as the Tigers' home. Known as "The Corner," it's the oldest home of professional baseball in the world. The Tigers played their first game there on April 28, 1896, when they trounced the Columbus Senators 17 to 2.

The Tigers' original stadium, Bennett Park, seated 8,000 people. As the Tigers' popularity grew, it became apparent that a larger structure was needed. Owner Frank Navin had Bennett Park razed and built a new stadium on the same site. Opening on April 20, 1912, Navin Stadium, as it was then called, was essentially the same Tiger Stadium that stands today. Twenty-six thousand fans crammed into a building designed to hold 23,000 and were rewarded with a 6-to-5 Detroit triumph over Cleveland in an 11-inning game. Despite the rousing success of the opener, the stadium was eclipsed in the papers the following morning by the sinking of the Titanic.

Navin Stadium went through a series of expansions throughout the '20s and '30s. In 1938, its seating was increased to 53,000 and the stadium was renamed Briggs Stadium by owner Walter Briggs. Tiger Stadium didn't officially become Tiger Stadium until 1961, under owner John Fetzer.

Along with Boston's Fenway Park, which opened on the same day, Tiger Stadium shares the distinction of being the oldest active park in Major League Baseball. In addition to serving the Tigers, Tiger Stadium was also the home of the Detroit Lions from 1938 to 1974, when they moved to the Pontiac Silverdome, their current home.

With the Tigers' final home game scheduled for September 27, Detroit watches as the rich history of Tiger Stadium draws to a close. Fans shouldn't miss this chance to come out and enjoy a game in one of the last of the grand old ballparks. It will be the final opportunity to experience this Detroit landmark. (For the Tigers' schedule, see the "Sports/Personal Recreation" section on Page 73, and for information on a money-saving discount Tiger package, see Page 72.)

Tiger Stadium
2121 Trumbull Ave.
Detroit
(313) 963-2050

Above: The corner of Michigan and Trumbull, home of Tiger Stadium
Inset: Tiger Stadium in 1969

Salute to Tiger Stadium
Detroit Historical Museum
5401 Woodward Ave.
Detroit
(313) 833-1805
September 25 through September 26

I have enjoyed my retirement. Sad to say, I was only four months into retirement when—as indicated earlier—Betty passed away April 8, 2000.

After my retirement, I was asked to join the board of trustees at Sacred Heart Major Seminary as well as the finance committee. I increased activity at our parish, St. Hugo of the Hills—Christmas decorator, volunteer, co-chair of the seventy-fifth-anniversary celebration, also chairman of St. Benedict Foundation, etc.

I maintained the daily physical-fitness regime that I have observed my entire life. This has been a physical and psychological benefit throughout my life—but particularly in retirement.

I also had the opportunity to travel a little more and visit with former associates at VALIC. Jim Costello and Todd Adams got together for golf and socializing.

Retirement has afforded more time to visit and help with the grandchildren. This is especially true as Jennifer's twin daughters—Keely and Natalie—joined Elizabeth, and of course, their older cousin, Christian, grows older.

During retirement in 2001, I began to see a friend of over twenty years at the parish, Cindy Dailey, who was St. Hugo's director of music and the widow of Tom Dailey, both of whom Betty and I knew well. It is rare and fortunate that you meet two wonderful women in your lifetime to whom you are willing to make a commitment of marriage. To their credit, Betty and Cindy shared many fine characteristics that their 100 percent Polish heritage endowed them with.

In any event, as our friendship grew, it flowered into marriage on October 18, 2002. Since both of us had so many friends at home in Bloomfield Hills, and not wishing to offend anyone with an incomplete guest list, we decided to celebrate the wedding at our surrogate family parish, St. Ninian's in Gourock, Scotland.

Msgr. Thomas Monaghan, our friend, officiated with our family present. Msgr. Tom had arranged for a Celtic harpist and young bagpiper to provide memorable music, and Ruth French (Cindy's best friend from Scottsdale, Arizona) and Kevin, my son, were our official witnesses. All of the flowers were "true" Scottish blooms—heather, thistle, white lilies acanthus berries, and clover greens. The ribbons were clan plaid, and many in attendance, including the groom, were dressed in kilts. The weather was lovely as was the bride. Our set pictures included scenes shot on the highest point (Lyle Hill) in

Gourock, overlooking the River Clyde. Afterwards, the entire group dined and enjoyed traditional Scottish wedding cake (secured by Myra, Andy, and daughters from Glasgow) at the Greenock Club where my cousin Andy Hanley was a sponsoring member.

Cindy Dailey

and

Jim Graham

warmly invite you to share in their joy

at the celebration of their marriage

Friday, the eighteenth of October

Two thousand and two

This celebration will begin at

Six o'clock in the evening

St. Ninian Catholic Church

7 Royal Street

Gourock, Scotland

A reception will follow the Nuptial Mass

at the Greenock Club

Greenock, Scotland

Your presence and love are cherished gifts,
We request no others

Extract of an entry in a REGISTER of MARRIAGES

(Section 37(2) of the Registration of Births, Deaths and Marriages (Scotland) Act 1965)

MG 0664273CE

MARRIAGE Registered in the district of	District No.	Year	Entry No.
Inverclyde	640	2002	261

1. When married: 2002 October Eighteenth
2. Where married: St Ninian's Church Gourock

3.	Bridegroom	Bride
Forename(s)	James Kenneth	Cynthia Elaine
Surname(s)	Graham	Dailey
	(Signed) James K Graham	(Signed) Cynthia Elaine Dailey
4. Occupation	Attorney at Law (retired)	Musical/Liturgical Director (retired)
5. Marital status	Widowed	Widowed
6. Date of birth	Year 1934 Month 3 Day 8	Year 1947 Month 2 Day 6
7. Country of birth	United States of America	United States of America
8. Usual residence	1744 Heron Ridge Drive Bloomfiled Hills, Michigan, United States of America	1161 Ivyglen Circle Bloomfield Hills, Michigan, United States of America
9. Father's forename(s) surname(s) and occupation	Robert Graham Millwright Foreman (deceased)	John Joseph Zerbiec Motor Vehicle Buyer (retired)
10. Mother's forename(s) maiden surname surname(s) and occupation	Hannah Boyle(ms) or Graham (deceased)	Wanda Mary Karpinski(ms) or Zerbiac (retired)
11. Person solemnising with designation	(Signed) Thomas J Monaghan Priest St Ninian's Church Gourock PA19 1PN	
12. Witnesses with addresses	(Signed) Kevin J Graham 1744 Heron Ridge Drive, Bloomfield Hills, Michigan, United States of America	
	(Signed) Ruth A French 6324 31st Street. Phoenix, Arizona, United States of America	
13. When registered	Year 2002 Month 10 Day 21	14. (Signed) Marion McNee Assistant Registrar
15.		
16.		

Extracted from the Register of Marriages on Twentyfirst October 2002.

(Signed) Marion McNee Asst Registrar

The above particulars incorporate any subsequent corrections or amendments to the original entry made with the authority of the Registrar General.

Warning

It is an offence under section 53(3) of the Registration of Births, Deaths and Marriages (Scotland) Act 1965 for any person to pass as genuine any copy or reproduction of this extract which has not been made by a district registrar or assistant registrar and authenticated by his signature. This includes any photocopy made by any other person.
Any person who falsifies or forges any of the particulars on this extract or knowingly uses, gives or sends as genuine any false or forged extract is liable to prosecution under section 53(1) of the said Act.
This extract is evidence of an event recorded in a register of marriages. It is NOT evidence of the identity of the person(s) presenting it.

Breathless Memories 291

Rehearsal Dinner in Gourock Scotland
October 17, 2002
L to R: Elizabeth, Jennifer, Christian, Jim, Cindy, Steve, Fr. Tom

October 18, 2002
Lyle Hill, Gourock Scotland following Cindy and Jim's wedding
at St. Ninian Church
Cindy and Jim with her two sons Phil Dailey and Rick Anderson

Dapper Jim and Beaming Cindy

October 18, 2002
Outside St. Ninian's Church in Gourock Scotland
as the young piper pipes the new couple

Cindy and Jim with family and friends
at their reception at the Greenock Club

Msgr. Monaghan presented us an exquisite papal blessing at the end of the Mass—so many great memories. It hangs in our home as you enter the front door.

The Holy Father John Paul II
cordially imparts the desired
Apostolic Blessing to
James Kenneth Graham and
Cynthia Elaine Verbiec Bailey
on the occasion of their Marriage
that their love consecrated at the altar
will be blessed each day with divine graces
St. Ninian's Church - Gourock, 18th October 2002

Upon returning to Bloomfield Hills, our pastor, Msgr. Tony, insisted that he bless our marriage in our home church of St. Hugo of the Hills. Further, his only condition was that we wear our Scottish wedding garb, including my kilts. The chapel was full of friends and family, and he toasted us at the reception he hosted at the rectory on November 1, 2002.

Cindy—as was Betty—has been a wonderful complement to my life. Hopefully, we will be blessed with good health so we can enjoy retirement and the fruits of our labors.

Wonderful Family Events

St. Hugo of the Hills Church
July 2004
Christening Day for the Twins
Keely Noelle and Natalie Elaine
Grandparents: Jim & Cindy Graham,
Granddaughter: Elizabeth Anne Nykerk (age 3)
Proud Daughter Jennifer (Graham) Nykerk holding Keely Noelle,
Grandson: Christian James Graham (age 10)
Proud Son-in-Law Steve Nykerk holding Natalie Elaine,
Son and daughter-in-Law: Kevin & Virginia Graham

St. Hugo of the Hills Church
Easter Vigil 2005
Rick Anderson, Steve Nykerk, Phil Dailey,
(the "three 'professional' Paschal Candle Bearers'")
Msgr. Tony Tocco, and Jim
At the center of the Easter Vigil Liturgy is the new fire
(represented in the lighted Paschal candle)
This candle is carried into the Church and moved to
various positions as part of the service—it weighs nearly 50 lbs!
Rick, Steve, and Phil have shared the role for over 8 years.

Celebrating Jim's 70th Birthday at home
March 2004
Jennifer, Christian, the birthday Boy—Jim, Kevin, Virginia, Steve

Easter Sunday, April 2010
After enjoying a delectable brunch at the "Kingsley"
Back: Kevin, Virginia, Cindy, Jim, Jennifer, Christian,
Curtis Clinton (Jim's nephew)
Front: Steve, Natalie, Elizabeth, Keely

September 2003
Jennifer and her Dad at the Fox & Hounds
Celebrating his 69 ½ birthday

Jim's 75th Birthday party at the Iroquois Club
March 8, 2009
Jim with Cindy's Family
Phil and Bernadette Dailey, Wanda Zerbiec and
Tim Hartmannszerbiec (Cindy's Mom and Brother)
Cindy & Jim, Jean Stieber and Rick Anderson

A friend's wedding at Subiaco Retreat House in Lake Orion
Back: Phil Dailey, Rick Anderson, and Jim Graham
Front: Bernadette Dailey, Theresa & Thomas Dailey,
Cindy, and Emily Dailey

Celebrating Anne (Cindy's Sister) Merenda's 45th Birthday
June 2005
Jim, Cindy, Tim Hartmanszerbiec (Cindy's brother),
Wanda Zerbiec (Cindy's Mom)
Anne Marie Merenda, John Zerbiec (Cindy's Dad)

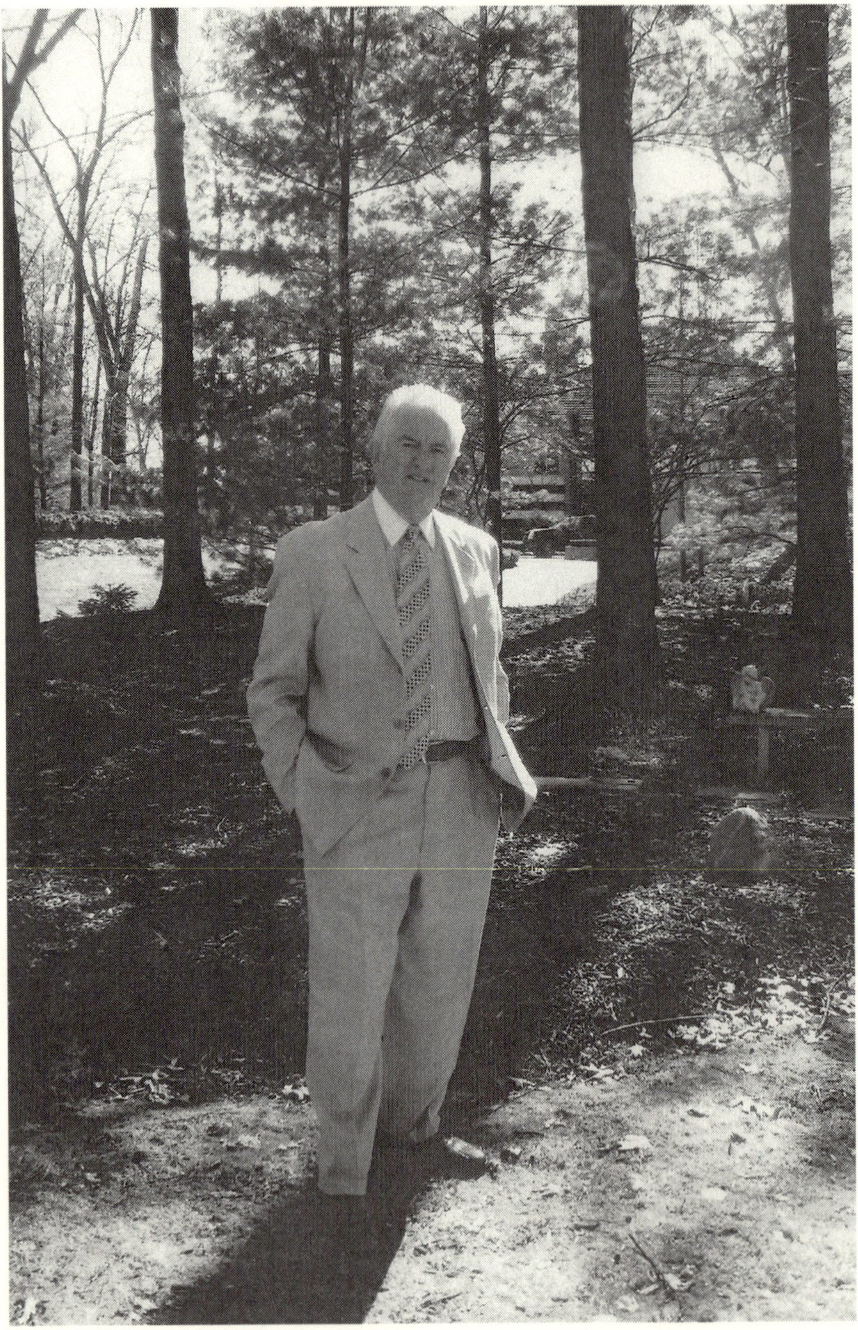

CHAPTER ELEVEN

Financial Accomplishments

As I indicated earlier, I always had a sense of earning—possibly my Scottish heritage. I began to learn the ropes as a six-year-old being pulled on the sled in winter snow, as my brother Billy took me on his Shopping News paper route. It was a free paper and the company paid the carrier direct—in other words, no time spent collecting.

Bobby followed Billy, but only for a short period did I accompany Bobby. The main reason for that was that Bobby tired of the winter delivery and started dumping the papers down a manhole rather than deliver them. That was a carefree Bobby—a kind soul, but sometimes too creative.

So much for background, from cutting celery at twelve for $.75 per crate with a scar on my right hand, at tip of third finger to prove it, I saved a little money. On to the Free Press route at twelve, peddling mail at the holidays, bookkeeping at the bowling alley, good-paying summer factory jobs, clerical work at the main Detroit Public Library (riding the streetcar down Woodward to Warren), and warehouse work at the Carling Beer Distributor at $2.75 per hour. I completed my High School College Prep diploma (1952), my bachelor of science (Economics major) (1956), and Juris Doctor in law (1959).

Upon completing military service in 1960, I applied to State Farm Insurance Company. They were hiring licensed attorneys as Bodily Injury specialists. I seem to recall the starting salary and cost of living as about $9,400 per year plus new auto—including full insurance—plus a liberal expense account. Since Betty was working as the head nurse for Dr. Leiberman, we were doing well for a newly married couple and were saving for a new home, as we lived with Betty's parents in their new home on Nunnelly and Weideman in Clinton Twp.

Kevin was born on November 6, 1960. As he was our firstborn, there was great joy. He was six weeks premature, but a beautiful blond baby. Kevin was born on an historic day, the election of our first Catholic President, John F. Kennedy. Our savings paid off, and we had a new home built at 13351 Iowa St., corner of Moulin in the city of Warren. Including custom brick, larger overhang, large corner lot, we paid $22,500—plus furnished it nicely with a finished basement and 2½-car attached garage. We paid it off by the time we sold it, without a realtor, in 1969 for $34,500.

While I was doing well at State Farm and was featured with picture in their national recruiting brochure, I wanted to gain experience. A friend told me about an opening at Chrysler Corporation as an attorney, so I went to work for Chrysler Corporation for about $28,000 per year. Betty continued to work into the late 1960s, so we were saving and doing well. I might say my dad and brother Bob also worked as millwright superintendents for Chrysler for a total of about sixty-five years.

Moving along, in 1962, a position I had anticipated opened up at Citizens Mutual Insurance Company as house counsel. Again, the salary, expense account, and trial experience were lucrative. But the ability to have my own law practice was an added feature. I worked there until 1966.

In 1966, I bet on myself confidant that Betty and I viewed this as a risk but also good opportunity. As I mentioned in the section on Working Career, I was solicited by a new pioneering company (VALIC) with its pioneering concept and innovative—but untried—product (the Variable Annuity financial contract).

The philosopher Schopenhauer once said, "All new ideas go through three phases: rejection, criticism, and finally acceptance as self-evident truism." So it was with the new unknown variable annuity. It was my good fate that I would look back as a proud trailblazer and pioneer in the financial services field.

In addition to retrospective pride in creating a new investment opportunity for investors, I reaped the financial benefits of this successful marketing venture. I smile when I look back to the 1960s and 1970s at our education of consumers, the IRS and competitors. This was an innovative venture that now ultimately is viewed—as the Schopenhauer philosophy generally predicted—as a concept that now is a "self-evident truism."

More importantly, to myself, Betty, and our family, the risk paid off. I accepted the offer of employment in September 1966 for a slight reduction in salary (but still had a car and expense account), but with a good incentive contract. We agreed I could continue a limited law practice.

I did negligence, probate, and free legal work for Bob Phillips, who hired me and was a good mentor. I might say I blazed a legal trail by being the first lawyer in Michigan, and I think nationally, by using the then-new video-recording camera to record and document the Last Will and Testament of my friend Bill Abercrombie.

This legal "first" was published in the *Detroit Legal News*, the *Detroit Free Press* (all with a photo showing Bill and I videotaping). ABC also covered it on their national evening news, and friends in Texas and California called to congratulate me upon seeing it.

Detroit Free Press

Redford Man Goes on TV To Bar Hassle Over Will

BY JIM NEUBACHER
Free Press Staff Writer

The hassles that arose last October when Bill Abercrombie's mother died convinced him that he wanted to go on television.

So Friday, the 52-year-old Abercrombie of Redford Township went before the cameras and became the first person in Wayne County to officially make his last will and testament on video tape.

He read the document — legal language and all — while a crew of technicians captured it for posterity.

"I had a few problems with some of the words, like 'executrix'," he said afterwards. "I wasn't the greatest guy in English."

ABERCROMBIE's attorney, James Graham, said he hopes to file the cassette transcription of the tape along with the traditional paper and ink will in Wayne County Probate Court next week.

Graham, whose Bloomfield Hills legal practice consists mainly of estate planning, said he thinks video taping of wills is an idea that will catch on.

"What better way to protect your estate?" he asked. If a question arises in court over interpretation of the will, or over the deceased person's frame of mind at the time of making the will, the video recording can be used as evidence, he said.

"A judge can look and see the demeanor, listen to the reading of the will, and see the person himself," said Graham. "This is a relatively new technique, but I just thought I had an obligation to utilize the latest techniques for my clients."

"It's something new, and I kind of like to see progress," said Abercrombie, a diminutive man with thinning red hair. "I think it will be better for the judge."

Probate Court Register Leonard Edelman said Friday, "If he brings the tape in here in an envelope with the document, well, we don't get involved in the contents, we accept it."

But Edelman said Wayne County does not currently have space to store cassettes for all persons making wills. "But this sounds like a good idea. Maybe it's an argument for more space," he said.

Abercrombie said that when his mother died last year, relatives "who contributed nothing for the last 20 years came out and wanted something. You can't believe it's happening until you see it. You find out how important a will is."

Now, says Abercrombie, he feels protected. "Although the people here, the witnesses or my attorney, might not be around when I pass away, the judge can see. Otherwise, who's to say I wasn't sound of mind when I did this?"

"I want to make sure that my loved ones, the people who have been good to me, are taken care of if I — when I — pass away," he said. "This is going to be a very, very authentic piece of legal document."

Brad Thompson, president of the Detroit Legal News, said his company employes three full-time crews to record legal statements on video tape.

Thompson said taping costs $175 per on-camera hour, with a minimum charge of one hour. Graham said that could nearly double the cost of making a will.

Abercrombie, who is retired from the Ford Motor Co., smiled as he finished signing his name to the written will.

The camera stopped rolling and Abercrombie looked up at his attorney and said, "All I've got to do now is die."

Attorney James Graham (left) and client William Abercrombie put the latter's will on a video recording.

5/10/75

In 1974, Bob Phillips felt he had a venture opportunity by moving to our home office now in Houston, Texas. In summer of 1974, Bob moved and I replaced him as regional manager—vice president. Bob had been director of sales, and I had been regional manager. Bob's title was extinguished, and I assumed the additional title of vice president. I now headed the Michigan-Ohio region. The promotion was gratifying personally, but the increased financial incentive was frosting on the cake.

My new contract called for increased sales-incentive commission and bonus on the asset base. The year (1974) Bob received a new position, we did about two million in annual sales with a few millions in asset base. My first year (1975) of complete control, we almost tripled sales to almost six million. With that, my compensation rose dramatically, and I won most sales awards and contests with national recognition at national conferences each year.

My compensation rose from $600,000 per year to $800,000 per year. One year, I paid taxes on earnings of over one million dollars. The compensation also leveraged up my fringe-benefit package with the company stock plan. We lived very well but never wastefully. I always paid off each of the five new homes we built, so we had no mortgage:

(1) 1959—*13351 Iowa, Warren, MI*
(2) 1969—*Stillmeadow Subdivision,*
    575 Woodway Ct., Bloomfield Hills, MI
(3) 1975—*Tamarisk Villas*
    #16 Frank Sinatra Dr., Rancho Mirage, CA
(4) 1984—*Tropicana Condo*
    15645 Collins, Suite 605, Sunny Isles Beach, FL
(5) 1984—*Southridge Mountain*
    2430 Southridge Dr., Palm Springs, CA
(6) 1993—*Heron Bay*
    1744 Heron Ridge Dr., Bloomfield Hills, MI

I planned our financial future following the same advice I offered to our successful client base.

Southridge Mountain Palm Springs

1984
Our home on Southridge Mountain
with a spectacular entrance

View of the swimming pool
House set on a promontory point overlooking the
Coachella Valley

An interesting aside . . .

In the February 2008 issue of Architectural Digest, the Southridge Mountain Palm Springs home was highlighted. Although it had changed hands since we sold it in 1992, and had been refurbished, much of the home was left untouched and many furnishings remain. The views of the valley and mountains are still incredible.

ARCHITECTURAL DIGEST
THE INTERNATIONAL MAGAZINE OF DESIGN FEBRUARY 2008

SPECIAL ISSUE: BEFORE & AFTER

Palm Springs
INFUSION SPLASHES OF COLOR AND SOPHISTICATION REVIVE A DESERT HOUSE

In 1992, Betty and I decided to build a new home. After looking at many sites throughout the Bloomfield Hills area we found a new development. The former "Greene Estate"—nearly 248 acres—which was west of Club Drive adjacent to Forest Lake Country Club was in the early stages of building. We looked at both 'treed' and 'lakeside' properties and felt it was like being in Northern Michigan while still in the city. The developer was David Johnson. After selecting acreage at 1744 Heron Ridge Drive, we closed the deal at David's home paying $800,000 for the property.

The architect selected was Bob Bryce and the developer Koch Development. Mark Morganroth was the Interior Designer. Our home cost $2.3 million dollars to build and complete. The Detroit Free Press ran a cover article after we moved in the fall of 1993. the article with photos is still fun to read today.

1744 Heron Ridge Drive—1993

HOMES & REAL ESTATE

SECTION K
Calendar, Page 4
Lon Grossman, Page 5
Robert Bruss, Page 5
Call Homes: 1-313-222-6614

Detroit Free Press

This striking new house has a series of stepped-down roofs, a horizontal beam and bold rose color with black accents.

NOT PINK
(wink, wink)

Striking new Bloomfield Hills home is a shade apart

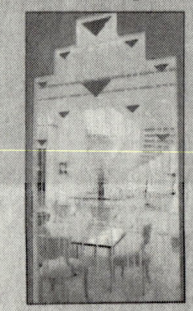

View through an etched-glass door shows the formal dining area.

Pink marble floors sweep through, framed by walls of glass. Furniture pieces are few and special.

CRAIG PORTER/Detroit Free Press

BY JUDY ROSE
Free Press Homes Editor

Jim and Betty Graham see the world from a rose-colored house.

It's not just any rose-colored house. This is a huge, original work of art — conceived, born and raised like a much-loved child — by the Grahams, the architect and a team of designers.

Jim and Betty Graham with Jennifer and Kevin, and the attentive Kimba. Kevin's wife, Dr. Virginia Graham, is on a medical fellowship in Louisiana.

In the Heron Ridge subdivision of Bloomfield Hills, where every new house is an individual monument, this one stands out for its handsome horizontal architecture — which suggests Frank Lloyd Wright's Usonian designs — and for its color.

That color is rose — vibrant, no-excuses rose. It was invented by the architect Bob Bryce, after the Grahams told him they wanted a house in a bright, happy, California-like color, like, say . . . um . . . pink.

There. The P-word is out. Today, no one involved in this house uses it. This house is visibly and officially rose.

But three years ago, the word lay there on the table, dangerous as a signed blank check. This isn't California, where pink houses may line a street; this is Michigan. Are we talking whisper pink here? English rose? Nursery pink? Pepto-Bismol?

To quote a Pink Panther movie: "Who pink? What pink? And how pink?"

Today the color is just one reason this is an unusually striking house in one of this area's most striking new neighborhoods. The silhouette, the roofs, the entrance are all more important than the color.

The Grahams, their architect and other designers created a house that could be material for the architectural magazines.

It was no accident. The Grahams are not in the homes business. Jim Graham is a lawyer; Betty Graham is a full-time homemaker who loves her job. But they picked professionals carefully, then "they really listened," says Bryce.

The Grahams spent a year picking the land, the builder and the architect. They brought Bryce a notebook of ideas, including the wide-overhanging roofs.

See PINK, Page 2K

Huge, walk-in closets, fine bathrooms are provided for each family member.

BY JUDY ROSE
Free Press Homes Editor

Jim and Betty Graham see the world from a rose-colored house.

It's not just any rose-colored house. This is a huge, original work of art — conceived, born and raised like a much-loved child — by the Grahams, the architect and a team of designers.

Jim and Betty Graham with Jennifer and Kevin, and the attentive Kimba. Kevin's wife, Dr. Virginia Graham, is on a medical fellowship in Louisiana.

Don't call it pink: New Bloomfield Hills house is a shade apart

Architect
Bob Bryce

Bryce, of Bryce and Palazzola in West Bloomfield, is known for one-of-a-kind, high-end houses, including about a dozen in Heron Ridge.

Once he had the basic plan, each step was shepherded by a team — Bryce, the builder Terrie Koch, the Grahams, their longtime interior designer Mark Morganroth and cabinetmaker Janice Morse.

For about a year, through cold weather and hot, these six met at the site each Thursday. No one tried to badger the others, they say; they decided things by consensus.

They stood inside the house while the circular stairs were being framed and decided to use clear glass block there, to preserve the view of outdoors.

They stood outside while black granite steps were being laid and decided where each step would go.

Bryce lost one argument because he went to Europe for two weeks. He'd designed the pink marble baseboard to fit flush under the drywall. But when he came back, the baseboard was over the drywall, jutting out.

"Oh no, there's a mistake here," Bryce said when he returned.

"I was told, 'No, it's not a mistake. We had our meeting while you weren't here.'"

Getting the right rose

The color of the house was Bryce's first challenge. He studied pinks, picked about five and had sample bricks made. One deep rose brick caught everyone's fancy, he says, except for the subdivision developer, David Johnson.

"He saw one brick, and said, 'Oh, God — pink.'"

No, no, no — rose.

To be sure they weren't messing up, Bryce had 1,000 bricks and matching mortar made in the color.

"We had the mason build a wall on the site," says Bryce. "We waited till a sunny day, when we all stood back and looked at it, and said, 'OK, now do we like it?'

"We all agreed that it looked as good or better than we thought it would." Even the developer liked it.

From the outside, though, the beauty of the lines is more important than the color. This house is very large, but wide, overhanging roofs descend in steps to make it feel low and welcoming.

Like a side-to-side exclamation point, a 39-foot beam stands on two pillars across the front. It ties the two wings together, encloses a courtyard, and marks the line where public space turns private.

"I like the layering," says Bob Bryce of the view from the street. "I like being able to see all the different spaces at one time," as the spaces grow more and more private.

The front door is a stunning design by Bryce with an oval of stainless steel suspended in a sheet of glass.

Bryce says this architecture also includes the fourth dimension — time — the way the house unfolds as you walk through it.

"Each piece is designed differently, so as you pass through, each one, it's a different joy."

Attention to detail

Inside, the house has wide-open spaces, floors of pink marble and white carpet, glass walls, glass block and the Grahams' favorite soft pinks and pastels.

Colored lights twinkle behind glass blocks in bathrooms, the kitchen and the dining room. They are a new fiber-optic light, cooler than neon.

Morganroth, who owns Sherwood Studios in West Bloomfield, and who designed the interior, found a special marble called Flor de Rose. Marble contractor Tony Pascucci traveled to Mexico to oversee the mining. A marble vein can change tones on different sides of the mountain, says Morganroth, and the Grahams wanted only the lightest. Pascucci sent back 4,000 square feet of the right stuff. The house used almost every scrap.

The rooms are designed to have a few large furniture pieces and no clutter.

"I don't have a lamp in the house," says Betty Graham, not to mention a lamp table. Every light has been built into the ceiling.

Completing the sweep is the built-in furniture by Janice Morse, who owns Designs Unlimited in West Bloomfield.

Each bedroom, for example, has built-in bed and storage, so there are no loose pieces of furniture, except perhaps a chair.

Morse's storage walls sweep through nine rooms plus all nine bathrooms — about 350 cabinet doors in all.

In the recreation area downstairs, there's a second kitchen, a bath, and a wooden dance floor.

There's an egalitarian note to the family house. The Grahams decided, "that we wouldn't have better than the kids had," says Betty Graham. So Jennifer and Kevin Graham each have a full master suite with sumptuous bathrooms, built-in furniture and huge walk-in closets.

Fits like a glove

To some this house may sound too large, but it suits the Grahams perfectly. Betty Graham loves taking care of the house. The interior is so simple, she's able to do most of her own housework.

"I love to cook, I love to clean and everything else," she says. Before this, the family lived in a four-bedroom quad-level they'd built in 1969, and Betty still did her own painting and papering.

Laundry and ironing are her favorite chores, so there is a 12-by-16-foot laundry room with a view of the woods.

"I love to fuss with laundry. I love ironing the shirts and having Jimmy say, 'That looks great.'"

And they are confident enough to put up their own favorite art — religious art — crucifixes in the bedrooms, Madonna and child paintings, a porcelain copy of Michelangelo's Pieta.

Close to the glamorous glass entry, old-time Catholic churchgoers would recognize a dressed-up statue of Jesus, called Infant of Prague. Traditionally, the statue's robe is changed to match the colors of the religious season. Right now, the color is white, passing next week into green. But Betty Graham keeps the statue dressed in her favorite color, pink.

Why build such a house? For the same reasons known to folks who work on a more modest budget.

They enjoy the creative process, says Jim Graham. They wanted to try today's modern building ideas. Finally, they'd always made money before on their houses. "Real estate has been a good investment for us," he notes.

This time they have more than an investment, they have a monument. And in the end it represents not a line from Pink Panther, but from Gertrude Stein: Rose is a rose is a rose .

Breathless Memories 315

This striking new house has a series of stepped-down roofs, a horizontal beam and bold rose color with black accents.

Striking new Bloomfield Hills home is a shade apart

View through an etched-glass door shows the formal dining area.

Pink marble floors sweep through, framed by walls of glass. Furniture pieces are few and special.

Jim & Cindy with Schimmel grand piano in background

We were blessed! Little did I think, when starting out and planning my future from high school, that I would achieve such financial success. I remember thinking early on that if I could accumulate a few hundred thousand in savings at my retirement, I would be fortunate. It pays to plan, dream ambitiously, and work hard consistently with some luck and fortuitous timing for good measure.

An interesting aside in the 1970's—I invested. with my high school friend—Larry DuMouchelle—for the creation of a new restaurant in Detroit. We called it "Rembrandt's Roadster". Our third partner was a successful restaurateur. Larry and I invested and our third partner ran it. While it was fun, we learned that it is not wise to let an experienced operator count the cash receipts. A lesson well learned.

In retrospect, it also pays off to be doggedly disciplined in saving part of your income. It tempts some people, particularly those earning big incomes, to think it will last forever and spend accordingly. Not so! Good financial planning and discipline are their own rewards. I look back with satisfaction that Betty agreed with my planning, and so we achieved financial security and a generous lifestyle.

August 2002
The Alaskan Inside Passage near Juneau
The always 'best-dressed' traveler ready
with binoculars for another incredible sight!

CHAPTER TWELVE

Travel

*F*rom 1948 (age fourteen), we spent summers at our cottage at 11 Conover St., Leamington, Ontario, Canada. It was great fun on the beach and swimming, boating, and fishing in Lake Erie.

We had the cottage until my dad died in 1965. We kids decided to sell the cottage. I also did much boating and water-skiing on Bill Abercrombie's Chris-Craft speed boat.

We did not travel like kids today have the opportunity. I went with my dad and brothers to Port Sanilac on Lake Huron for Boy Scout camp.

When Betty and I married, we traveled quite frequently. For brevity's sake, I will enumerate to the best of my recollection:

(1) Many summers and weekends to my parents' Leamington home.
(2) Our honeymoon in November 1957 was to Niagara Falls, Ontario.
    We drove and stayed a week at the Fallsway Hotel. We returned a couple of times in the 1960s.
(3) We traveled to Florida, driving and flying many times.
    On personal trips, we stayed at the Olympia Motel many times with Betty, her mom and dad, kids, and relatives.
    In 1984, on a family vacation trip with Betty, Kevin, and Jennifer, we noted the new Tropicana condo building being

erected. We went to look at the model and bought #605 on the spot. We've had many great trips there.

(4) We also attended company trips to Florida, i.e., Naples, Boca Raton, Palm Beach, Marco Island, Doral Country Club, the Breakers, etc.

Many company conventions were in great places with first-class accommodations.

Some are as follows:

a. Palm Springs, a number of times; San Diego, Pebble Beach, San Francisco, Las Vegas, Puerto Rico, Nassau, Vale, Colorado, Lake Louise, British Columbia, Canada, Switzerland, the Orient Express Train to Montreaux France, Austria, Germany, and Hawaii; a number of times to Oahu, Kawai, Maui, Hawaii Island, Mexico Cabo San Lucas, the Princess in Acapulco, New York City, Houston Texas, and Seabourne Cruise to Spain and the Mediterranean—about forty lavish company trips in all.

b. It was on one of the trips in the 1970s that Bob Phillips interested us in a new home at Tamarisk Villas #16 on Frank Sinatra Drive at Duval in Rancho Mirage, California. In the 1980s, we bought a home at 2430 Southridge Drive on Southridge Mountain in Palm Springs, California. It had a beautiful pool overlooking the entire Coachella Valley to go with the fabulous home. We sold it in 1992 because we sold the Polo Stores, had the Miami Beach condo, and were building our new 1744 Heron Ridge Drive home in Michigan.

(5) We took many personal trips: Many trips to Europe, particularly Scotland and Ireland. On our twenty-fifth anniversary, we took, as our guests, Catherine and Bill and Bill and Pat. (Lorene was afraid to fly, and Bobby could not get convenient time off from a busy season at work.) However, he did accompany us on a later trip—Maureen McDevitt's wedding.

Cindy and I traveled to Scotland for our wedding (October 18, 2002.). We also toured Loch Lomand, Edinburgh, Glasgow, and other places of interest. It was a marvelous trip for our honeymoon.

Insofar as cruises, Betty, Kevin, Jennifer, and I cruised the Caribbean Sea on RNC to Puerto Rico and many ports of call. We traveled to the French island of Martinique. It was funny because Betty would ask for chocolate milk for Jennifer (at the time about six years old). The wait staff would always say, "No chocolate milk." So Betty would smile and say, "Bring us a glass of milk and chocolate syrup." They would look puzzled but go and get the ingredients, and Betty would make "Chocolate milk." They never learned, and this became a daily joke.

We cruised Italy and the Mediterranean on Costa Lines with the O'Sullivan's. We also cruised the Atlantic ports of call down through the Caribbean and Gulf of Mexico, including Costa Rica, through the Panama Canal—while the Queen Mary was going through the opposite way. In the Atlantic—apparently where the oceans merge—we hit eighteen-foot waves for about eight hours. Really rough seas!

From the Panama Canal, we cruised and disembarked in Acapulco, Mexico. When we flew out of Mexico, it was January and eighty-four degrees—we changed planes in Chicago enroute to Detroit. The Chicago temperature was minus-eight degrees. What a wake-up!

Another memorable trip was January 22-29, 1989 with the entire family. Accompanying us were many friends including the Scotella's, Machiorlatti's, etc. on the cruise. We sailed on the M/S Seaward of the Norwegian Cruise Line. Our ports of call included Ocho Rios, Grand Cayman, Playa del Carmen, Cozumel, and NCI's private island. The prime attraction was our mutual friends, The Gaylords, aka Gaylord and Holiday with private shows. Some of the gold records were: "The Little Shoemaker". "From the Vine Came the Grape", "Isle of Capri", and "Arriverderci, Roma". It was a great trip!

Second Annual
"Festival at Sea"
January 22-29, 1989
M/S SEAWARD

"Spend a week with us cruising the Caribbean.
You'll be invited to 2 very special private shows and a private cocktail party
as well as the shows we will be performing for the entire ship."

Ron & Burt

Burt and Ronnie Gaylord were featured entertainers on the 'Seaward' Cruise

Jim Graham, Burt Bonaldi of the 'Gaylord's',
Joe Machiolatti, and Sam Scotella

Betty and I (as well as Cindy with her late husband, Tom) traveled with Fr. Tony and the St. Hugo group in 1993 to tour Italy: Monte Casino, Assisi, Sorrento, Rome (including a special personal audience with Pope John Paul II with photos we still have).

In 1995, Jennifer, Betty and I (also with Cindy and Tom) toured the Holy Land (Jerusalem, Bethlehem, Tiberius, the Sea of Galilee, Cana (a renewal of marriage vows), and the Jordan River (the waters of baptism)). Then, we flew to Egypt to see the pyramids and travel the Nile River on a river barge. Two great trips!

We had traveled to Las Vegas, California, and Arizona many times. We visited New York City (shows), Boston, Philadelphia, and Nantucket and Ocean City, N. J., with the Costello's. In Las Vegas, we had seen virtually every entertainer of the times, for example, Johnny Carson, Frank Sinatra, Tom Jones, Dean Martin, Sammy Davis Jr., Engelbert Humperdink, Jay Leno, etc. We had stayed at almost every hotel in Las Vegas in our forty or so trips. We did all the tourist attractions: Boulder Dam, Red Rock Canyon, etc. We had also purchased artworks (Xavier Cugat), jewelry, fur coats—especially the Liberace full-length mink coat. A good story!

We were good friends of Anna Nateese and her husband Ray LeNoble. They made all of Liberace's large showpieces. When we would visit one of their stores, they would bring out new showpieces, i.e., forty-foot train on a chinchilla showpiece for his concert. They would have me try it on and take pictures, commenting that I was his size.

Around 1988, we were in Las Vegas and went to their salon at the then Dunes Hotel. They told us that Liberace was terminally ill. They said he had visited the store six months before and picked out fifty female skins for a new personal coat. Now, he would die soon, so he instructed them to keep his down payment.

They said, "Try it on." I said, "Has Liberace ever worn this?" They said, "No." Anna said she could remove his emblem and signature. I said, "No, leave it in for fun and put mine on the opposite side of the coat lining." So for $12,000, I got a $24,000 new coat. Some stories about Las Vegas!

Christmas 2005
Cindy (in her special Christmas gift from me) and
Jim (in his "Liberace" *new* mink coat 'gifted' to myself!)

One interesting evening in Las Vegas was about 1969. Betty's parents accompanied us with Kevin, age nine. We went to the dinner show at Caesar's Palace, which featured the Tom Jones show. We then went to the Hilton International for the 10 PM show starring Elvis Presley.

At that time, they had the largest showroom seating thirty-two hundred people. It was packed. Elvis put on a great show. With our good seats, we really enjoyed it, especially Kevin.

Also, Betty, Jennifer, and I went to the old Sands in the early 1990s to see Frankie Valli and the Four Seasons, while Betty worked the slot machines. Cindy and I went to the Andiamo showroom in Warren in 2004 and saw Frankie Valli with a "young" Four Seasons backup group. He is still performing well. Cindy and I again saw Frankie Valli at the Flamingo, while staying at the Bellagio in the spring of 2005.

Besides Scotland, in 2002, Cindy and I have traveled to Scottsdale Arizona, Palm Desert, and Sedona Arizona. We visited the red-rock formations and jeep-toured the plateaus in the surrounding areas. We also traveled to Las Vegas and many times to Florida.

A highlight trip was a motor trip through Washington State, Montana, Idaho, and Wyoming, Utah (including the Mormon Tabernacle in Salt Lake City). This trip also included a cruise on Holland America's Zaandam from Victoria, British Columbia, Canada, through the inside passage to Juneau, Skagway, Ketchikan (where Cindy purchased my gorgeous black-and-white diamond wedding-band set in platinum—wow!), and other Alaskan Glaciers and cities.

We cruised the "great" rivers of Europe with the Nomads in summer of 2002. Starting in Budapest on the Danube, we traveled through Hungary, on the Maine River into Germany (Reggenberg, Rudescheim, Koblenz), through the canals of Mainz, castles, and vineyards in the wine country of Germany. Also, we traveled to Vienna, Austria, and Passau, Germany.

In 2003, we joined another St. Hugo group to tour beautiful northern Italy, beginning in Lake Como at the Ville d'Este, shopping and lunching in Bellagio, sightseeing in Lugano, Switzerland, and several days in Venice. Boarding a Costa Line ship, we toured Adriatic Sea ports of Dubrovnik, Montenegro, Crete—several Greek islands—and celebrated our first anniversary with a blessing shared with Fr. Tony and friends.

In late summer 2004, Cindy and I took a motor-coach tour of New England: Philadelphia, the Concord Trail, Boston, New York City, the Mohegan Sun casino in Connecticut, the Huron River Valley, and Lake Geneva, New York. Then to Montreal, Canada, with tours to St. Joseph's Oratory and St. Anne de Beaupre, before boarding the Holland American Maasdam for a tour of the St. Lawrence River up into the Maritime provinces of eastern Canada, including Prince Edward Island, Nova Scotia (meaning New Scotland, as Scots settled this area), and Halifax. We finished at Bar Harbor Maine and flew home from Boston.

Fall of 2005 included another St. Hugo pilgrimage to Italy (a Seventy-fifth St. Hugo Anniversary event with Cindy and me as tour leaders)—this time with forty-seven parishioners and Fr. Bill Herman in Msgr. Tony's place as spiritual leader. We started in Venice, Florence, Sienna, Assisi, Tuscany, and concluded in Rome with an audience with the new pope, Benedict XVI, on the dais in St. Peter's Square.

Summer 2006 featured Scotland and Ireland with their incredible scenery and Celtic colors—the military tattoo in Edinburgh was a particular highlight.

We have also enjoyed a trip to Nantucket with the Costello's and Brobyn's, with extensive touring Boston and the surrounding area.

The family has had expansive and fun travel experiences. People often remark that "travel broadens you." It does that, and sometimes broadens your waistline!

Fall 1995
Jim & Betty
In the shadow of the Sphinx
Cairo—Egypt

Breathless Memories

River Nile Cruise in Egypt
In costume for a "Drama Skit"
Created by Joe McGlynn and Tom Dailey
Jim in the center front row (Caesar)
Above Jim's head L to R: Betty, Jennifer, Cindy
St Hugo Travel Group
Fr. Tony is the 7th in the top row above Jennifer

1995
Fr. Tony's Holyland-Egypt Group
The Great Pyramid
Cairo, Egypt

Breathless Memories 333

After dinner on the River Nile Cruise
Caesar (Jim) enjoying a dance with daughter Jennifer

December 2001
Palm Desert,
Marriott Spa and Resort

September 2005
On the highway along the Hudson River
In up-state New York.
Lunch at an authentic 1940's Diner

August 2007
"GRAHAM" Park
outside of Sebawing, Michigan

October 2007
Assisi, Italy
Cindy & Jim celebrating their 5th anniversary and 'Sweetest Day'
Hand-painted and Glazed ceramic Madonna in an antique frame

September 2005
The "Liberty Bell"
Outside Independence Hall
Philadelphia, Pennsylvania

July 2002
Nomad European River Cruise aboard the Amadeus classic
Frankfurt Germany
Half-timbered houses of Alstadt style

**Summer 2003
Juneau Alaska
Jim with the 'Lumberman'**

August 2009
Simi Valley California
The Ronald Reagan Presidential Library and Museum
Jim and Cindy with Air Force One

Summer 2003
Jackson Hole Wyoming
Jim under the antler arch in the town square
Each year the residents collect abandoned elk and moose antlers
from the frontier landscape

September 1995
A beautiful day cycling around Loch Lomond Scotland
L to R: Jennifer, Dick McDevitt, Jim, Virginia, Kevin

1985
Greenock, Scotland
Jim and 'ladies' on a bench!
L to R: Aunt Jenny Graham, Aunt Maggie Ward, cousin Moira Flanagan,
My wife Betty, Aunt May Graham, Jim, and daughter Jennifer

1995
St. Andrews, Scotland
Jennifer 'steals' a moment with
Actor Sean Connery ('007) in the Clubhouse

James Kenneth Patrick Graham J. D.

August 2006
Jim—the dapper Scotsman
St. Andrews Bay in the background

Las Vegas, Nevada

2005
Inside the gardens at the Bellagio Hotel

2003
The lobby of the Venetian Hotel
On Center Strip

**September 2005
Jim in the lobby of World Headquarters of AIG—
At the time the world's largest insurance company
70 Pine St. New York City**

June 2000
Barcelona, Spain
VALIC Mediterranean cruise
Jim, with long-time friend Jim Costello from BlueBell
Pennsylvania and long-time (Ho! Ho!) son Kevin Graham

Fall 2003
Ancient Roman Catacombs along the Appian Way
All entrances today are obscured by beautiful gardens which are tended by monks who live off the land.
This catacomb had thousands of crypts in its tunnels and levels.

July 2009
Islamorda, Florida along the Florida Keys
In the shade of Ernest Hemingway
A sunset dinner with Kevin, Jennifer, and Dad (Jim)

July 3, 2010
Dublin, Ireland
Jim and special friend "Mr. Blarney"
Wishing all of us the "top of the morning"

1980's
Palm Springs, California
Jim and Betty at home on Southridge Mountain
Many beautiful memories in a most beautiful home . . .

August 2009
Ventura Harbor, California
Before a sunset dinner at a Greek Restaurant
complete with Belly Dancer!
L to R: Keely, PAPA (Dad), Natalie, Jennifer,
Elizabeth and Steve

James Kenneth Patrick Graham J. D.

"SNOOPY" the World Traveler!

Fall 2005
COSTA Cruise—Italy and Greece
In the belltower overlooking the Duomo
of the Cathedral in Florence, Italy
The carillon tower had over 200 steps to the top!

June 2010
Kylemore Abbey, Ireland
Beautiful country home, built as a wedding gift
for an Irish lass (the bride of the owner),
bought by the Benedictine Sisters
in the beginning of the twentieth century
to be used as a convent and boarding school ...
The original owners are buried there with their families
as well as many Benedictine nuns who spent their lives there.

June 2010
Northern Ireland
The "Giant's Causeway"
The '8th' Wonder of the World
at the top of Ireland on the North Channel
. . . enormous basalt and volcanic rocks the size of buildings!
Jim sports his "English D"

**August 2009
Santa Barbara, California
Outside the Historic Courthouse**

Views Along the Water

2003
On the balcony of our Tropicana Condo overlooking the
Atlantic Ocean, Haulover Beach, and the Intracoastal Waterway

Summer 2006
The Lighthouse at Whitefish Point,
Lake Superior, Michigan
Michigan Maritime Museum had an extensive display of shipwrecks including the "Edmund Fitzgerald" which broke into two sections just north of this location

Summer 2006
The pier and lighthouse in Petoskey, Michigan

October 2005
Costa Cruise Line—Tropicale
Mike and Dolores Mutchler, Fr. Tony and Jim
at the Adriatic Sea Port of Montenegro

July 2002
'Nomad' Danube-Rhine River Cruise
Traveling the Danube, Rhine and Main Rivers
from Budapest, Hungary north through Germany and Austria
into wine country in France
Jim along the walled walkway around the town of Regensburg German
in the center of the European waterway
stretching from the North Sea to the Black Sea

September 2004
Holland American Cruise—"Maasdam"
Jim and Cindy—Formal night on the St. Lawrence Seaway
On our way to the Canadian Maritime Provinces
and the northeast United States

July 2010
'Close to home' Gordon Follmer Ranch
Camp Tamarack
Jim—the 'urban' cowboy!

At the edge of the Ocean . . .

September 2004
New England Cruise
Acadia National Park
The "Red Rocky" shore of the Atlantic Ocean
near Bar Harbor, Maine

June 2010
Spanish Point, just south of Galway, Ireland's west coast
The Atlantic Ocean
Rocky, moss-covered shore where nearly a hundred
Ships of the Spanish Armada crashed
in their attempt to make shore over 500 years ago

January 2003
Jim and Cindy poolside at the Tropicana Condo
Sunny Isles Beach Florida
The calm Atlantic Ocean in the background

August 2009
Jim, with the Pacific Ocean in front of him . . .
the picturesque, tranquil, and temperate city of Santa Barbara,
California relaxing after a day at the Polo Grounds as
the guest of Ambassador Glen Holden
. . . our Hotel—the Oceania—recommended by his daughter,
Gina . . . as the "ideal spot for a vacation"!

June 2010
Fr. Eoin Murphy and Jim outside out hotel
in Trim Ireland

James Kenneth Patrick Graham J. D.

October 2006
Lugano, Switzerland
After spending several days in the Lake Region of Northern Italy, Fr. Tony's travel group ventured to Switzerland—home of "Watches" and "Watchmakers"

March 2006
The courtyard of St. Patrick Catholic Church
Miami Beach, Florida
The Spanish style belltower in the background

Up in the Clouds and Sky . . .

November 1993
Almost above the 'clouds' at Monte Cassino, Italy—
Jim standing on the steps of the Benedictine Monastery
in total silence!
This mountaintop cloister, reached by a winding steep road,
is often obscured by clouds from the bottom countryside.

August 2005
The twin spires of St. Anne de Beaupre Basilica
reach towards the skies above Quebec, Canada
Jim's height of nearly 6 feet, is only a fraction
of the towers height behind him, which soar nearly 200 feet

July 2010
'Up, up, and Away . . . in my beautiful balloon!'
Jim and Cindy ascend above the grounds of
Camp Tamarack in Brighton-Hartland, Michigan
This 50-acre property was purchased
and restored by Gordon Follmer, Jim's accountant for nearly 50 years
Gordon hosted a western round-up and provided
balloon rides, as well as caricature drawings, hay rides,
western grub and, mechanical bull-riding!
Lots of good old-fashioned fun.

**Jim and Cindy safely back on the ground
after a trip up in the sky!
Great balloon experience . . .**

In the 1980's
Betty and Jim outside the Casino in Monte Carlo

Summer 2007
Jim and Cindy collecting 'sparkling flat stones'
in the frigid surf of Lake Superior . . .
Air temperature—85 degrees,
Water temperature—58 degrees!

March 8, 2004
70th Birthday celebration at our condo
in Sunny Isles Beach Florida

A relaxing summer day at home
In Bloomfield Hills on the back deck

Butchart Gardens—Vancouver Island, Canada

CHAPTER THIRTEEN

Hobbies

I guess I never had the patience for intense, time-consuming hobbies. I was never as intensely engrossed as some people are.

However, over the years, Kevin and I accumulated some interesting memorabilia. Kevin and I went to the 1981 Super Bowl at Pontiac Silverdome (Cincinatti Bengals vs. San Diego Chargers). I secured for Kevin a Leroy Neiman Limited Edition artwork, depicting a goal line stand of the game, which Kevin hung in his room. This goal-line stand was directly in front of our seats.

At a VALIC convention in Las Vegas at Super Bowl time, George Blanda—Hall-of-Fame NFL quarterback—autographed a football for Christian and a helmet. Also, New York Yankees manager Joe Torre autographed a baseball and his book.

At a "Jimmy Fund" charity at Reedy's Pub, Kevin and I paid $1,000 for Ted Williams' bat, which he signed, and we took our picture with him.

IN DETROIT
REEDY'S SALOON
1846 Michigan Avenue
Detroit, Michigan 48216
(313) 961-1722

1990—Reedy's Saloon, Detroit, Michigan
Fundraiser for "Jimmy's Fund" (a children's cancer research fund created by Boston Red Sox owner Tom Yawkey and Hall of Fame player Ted Williams)
L to R: Kevin Graham, Ted Williams, and Jim Graham witness Signing a Ted Williams bat (still ours today)

I would say clothes, artworks, watches, pens, and rings were a fun hobby. I always enjoyed fine clothing of which I admittedly have too many. But I could always afford it, and I never spared the family and home because my income was fortunately large enough to cover first things first, i.e., family, good lifestyle, charity, savings, vacations, etc. Although I have hundreds of suits, sport coats, and shirts, I enjoy different outfits, and I know my appearance helped me to be successful in my career.

Because I enjoy artful creativity, I have collected watches. I have about 125, varying from inexpensive fun watches to valuable pieces ranging in the thousands, including Rolex, Tiffany, Chopard ($10,000 for the skeleton Chopard), Silberstein, etc.

Likewise, I have collected over one hundred pairs of cuff links from relatively inexpensive fun cuff links to $7,500-quadrillion diamond cuff links from Robann's in Palm Springs, California. Of course, these various styles and colors complement my wardrobe.

However, the two watches inherited from my dad are priceless. They are an Elgin wristwatch and a Waltham pocket watch, both almost a century old. Always a great feeling and thoughts of my dad while wearing them . . .

Additionally, the single, most expensive "fun" acquisition was a harvest yellow Rolls Royce Corniche convertible. The tan Connolly leather hydes (seat coverings) were pure quality. Automobiles are enjoyable conveniences. In 1984, while driving down Palm Canyon Drive in Palm Springs, CA, I noticed a beautiful 1984 Rolls Royce on display. To make a long story short, we purchased it and enjoyed many pleasurable drives in Palm Springs and the Bloomfield Hills areas.

Our new 1984 Rolls Royce Corniche Convertible purchased at Epstein Motors in Palm Springs, California parked in front of St. Hugo of the Hills Chapel in Bloomfield Hills, Michigan

    A whimsical note goes with the story. Kevin was in his early twenties, and Betty and I were going to buy him a red Camaro sport coupe for his next birthday and graduation from law school. We told him to go to the then Chevrolet dealer at Telegraph at 12 Mile in Southfield. He drove there in Betty's car. Because he was a twenty-four-year-old, no one approached him and he could not get a salesperson to help him. In short, he came home crestfallen. However, he had an idea to go back in the Rolls Royce. We gave permission. When he drove back, the sales staff gave him special attention. Who says appearances don't matter?
    I also collect rings of various types and styles. The most expensive is a $24,000-quadrillion diamond from Robann's on Palm Canyon Drive in Palm Springs, California. When we owned homes on Frank Sinatra Drive in Rancho Mirage and Southridge Mountain in Palm Springs, we were a good customer of Roger Robann and his dad. Rings also complement your wardrobe and appearance.

I enjoy writing and may have acquired this interest from my mom and uncle Charlie Boyle. A well-composed writing is a pleasant experience to read. Also, I enjoy reading as a hobby and pastime. I particularly prefer reading biographies and Western tales, detective and spy fiction novels. Music is a pleasant hobby—all types—especially when Cindy plays the piano for me and others. I also enjoy writing poems or more accurately whimsical rhymes—especially for special occasions for friend and family. Uncle Charlie always wrote his Christmas cards. Please see the Appendix for a sample of my endeavors.

My last avid interest (hobby) was the homes we built and owned in Warren, Michigan—two in Bloomfield Hills, two in California and Miami Beach, Florida. Homes are a work of architectural art and an extension of the people who reside there.

From furnishings, sculptures, glassware, Schimmel acrylic and brass piano, wall hangings collected on trips, there are many works of art and jewelry purchased for its beauty and remembrance of the trip.

Included in the collection are a Diego Rivera, a number of Leroy Neimans, Xavier Cugat oils, beautiful Daum and Waterford crystal, priceless Fontini Roman Mosaics, etc.—almost all reflective of a time and memory place.

Hobbies, then, are the pleasures of your life and a reflection of one's interests.

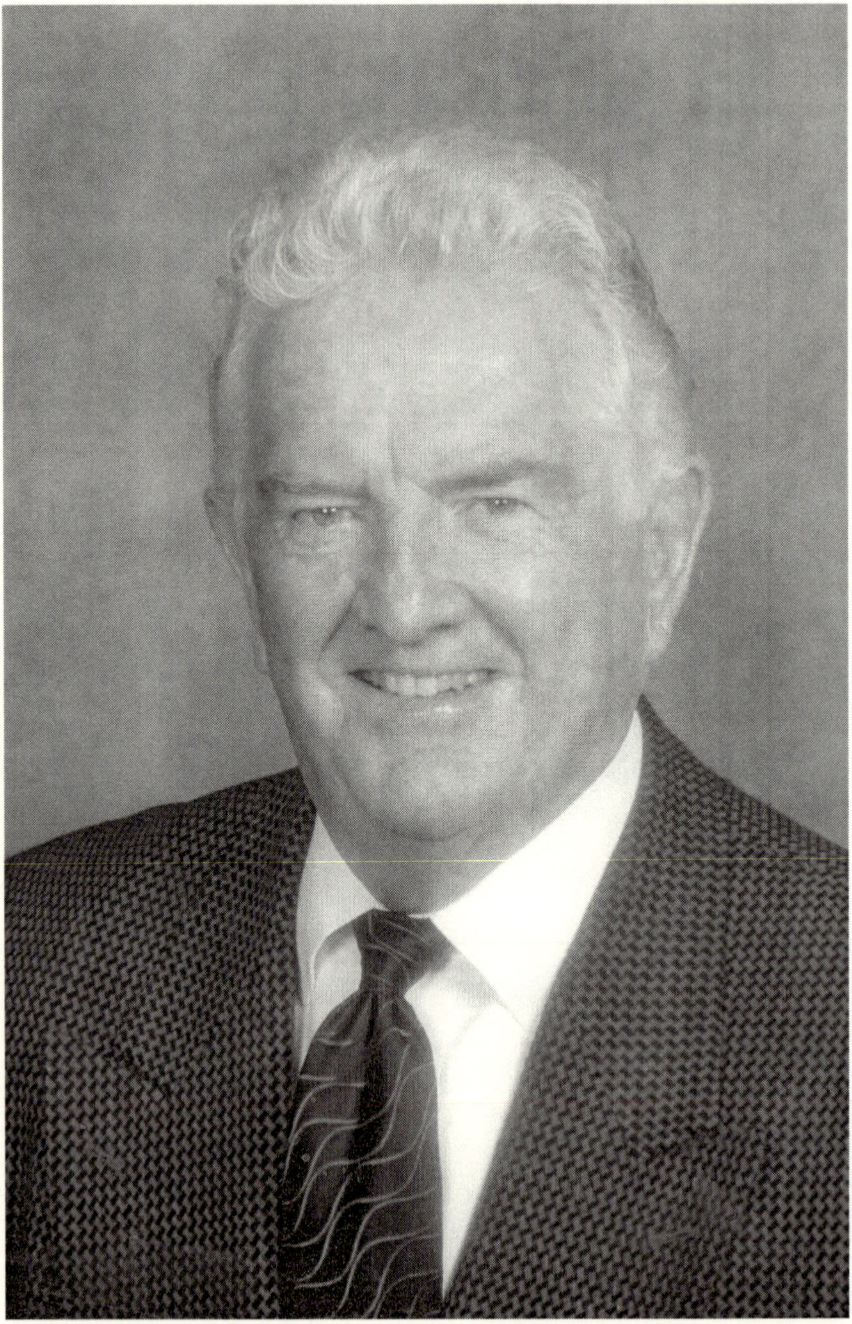

CHAPTER FOURTEEN

Discipline

*D*iscipline—while sometimes unwelcome and possibly unpleasant—is an essential ingredient of a well-balanced life. You cannot be happy, well adjusted, and productive without discipline. Discipline is a characteristic that one builds as you live your life. Discipline assists you in being on time and organized in your life's pathway. Without disciplined organization, your life is chaotic and therefore unrewarding.

My philosophy professor, Fr. Belleperche S. J., taught that the philosophy of a balanced life was "Always strive for the mean between extremes," still good advice, fifty years later. Too little or too much of anything is usually—on major things—not as fulfilling as the middle ground.

Not true what actress Mae West said, "Too much of a good thing is a good thing." Ho! Ho!

For example, too much food or sweets is not healthful and distorts your body with weight. The wisdom of moderation is self-evident. Again, discipline plays a significant part in moderating your lifelong behavior.

On the light side, one discipline I have practices since childhood—starting with my Dad's car—is keeping my auto's clean. While I no longer work on my own car, one of my fun disciplines it having a full-service car wash daily at one of the Jax Car Wash facilities. A clean car goes faster . . . really?

So! Always be disciplined and strive for the mean between extremes for a better life.

Outside St. Patrick's Cathedral, New York City

CHAPTER FIFTEEN

Spirituality and Core Values

*T*he late great Hall-of-Fame Coach Vince Lombardi said his formula for success—which he certainly achieved—was to have a priority of God, family, and country in your life. His son, fellow attorney, Vince Lombardi Jr., discussed this at a meal when I engaged him to be a motivational speaker for my sales meeting. I still have his signed book in my library, which expands on his dad's format for life.

If we do not have a spiritual belief in an "Uncaused Cause," a supreme being, i.e., God, then we lack a moral compass. My Roman Catholic faith—Faith of my Fathers—has been an essential foundation.

From this foundation emanates a set of core values that has been time tested over the millenniums. This faith principal becomes more apparent as one lives life and gains a perspective that only experience can impart. That is why more converts—particularly to Catholicism—occur as they grow in their knowledge of life.

For example, Cardinal Newman, Malcolm Muggeridge, Hillaire Belloc, and G. K. Chesterton converted late in life. In fact, G.K. Chesterton is his writing "The Hound of Heaven" lyricizes how God is the hound that pursues our immortal soul through life.

A strong spiritual belief fortifies you in good time and bad times. I have prayed daily throughout my life. One beseeches spiritual guidance in school tests, career decisions, life's path, health help and overall guidance, and the afterlife. Or as a saint said, "Faith cushions despair."

Prayer should not be for just in times of stress although it is especially comforting in those stressful points in life—as in the death of a loved one, i.e., parent, spouse, etc. If one thought that this mortal life was the be-all and end-all. it would not be fulfilling. As once was said to me, "Even if I was not a strong-believing person, I would still believe in a heaven, because it beats the alternative and I would not want to be wrong."

From my earliest days from my mom and dad, my Catholic training at St. Benedict Grade School, and as an altar server, I prayed daily, notably morning, night and through the day. In July 1984, a despicable group of employees, to get a bonus from E. F. Hutton and with no notice, jumped to a new company—with hopes of stealing the business I had helped them acquire and build up since they had applied for jobs and been hired by me.

Throughout my existing prayer habits, I survived the stress of this Pearl Harbor backstab. I began at that point in 1984, years ago, to recite the rosary every day. My prayers fortified me, and I prospered beyond my expectations without the traitorous malignants who premeditatively plotted this secretly over months. My point is I have supported and helped many people—including the gang of six. If a person can get a better job, more power to them. However, if one does you a favor hiring, training, and loyally supporting you, leave honorably. Give notice, don't plot and sneak around planning a Pearl Harbor. Ironically, what they dishonorably gave out came back to all of them. Just desserts!

What saddened me even more, as a loving brother, was the shame and embarrassment that my loved ones—who recommended helping and hiring their children in need—expressed after Pearl Harbor.

In fairness, one of the relatives had a conscience awakening. Some months later, he came to apologize for his part in the wrongful act. He asked me to rehire him back with the explanation that what was represented did not pan out and he did not have the expensive support staff or system that I had developed. Recognizing his ethical repentance and after his apology to the staff, I rehired him. His subsequent good deed was rewarded—after all these years, he remains employed with the successor company to this day.

I smile when I think of the Irishman who, having been grievously wronged, toasted the wrongdoers with an old Irish curse as follows:

> "May those that love us, love us;
>   and those that don't love us,
>   may God turn their hearts;
> if He can't turn their hearts,
>   may He turn their ankles,
>   so we'll know them by their limping."

No! I did not begrudge them, but it was ironic what befell them in deaths, bad health, and broken careers. None of them stayed with Hutton beyond a couple of years—as opposed to the decades I had employed them. The main point is my spiritual core values helped me and their lack of them defeated them. A good lesson!

As a P. S., the person who recruited them into the plot died young of a sudden heart attack. I take no pleasure in the tragedies that befell the conspirators, quite the contrary. However, it makes one wonder about the old maxim, "What you put out, comes back ten-fold."

In addition, it is ironical that after decades of successful business, the company E.F. Hutton died also. E. F. Hutton ceased to exist as the large financial conglomerate that it had been.

One contemporary of this premeditated debacle humorously suggested it was the first case of corporate fatality by being infected by swine flu.

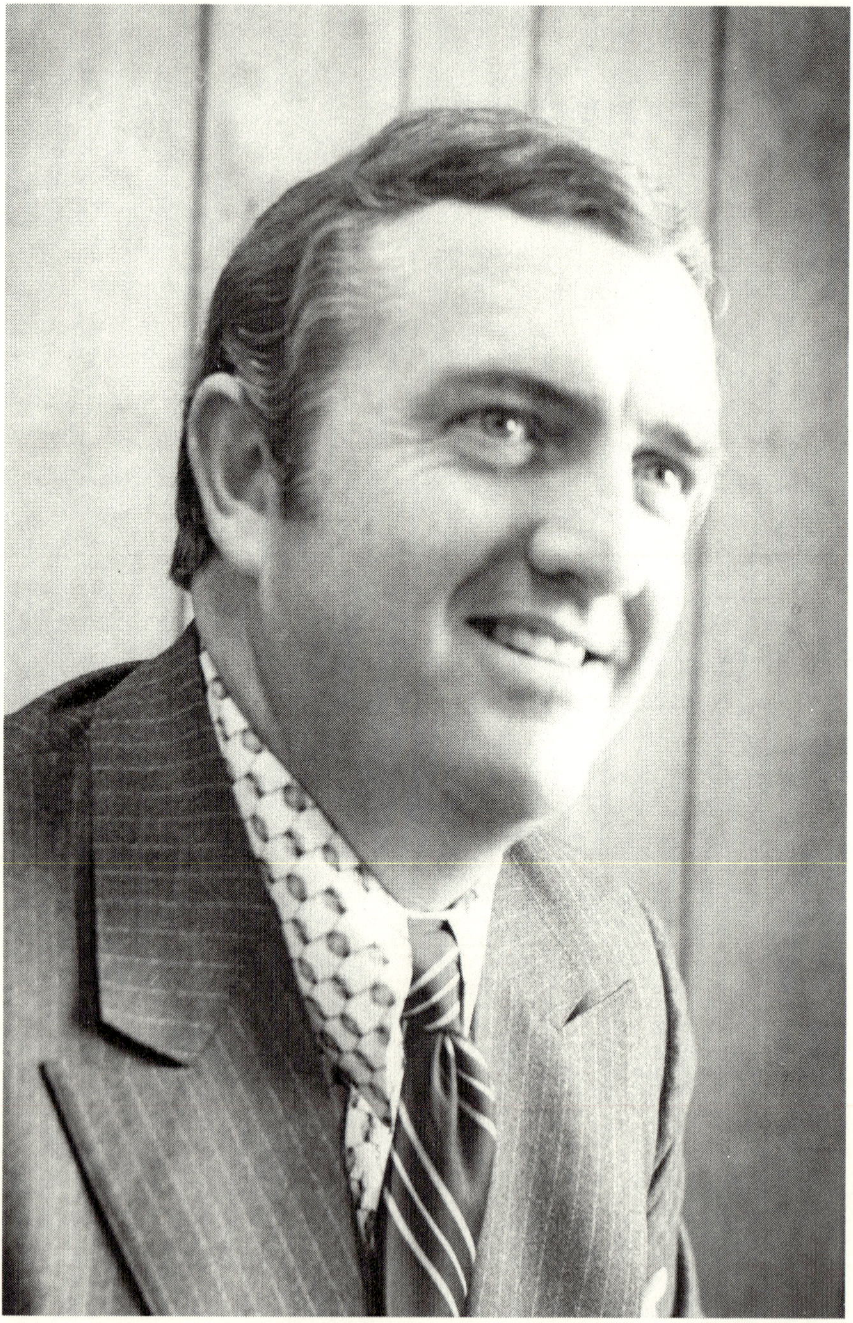

CHAPTER SIXTEEN

Loyalty—God, Family, and USA

In my view, *loyalty* should be one of the most cherished principles of life. Loyalty is an elevated extension of appreciation. Loyalty to God, family, and country are simply acknowledgement of the blessings flowing from these main sources in one's life.

Unfortunately, the perverse side of loyalty (appreciation) is selfishness. There is a growing display of disloyalty in the world. The "me-first" syndrome works against recognition of favors received.

For example, every person or entity that has blessed me in life deserves—and has gotten—my loyalty and support. My loved ones, my church, and my country have unswervingly received my commitment of loyalty. While somewhat extreme at first, hearing the saying "My country right or wrong, my country" conveys this sentiment. I would rather err on the side of too much loyalty, than too little.

One can be tested in life, because some unprincipled people will exploit your good acts of loyalty. Some will not reciprocate loyalty. As you live life, you must be prepared to be backdoored by some friends or business associates—out of greed or envy.

Again, as is said, "Keep your friends close, and your enemies closer."

Prior to 1984, I hired people—some relatives and some down and out at their parents' urging—and gave great opportunity for them more than me. They made more money than they ever had before, and their training and experience with me made them more valuable in the marketplace. As a result, when tempted by a bonus, they became "Judas." It was not just the scheme to raid my business, but the sneaky, devious way the six pulled it off.

My point is loyalty is valuable and should be prudently practiced even if there are potential pitfalls. Loyalty—it can be said—is its own reward.

Conversely, on the opposite end of the disloyalty scale, there is the 24K loyalty principled person. Growing up in a 1940's-1050's middle-class neighborhood, one had to be respected as one who would not be bullied. I did not look for fights, but had to be ready in those times to stand up for myself. Generally I tried to be friendly with the various neighborhood groups, i.e. St. Benedict Highland Park classmates, Greenfield Park Detroit grade school neighbors, pool room guys on John R, Antior's Gas station, Palmer Park Bowling Alley and Bar, etc.

On one of my occasional visits to the John R Pool Room (where the "John R Special" was created) defined as a swift kick between the opponent's legs which left him as a soprano candidate for the Vienna Boys Choir. I encountered an outsider. I was about 17 years old and this slightly older guy named "Rocky", if you will, started to hassle me. The Pool Room proprietor John Mafasoli said "Take it outside."

So onto the sidewalk on John R—across from the Ambassador (later Temple) Theater we went. Fortunately, I was faster afoot and Rocky went down three times (two stumbles and one punch). All the guys from inside the poolroom encircled us. Tough Rocky was getting fatigued and desperate, so he called to his slug buddy, Bobby Ward, "Help me."

I glanced to see Ward starting to come behind us. Suddenly a tough voice said, "Bobby, don't even think about it." Bobby stopped in his tracks and Rocky quit the fight he started. The welcome voice was my kindergarten and grade school buddy, Mike Van (Vanderlinder). Mike was poolroom regular and tough as nails. Mike, a good athlete, loved to fight for fun and had a reputation for winning his fights. In short, Mike's well-earned reputation stopped the potential back stabber, because he knew a severe whipping would result.

I smile to this day—all these years later, and at his funeral a few years ago—at this terrific display of friendship and loyalty. Mike's spontaneous expression of loyalty causes me to cherish his memory and pray for his soul.

This act of friendly reciprocation, for my assistance in school work, stands in stark testament to his virtue, as opposed to the non-virtuous disloyal payback for my good deeds by the "Gang of Six". Proving again, that good deeds define one's life. God bless, Mike. He was true "family".

A Sad Day of National Tragedy

We are blessed by living in such a beautiful and bounteous United States of America. Thank God for country and the super heroes who built it so democratically well and bequeathed it to us—the future generations to enjoy. It is why immigrants—legal as well as millions of illegal—leave what they have created and enter the USA by any means necessary.

It is also a backhanded insult to our great country that the liberal media and the U.S. bashers in education—mainly higher education—make a good living with short work years and lush pensions and yet hypocritically never leave America, thereby enabling the terrorists and haters of our beautiful nation.

Wasn't it the Communist Lenin who hatefully said, "We will destroy America from within?" Well, these malcontents, closet leftists, are hoping to achieve their mentors' admonition. These same traitors—or quislings in WWII terms—achieved "change" in Cuba fifty years ago, and Castro dealt with these bashers in a way only another Marxist can, i.e., Putin. Unfortunately, this started the flooding of our country with millions upon millions of refugees escaping this left-wing tyranny. In fact, yesterday, June 5, 2009, two of these same types were arrested for living in New Jersey, working in America, and being paid spies against America by Castro. This mirrors a Florida Cuban living off America and being a paid spy for Communist Cuba and Castro at a Dade County University.

Thanks, you U.S. bashers in the mainstream America "free" media. You also serve Castro and Chavez but hypocritically will not go there. You hate America because of its goodness and sell your soul for celebrity and money. You live a capitalistic life but promote your Marxist philosophy.

The hate and lies promoted by these closet anti-Americans has enabled terrorism to flourish. Fraudulent voting organizations such as ACORN—funded by capitalist George Soras—promote unrest for their own power and enrich themselves. They steal elections, demoralize unthinking voters, slant the truth, distort or hide facts in order to achieve their perverted control of the American body politic whose vote is to be manipulated. Then these elected bureaucrats enrich themselves off U.S.A. taxpayers' money appropriated by liberal-left politicians focused on being re-elected. For example, beneficiaries of organizations like ACORN (Bill and Hillary) came into office financially flat. Now they are worth over $100 Million. Who says being a politician in American doesn't pay?

It would be interesting if each college teacher and media orchestrater were compelled to honestly—is that possible—list their credentials, i.e., military or service type to the USA, then voting preference, previous or current affiliation, their biases, etc., so one knows the slant that their "sale" is coming from.

The anti-American left follows the political mandate of Mao Tse-Tung, "You must endure a thousand no's, to get one yes."

So too, the so-called "American" left enables Islamic terrorism in the world. By bashing the country they parasitically feed on, they encourage and enable the terrorism of the Islamics around the world. Again, the fanatical Islamics love their Islamic nations' benefits so much they immigrate to America but bring their hate-filled culture in order to poison our well.

As a result, the left (ACORN, etc.) have elected a Kenyan rooted, biracial, Islamic-raised immigrant who refuses to furnish a birth certificate and brags to the anti-American left about "Dreams of My Father," Read the truthful facts about who they say his father is, and it is truly a "nightmare" rather than a dream.

Barack Hussein Obama sat in a church for twenty years listening to a "reverend" who is a white-race hater and has a foul mouth, using "Goddamn America." Some mentor!

Therefore, my love and loyalty to America brings me to the "sad day of national tragedy." Thanks to our U.S.-enabling left and their Islamic-enabled terrorists, over three thousand innocents were violently murdered in the name of Islam. Some of Obama's supporters even said America deserved that and worse. Have you ever heard an apology from the "religious" Islamic and their so-called American apologists? They can bash America—never leave—but never honestly criticize the Islamic terrorists. Rather they coddle and support them, i.e., whining about the U.S. military and a Guantanamo that has saved U.S. lives.

Meanwhile, back in good-old Islam land, girls were mutilated in the name of Islam, women murdered for breaking Sharia law, and terrorist bombings (murders) in houses of worship (Sunni vs. Shite) and the left media and left-wing teachers never uttered a word. Are they believers in Islamic ways or just collaborators? What kind of belief "theology" teaches hateful Jihad in the name of religion and God?

In any event, my longtime friend and business associate for years in VALIC—Todd Adams—invited Kevin and me to play golf at his club designed by and founded by Jack Nicklaus—the golf great. Kevin and I drove to Muirfield CC in Dublin, Ohio (quite Irish, all around,) to meet Todd on September 11, 2001.

It was a lovely day and so was our golf camaraderie. At the first nine turnaround, we went into the clubhouse for a break. We noted a sense of tension with everyone watching the TV showing smoking buildings. We were flabbergasted when told there were multiple terrorists. It is incomprehensible to this day. Have the Islamic countries or all these terrorist cells been made to pay? Oh no, left-wing apologists say it's our fault. Just appease them and let the Islamic terrorists around the world kill and maim innocents, and maybe, they'll leave us alone. In the meantime, get a closet Islamic, Kenyan-rooted president to apologize to the world for us and then they attack America.

Just as the left-wing appeasers in WWII groveled at the terror of Hitler, so do the liberal left love anything perverted or terrorist. As the great statesman, Winston Churchill, whose patriotism helped save England (and eventually the USA saved the world), said that Neville Chamberlain groveled to Hitler to secure peace and he secured war. Do appeasers ever learn? Apparently not!

In any event, that day of September 11, 2001, at Muirfield CC will, as FDR said concerning December 7, 1941, will forever live in my memory as a "day of infamy."

Contrary to the anti-American contingents who live off our nation, may God Bless America and the fallen heroes who stood up and died as valiant patriots against the traitorous liberal left.

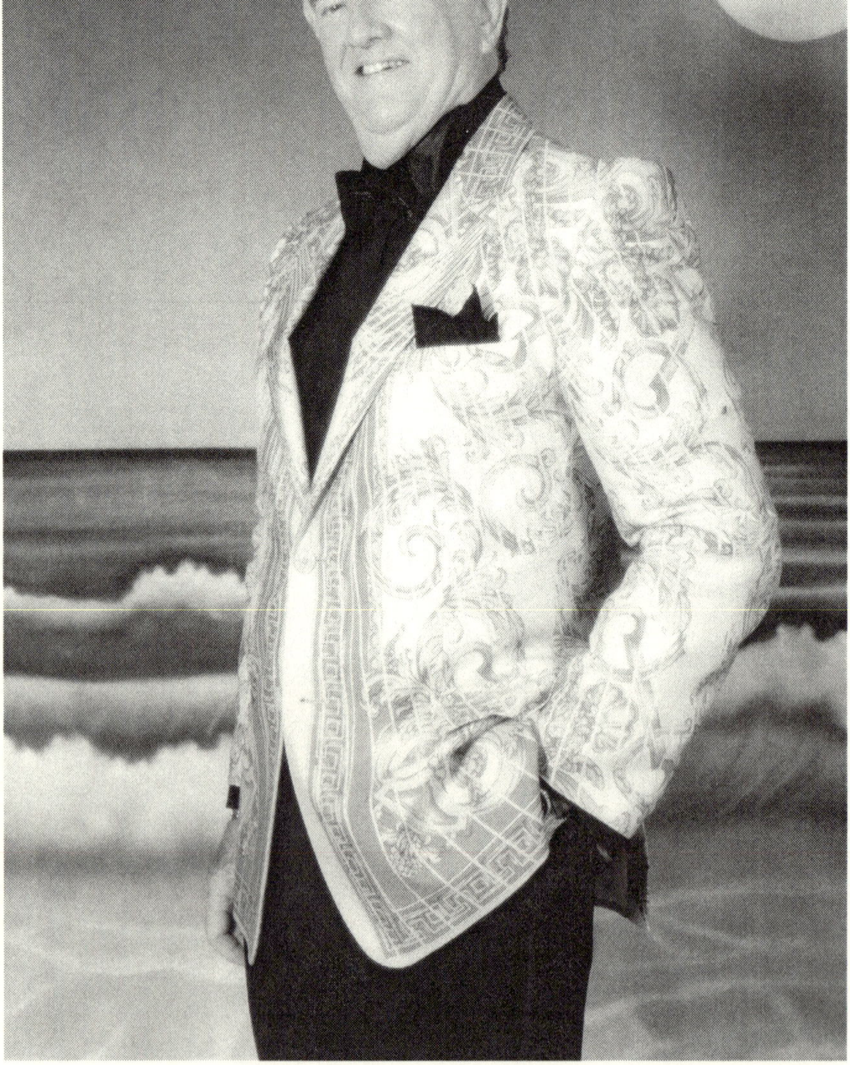

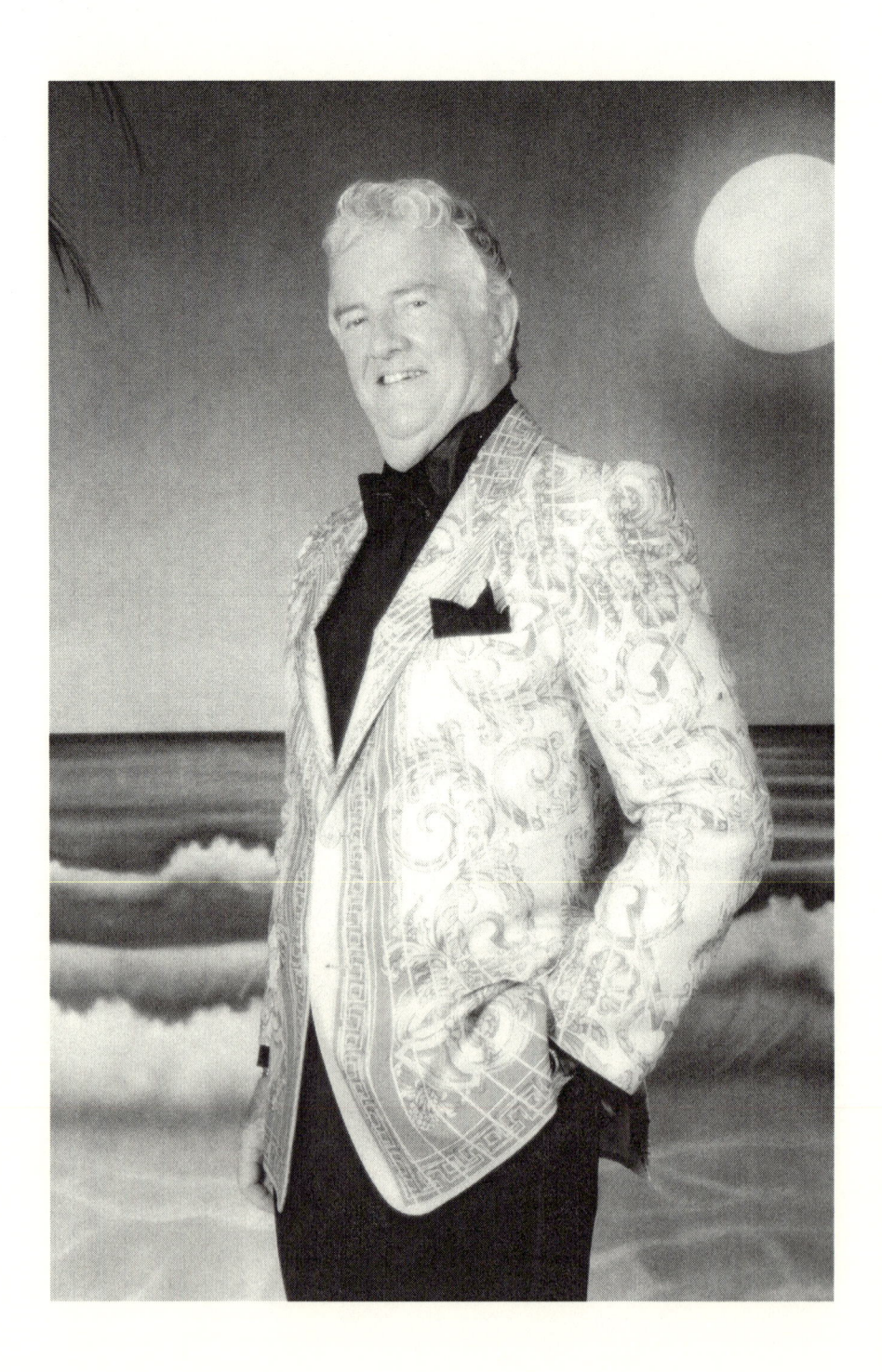

CHAPTER SEVENTEEN

Luck—(Blessings)

It is said the "harder you work the luckier you get." While truthful in some respects, virtually every success has an element of a blessing—or in street parlance—luck. Many people work very hard but never get a breakthrough. One is fortunate to be in the right place at the right time to exploit an opportunity. Again, timing is an essential ingredient. Said another way, I would sooner be lucky than good.

The Boy Scout motto "Be prepared" is a good one. You must be prepared with credentials in order to answer the call of opportunity. Then, by practicing your values, you will hopefully be blessed to have good timing come your way.

Again, I believe good discipline, awareness, credentials, and a prayerful life will help achieve your success goals—whatever they may be. As the cliché goes, "You must buy a lottery ticket if you want to be lucky enough to win the lottery."

So the message is do your part in your life's plan and pray for the best.

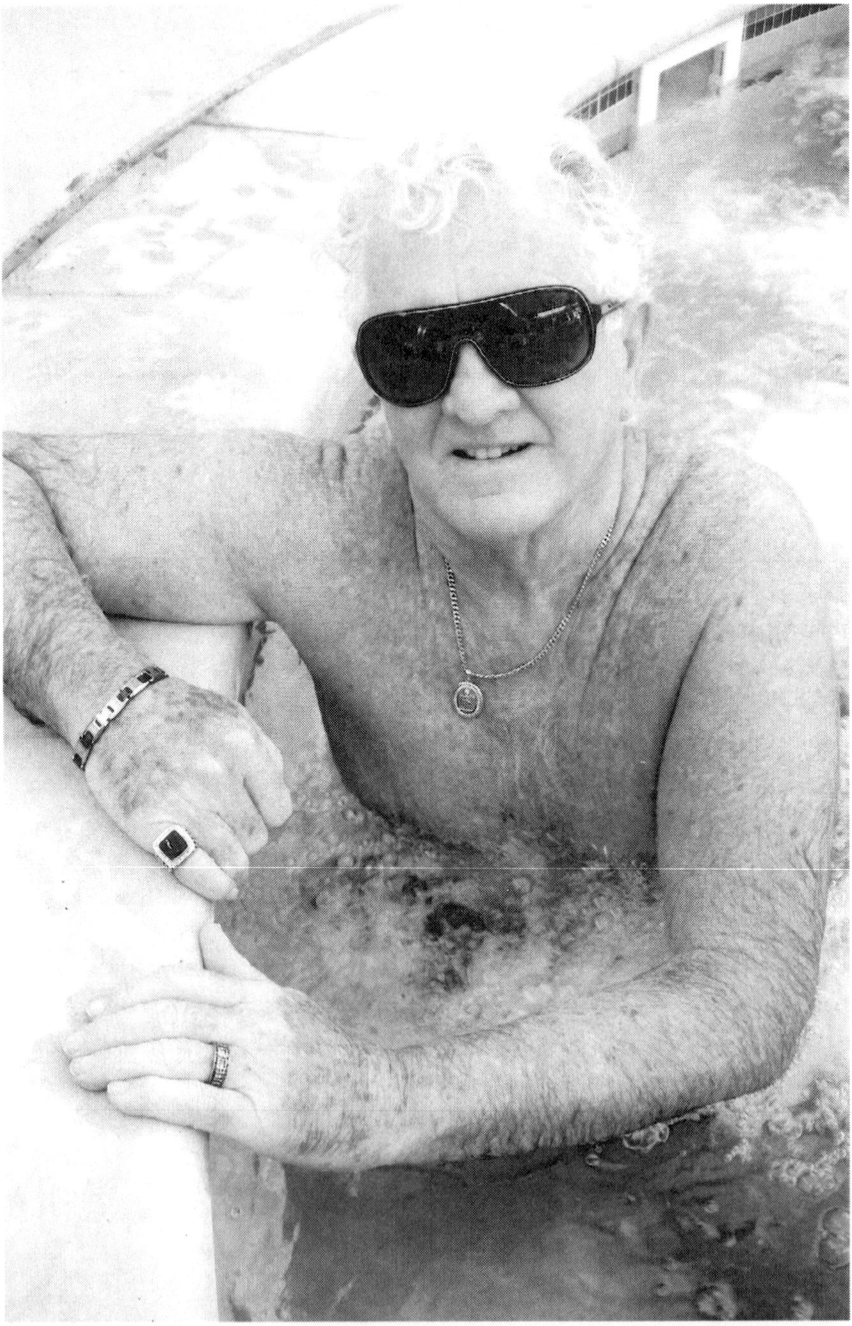

CHAPTER EIGHTEEN

Diet—Physical Fitness

*T*hanks to my mom, as a child, I had a good diet. This made a lifelong habit of wholesome eating. As a child, we had oatmeal most mornings. Hot teas and glasses of milk were a staple. My mom was a good cook and made wholesome meals. She also was vitamin conscious before it was a fad.

In fact, Mom started me on liquid cod-liver oil—ugh (before capsules)—when I was about eight years old. I have taken cod-liver-oil pills every day since then. Cindy is good about putting out my vitamins and small aspirin both AM and PM. The point is a good diet and supplements are essential for lifelong health.

At age 12, I had my first operation—a T & A (tonsils and adenoids removed)

I always liked fruits and vegetables since childhood. I eat them regularly. I have, since childhood, gained a growing taste for fish. Some foods like asparagus, I am not crazy about, but I eat them because they are good for me. We must do this and maintain a balanced diet.

I have always tried to eat moderately, so it has helped me maintain my weight. I enjoy desserts, especially chocolate. Fortunately, now science is saying some chocolate is good for you. Yea!

However, while I do partake in desserts, physical fitness has been a saving discipline. From athletics in school, I continued a physical-fitness regimen into adulthood. After my honorable discharge from the military in 1960, I bought a lifetime membership to American Health Studio/Fitness, USA. Then, I joined the Southfield Athletic Club, the Hamilton Place, which became CMI Tennis Club. When CMI closed, I accepted the invitation of friends to join the JCC (Jewish Community Center) where I currently work out daily. I have continued these workouts almost every day. I try to allocate my time to one and one-half hours so I maximize my workout and don't use up my entire day.

In June 2008, I joined the Oakland Athletic Club. Now, I have the convenience of Jax Car Wash (a daily ritual) and my workout club, because they are side by side! Now the OAC closed and I exercise at the Franklin Athletic Club. Each club I join, closes on me!

My routine is ten minutes on the treadmill or bike, thirty minutes on stretching and weights, and then the balance of the time on pre-workout sauna and after workout steam and shower. On alternate days, I swim several laps in the pool. This "must" discipline keeps me flexible, hopefully healthier, and my blood pressure at 118/78, my cholesterol at 161, and my other numbers in good norm. Now, I must be lucky enough to avoid being run over by a truck. Ho! Ho!

Physical fitness dictates maintaining a regular stable of good doctors. Also, regular visits, physicals, and blood work to have a good medical history as you age. For example, a preventive physical caught a carcinoid on my lung that I had removed about 1991 at Beaumont Hospital by Dr. Stuart Pursel. Further, in about 1998, my PSA suggested further tests. My general practitioner, Dr. Harold Rodner, said 3.8 PSA was OK for my age. However, being proactive, I insisted on further tests, which detected very early-contained pre-cancer in my prostate. I arranged—thanks to my Baltimore pal, Paige Davis—a Hopkins board member—to get an appointment at Johns Hopkins Medical Center in Baltimore. Kevin and I met with Dr. Patrick Walsh, the then number-one proctologist in the USA, who had developed a nerve-saving technique.

After seeing him, we set a surgery date for November and Betty, Kevin, and Jennifer insisted on going. The head anesthesiologist was the brother to a friend of mine, so I received first-rate care. The surgery was successful taking place on a Wednesday. We flew home on Friday, and I went into the office that Sunday—pretty good, if I say so, myself!

Therefore, as I approached my seventy-first birthday this March 8, 2005, I felt fine. Thank God and I pray that my good health continues.

My medical history also includes unexpected circumstances that sometimes intervened. On September 25, 2006, Cindy and I flew to Ft. Lauderdale to spend a couple weeks at the Tropicana condo in Sunny Isles Beach.

During the night, I experienced cramping on my right side. Cindy drove me to Mt. Sinai Hospital in Miami on September 26. Tests confirmed I had a gall bladder inflammation. On September 27, 2006, I had a laparoscopic removal of my gall bladder performed by Dr. Gary Glick. After being discharged two days later, I recovered nicely.

Unfortunately, some minor scarring at the sight where the bladder and urethra connect had developed after my prostate surgery; this complicated the insertion of a catheter during the gall-bladder removal. On a follow-up visit to the Miami urologist—Dr. Alan Neider—Cindy and I decided to return for a minor outpatient surgery to alleviate this scarring. This surgery was scheduled at Mt. Sinai on April 17, 2007 (tax-filing day in 2007—an omen!).

The surgery was an immediate success. But during the wake-up period after the three-minute procedure, an incident occurred. For some undetermined reason, I stopped breathing and my heart started racing, causing some ballooning of the heart, with a blood pressure drop. Although this incident was momentary, emergency procedures were immediately begun in the post-op area. After many tests, including a heart catheterization, no permanent defects were detected or ascertained. Within a couple of hours, I was progressing back to normal pre-op levels.

Prior to this scheduled surgery, I had a complete physical in Michigan, including cardiac, pulmonary, and internal medicine labs. My cardiac stress test had included twelve minutes on the treadmill. Nothing indicated any physical problems.

The doctors kept me hospitalized for observation and further tests, but could not determine any specific cause for the incident. After returning home to Michigan, Cindy and I continued follow-up visits with Dr. Vicki Savas, my cardiologist. After repeated echo-cardiograms and EKGs, she determined that there was no permanent damage to the heart, and continued daily routines, including good diet and exercise, continued routine doctor visits, and common sense would contribute to my continued good health. Dr. Savas contacted Mt. Sinai for the complete medical record—there never was a conclusive finding. Could the anesthetic propofol been a factor? We will never know.

Hopefully, all's well that ends well. While a scare, the medical staff was apologetic and unable to pinpoint the cause of the reaction—again proving, "No surgical procedure is minor." Thank God for the blessings of health.

For longevity advice and quality of life, I recommend—as do experts—disciplining one's self into a firm regimen of good diet and eating habits, vitamin supplements, moderation in all things, a regular physical-fitness program for cardiovascular health, and general well-being. You will lead a physically, mentally, emotionally, and psychologically better quality life. One last piece of advice—floss your teeth daily before you brush. Experts say decaying material in the teeth crevices can poison the body gradually over time.

Again, the mean between extremes.

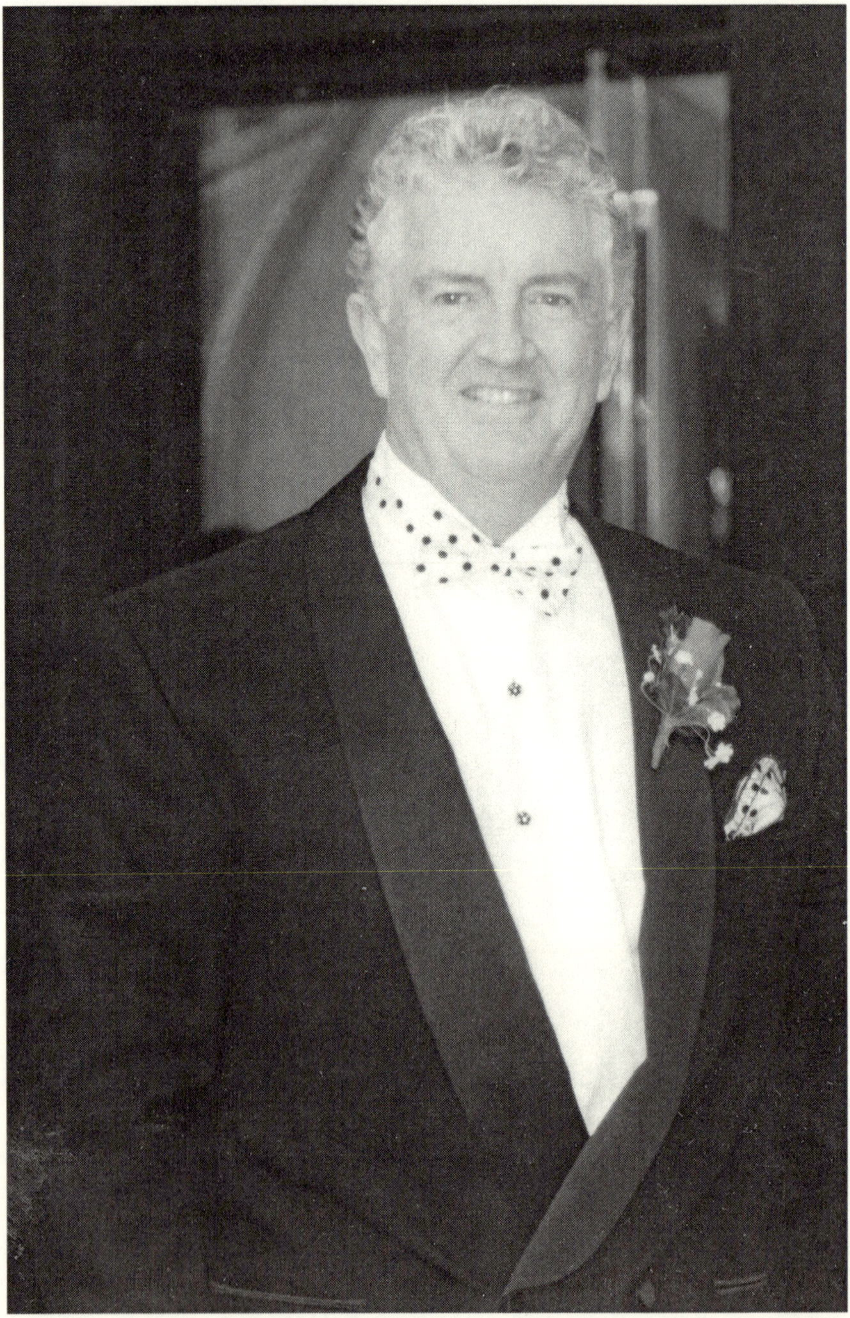

CHAPTER NINETEEN

Life's Strengths and Shortcomings

As the saying goes, "Do you want the good news or the bad news?" Well, I don't feel there is any bad news. From a general viewpoint, one wonders what initiates a person's traits in life.

Is it genetic? Is it learned? Is it from your environment growing up (family, school)? Is it from your friends and associates? Is it from books, media, or TV?

It is from all of the above, although some are more important than others.

For example, mom, dad, and family are number one; early school and selection of friends is another. Religious faith is also important.

One is blessed to have good parents and siblings as I had. Good values spring from this influence. Further, good value-based teachers are important, particularly early on. That is why we hear so much about American-bashing teachers at the college/university level. While these ingrate educators are to be despised, I feel that those who are fortunate to have the good foundation I have described above, usually, are not deviated by these Marxist-oriented teachers.

I believe my good fortune to have good ingredients in my young formation made me stronger in confronting life's hurdles and, certainly, far less likely to be adversely influenced by the negative influences in life's journey.

As for myself, my partial shortcoming was a tendency to impatience, sometimes annoyed with wasteful inefficiency. Life's experiences help you to realize that patience is at times a virtue. Impulsiveness stemming from impatience can be counter-productive. So I have learned to improve on being patient. Not perfect yet!

On the other end, my drive for good results (impatience?) has been a productive force that helped me to succeed. Again, striving to achieve the best you can be can be a positive factor in your life's path. Not being content with the status quo helps you to improve yourself—and hopefully help others.

Again, striving for the mean between extremes. This philosophy also leads to a more contented existence. Within this context, you achieve the "mean between extremes" in life by rational discipline. This has helped me and others who are disciplined to avoid the pitfalls of smoking—a habit that I never participated in because I always felt it was a dirty habit and unhealthy. Also, avoid the detrimental affects of alcohol and drug abuse that some succumb to in life. Good discipline saves oneself for a better life, family, and career. Be strong throughout life and always be your own person.

To frame it into a life-long perspective:

> "Yesterday is history
> Tomorrow is a mystery
> Today is the present
> A present to live life to the fullest."

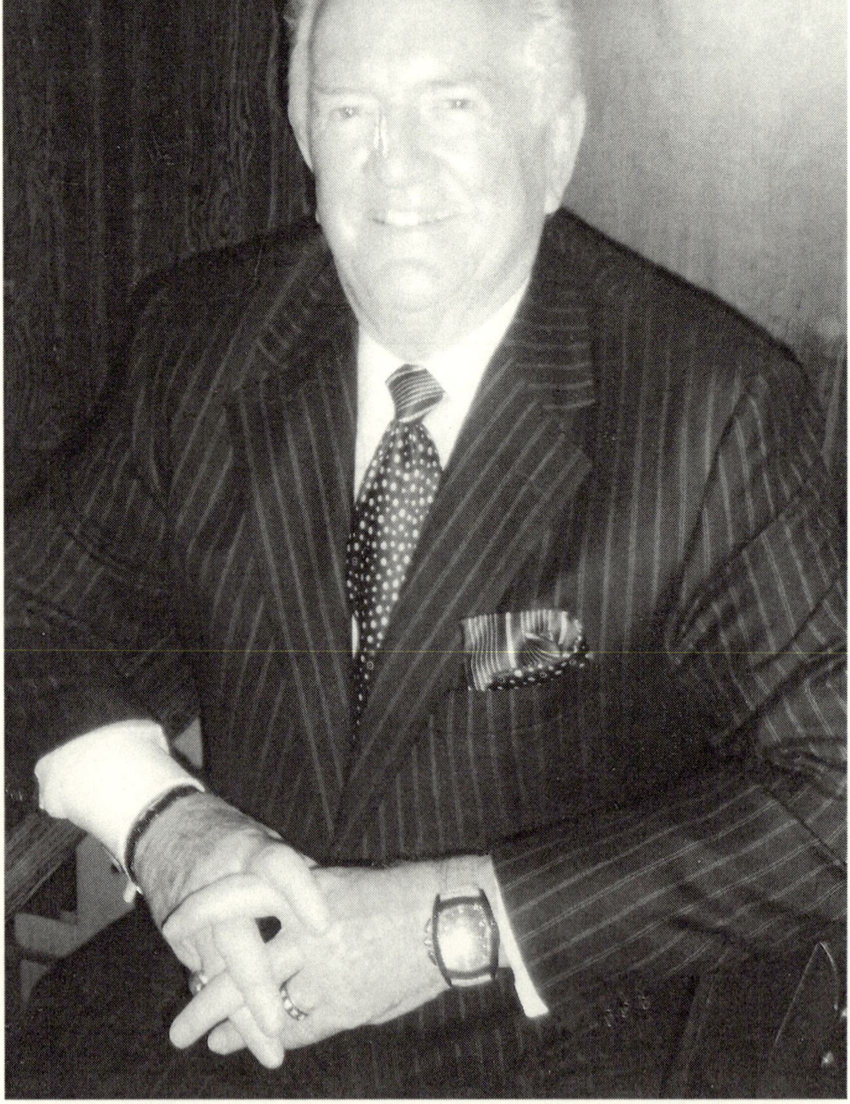

CHAPTER TWENTY

Favorite Sayings

I have always enjoyed "sayings" as they said years ago. My mom and dad had lots of "sayings," perhaps from their upbringing. A "saying" is a rather brief phrase or sentence that is so well crafted linguistically that the "sayings" express a powerful message with a few words. In other words, you say a lot to convey your point with an economy (few) words.

For example, my mom used the expression, "A stitch in time saves nine." This short expression very neatly communicated in an efficient and pointed manner the truism that "timing in life" is important. You could construct an entire paragraph and not get your thought across as effectively as this saying.

My dad and mom liked to use the saying, "There's many a slip between the cup and the lip." In other words, while socializing with tea, gossip or loose talk can carelessly slip out. The same theme used in WWII was "loose lips sink ships." Point made, well-constructed sayings can say a lot in a few words.

Since communication is vital, sayings can help one to be persuasive. Not to say you should overuse them, but they are fun to occasionally work into your communicative conversation.

Some of my favorite additional sayings are as follows:

(a) *A fool and their money is soon parted.*
(b) *A penny saved is a penny earned.*

(c) It's too late to close the barn door after the horse is gone.
(d) Hate can corrode the soul to disintegration.
(e) There's a hell to every heaven.
(f) If you were accused of being Christian, would there be enough evidence to convict you?
(g) It is more important to know where you are going, than the speed you are traveling to reach your destination.
(h) Act in Haste, Repent in Leisure.
(i) "Please leave this place better than you found it," a sign in beautiful nature trails in the Muirwoods, but a good saying for life in general.
(j) Some days, you are the statue; others days, you are the pigeon.
(k) If is isn't broke, don't fix it . . .
(l) Life is fragile, handle with prayer
(m) Sometimes the memories find you.
(n) We plan, and God laughs

Please see Appendix 1 "Whimsical Words—Sometime in Rhyme" for more interesting and useful "sayings" or concise thoughts

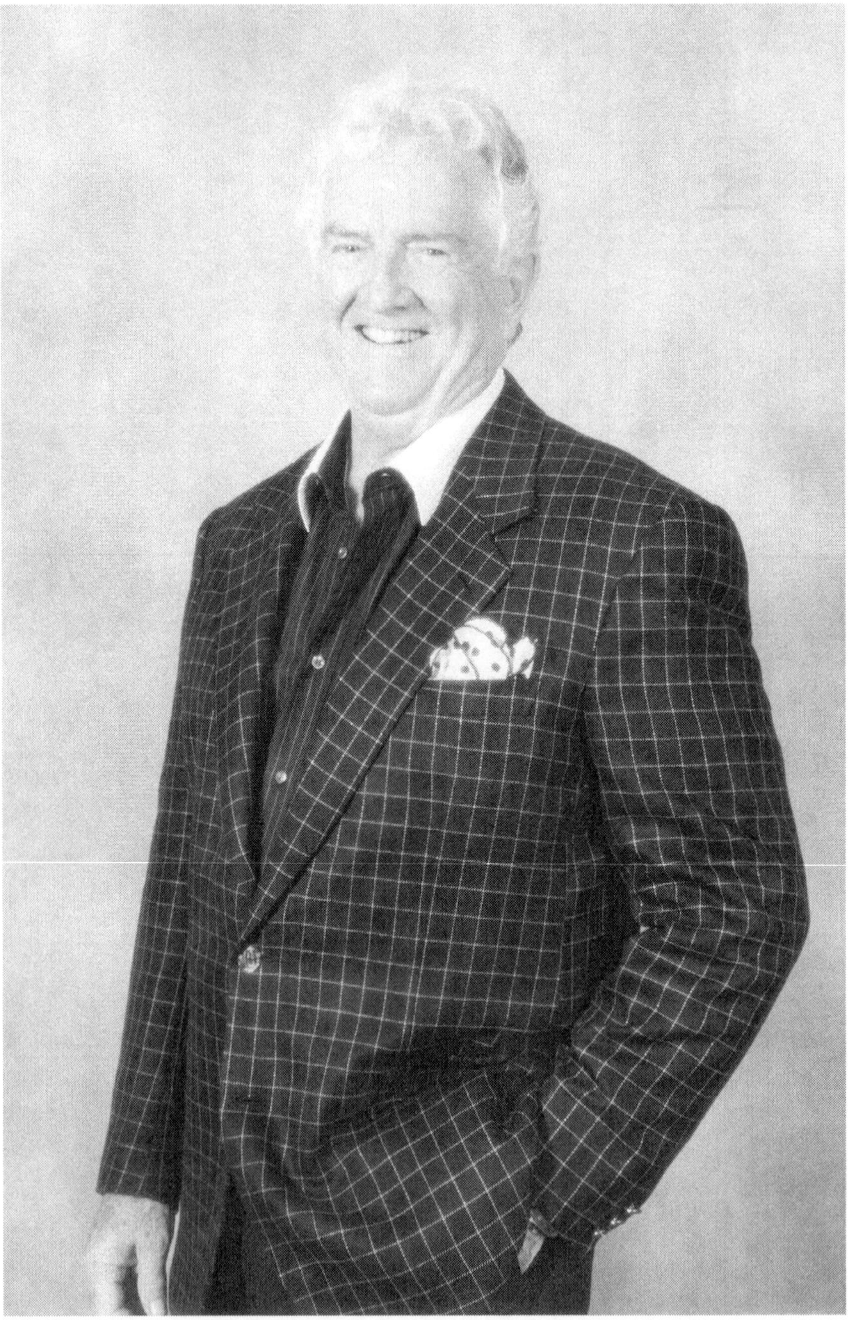

CHAPTER TWENTY-ONE

Sense of Humor

*I*t is said, "When you laugh, the whole world laughs with you; when you cry, you cry alone."

While possibly an overstatement, there is truth in it. My take on the moral of the adage is while life can be difficult, everything, when possible, is lightened by an appreciation for the lighter side of occurrences. Conversely, we have had the last few years of incidents of "road rage" by drivers losing control. Whether rightly or wrongly instigated, this is an example of being too tightly wrapped. Not to suggest that to be constantly a jokester or clown is the recommended image to project; it is not, because everyone perceives you to be a fool and never takes you seriously.

However, the point is that in personal or business dialogues, one can develop a pleasant demeanor with kind, light humor that puts others at ease and enhances your friendship or business pursuits.

I have enjoyed good entertainment and in particular good comedy. One can adapt this into one's persona. For example, cousin-by-marriage Andy Hanley was driving me to a relative's home in Scotland while on a trip there some years ago. We were staying at the Gantock Hotel in Gourock, near the Castle Levan on the River Clyde, which had a weight scale in the lobby with a printout fortune card when you weighed yourself. When Andy picked us up one day, he said, "Let's weigh ourselves." I got on the scale, and the fortune card popped out, saying some usual cliché about "you will have good luck."

Andy got on the scale, and his card popped out. He looked at me, smiled, and said, "It says for my weight I should be seven foot tall. Since Andy is short—about 5'4"—this was an example of quick creative wit. The point is these impromptu quips make one a more-pleasant person to be around. In business, this can translate into success, although this alone is not why one should strive to achieve a sensible "sense of humor" as opposed to the unpleasant sometimes-mean practical-joke approach.

Lastly, I think—as I said at the onset of this section—one copes with life's journey, especially the rough spots, if you can develop a keen wit, which is sprinkled with kindness.

CHAPTER TWENTY-TWO

Staying Alive at Seventy-five

Staying Alive At 75

James K. Graham
March 8, 2009

The 36th Anniversary of My 39th Birthday

STAYING ALIVE AT "75"
"The 36th Anniversary of My 39th Birthday"

Welcome to the 36th Anniversary of my 39th Birthday . . .
That having been said, please let me have my birthday say,
Thank you for the blessings of family and friends
Your loyalty in my life is constant and not the whim of trends,
I am thankful for the gift of loved ones passed on—
This gives me a greater value for those loved ones who do live, on.
So when this aging body starts to ache and pain
I am confronted by the good vibrations from you stalwarts who remain!
Therefore, I contemplate this Dean Martin adage from the book on the shelf
"If I knew I would have lived this long,
I would have taken better care of myself."

Thanks for the Memories at 75

Jim Graham

COME CELEBRATE this ANNIVERSARY
On Sunday, March 8, 2009
From
3 PM 'til 6 PM with DINNER served at 4 PM

We're gathering at the Iroquois Club
43248 N. Woodward Avenue
Bloomfield Hills, MI 48302
(just north of Square Lake Rd on Woodward Ave)

Please RSVP no later than February 25th
cindy1161@sbcglobal.net or (248)909-1202
(No gifts, Please)

"The Graham Family"
Steve & Jennifer Nykerk, Elizabeth Nykerk, Cindy & Jim Graham,
Natalie Nykerk, Keely Nykerk, Kevin, Virginia & Christian Graham

"Musical Joy!"
Rudy's Trio entertains Fr. Eoin, Jim and Cindy

Remembering March 8, 2009
While I am Seventy-five!

March 8, 2009, marked the "36th Anniversary of my 39th Birthday," as noted in my limerick on the invitation to the party. Cindy, Kevin, and Jennifer mentioned, at various times, that we should have a special party—and party we did!

We—almost ninety guests—gathered on my birthday, Sunday, March 8, 2009, at the Iroquois Club in Bloomfield Hills, Michigan. The guest list included family and friends from virtually all phases of my life: grade school at St. Benedict to the present.

Cindy, the party "producer" did a great job of putting the celebration together, including a musical program that was as varied as the guests:

(1) Scottish Bagpiper, Patrick MacDonald, in full Highland regalia piped the guests as they arrived and continued his lilts throughout the entire party.
(2) The Ron, Rudy, and Andy Trio (strolling musicians) played requests at every table tirelessly all afternoon.
(3) "Cindy's Ensemble," including Ed Guay vocalist, trumpeter Bill Beger, and 'herself' Cindy on piano with Sinatra Favorites, my favorite new choral piece—"The Best of Gifts," and a parody of "Jim's Favorite Things," as a lovely musical tribute to me.
(4) Special guest, Fr. Eoin Murphy, wowed the crowd with his rendition of Danny Boy!
(5) Concluding the program, I then offered my remarks for several minutes . . . all in all, it was great fun. My thanks obviously included Cindy, Kevin, and Jennifer, and I joked about the honest, youthful remarks made by Christian, Elizabeth, Keely, and Natalie about my aging.

I would be remiss if I did not reiterate the terrific job that Cindy and our friend, Julie Husak, did in transforming the club into the Scottish Highlands. The full-size flags of the USA, Scotland, and Ireland; plaid runners, bows, and miniature flags; flower arrangements with thistle, acanthus berries, heather, red roses, wild flowers, and gerbera daises on the tables—all superb.

Additionally, the photos and yearbooks, etc., from my entire life were nicely displayed. An outstanding photo—from a vacation cruise through New England and Canada—that Cindy had enlarged and hung over the stone fireplace drew raves. Needless to say, the Iroquois Club food and service were impeccable.

When all was said and done, it was a marvelous seventy-fifth birthday with thanks to all! However, a caveat, how do we top it for my one hundredth birthday?

"Jim's '36th of his 39th' Anniversary Celebration"
March 8, 2009—The Iroquois Club
Jim and Cindy Graham

M/M Thomas Abele
Mr. Ross Ainley
M/M Edward Alexander
Mr. Richard Anderson—Jean Stieber
Mr. William Beger
M/M Frank Boyle
M/M James Boyle
Dr/M Thomas Brobyn
M/M Richard Burke
M/M Jack Caradonna
M/M Thomas Chisholm
M/M Steve Cicchini
M/M Curtis Clinton
Mr. James Costello
M/M Larry Cremen
M/M Walter Czarnecki
M/M Phillip Dailey
M/M Daniel Devine Jr.
M/M Daniel Devine Sr.
Ms. Mary Drake
Fr. Charles Fox
Dr/M Michael Geheb
M/M Joseph Genovesi
M/M Julius Giarmarco
M/M Alan Graham
Mr. Brian Graham
M/M Bruce Graham
Master Christian Graham
M/M Kevin Graham
Mrs. Patricia Graham
Mr. Steve Graham
Mr. Robert Graham
Mr. Ray Grattan—Janet
M/M Edmond Guay
M/M Marty Halloran
M/M/ Lee Halsey
M/M James Hutton
Ms. Julie Husak
Mr. William Jordan
M/M William Jordan

Mr. Barry Kadans
M/M Matt Keil
M/M Joseph Knollenberg
Dr. Newman Kopald
M/M John La Framboise
M/M Daniel Lorigan
M/M Thomas Lynch
Sr. Maria Magrie and Pat Miller
Cardinal Adam Maida
M/M Remo Mancini
M/M Larry Marion
Mr. Patrick MacDonald
Fr. Robert McGrath
M/M Gerald Millen
Msgr. Jeffrey Monforton
Fr. Eoin Murphy
The Nowakowski Family
M/M Steve Nykerk and Family
M/M Robert Ortolan
M/M John O'Sullivan
M/M Michael Papista
M/M David Patton
M/M David Payne
M/M Thomas Radascy
Ms. Barbara Reed
Ms. Kay Reilly
Ms. Chris Rekowski
Ms. Virginia Rozman
Mr. Donald Ross
M/M Robert Ross
M/M Sam Scotella
M/M Thomas Soma
M/M William Slowey
M/M Chuck Sowers
M/M Charles Tines
Msgr. Anthony M. Tocco
Archbishop Allen Vigneron
Mrs. Wanda Zerbiec—Tim Zerbiec

Our fine bagpiper, Patrick MacDonald

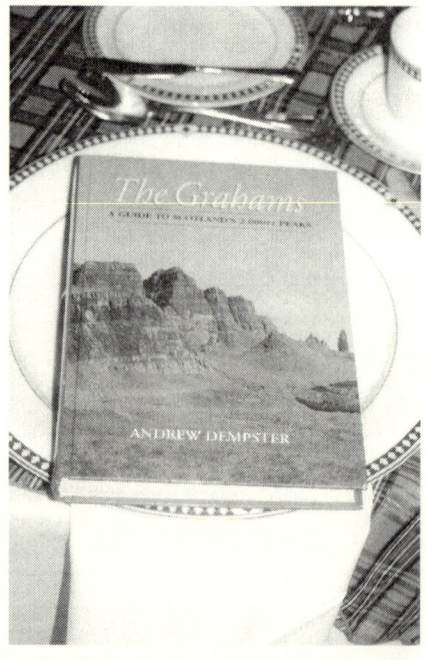

A special gift from Pat MacDonald—the story of the Graham Mountains in Scotland

The Nykerk family with Jim—
Steve & Jennifer, Jim (PAPA)
Granddaughters: Natalie,
Keely, and Elizabeth

A proud daughter,
Jennifer with her
Dad

Grandson, Christian with his Papa;
and Mom and Dad—Kevin and
Virginia Graham

Jim with the next generation:
Jennifer, Bruce Graham (nephew) Jim, Marianne Abele (niece), Kevin, Brian Graham, (nephew), Bob Graham, (nephew)

Kevin Graham (son), Kathleen Cicchini (niece) Steve Cicchini, Jennifer (daughter), Virginia Graham (daughter-in-law)

St Benedict Grade School friends
Back: Ray Grattan, Jim, Marty Halloran, Diane Halloran, Jerry Millen, Sandy Millen;
Front: Cindy, Barbara Reed, Kay Reilly

Special Friends
John & Margie La Framboise
enjoying Jim's portrait

Msgr. Anthony
M. Tocco, Pastor, St. Hugo
of the Hills Church

Mary Drake and Chris
Rekowski (Hair Studio)
pictures and memorabilia

Enjoying the "Golden" trumpet
of Bill Beger

Three generations from U of D High School
Tim Hartmannszerbiec '70 (Cindy's brother),
Christian Graham—hopeful graduate in 2012
(grandson), and Jim '52

Jack & Lorraine Caradonna (Virginia's parents),
Grandson, Christian and his Mom, Virginia,
Jean Stieber, and Rick Anderson (Cindy's son)

Lorraine Caradonna, Catherine Alexander (Jim's 1st cousin),
and Nan Jordan (niece)

The "Girls"—
Natalie Elizabeth, and Keely

Natalie Nykerk,
Son-in-law, Steve Nykerk,
and Keely Nykerk

Jim and granddaughter Keely

Cindy with her Mom—Wanda Zerbiec at "90",
Jean Stieber, and Cindy's Son—Rick

Cindy and PAPA with
Keely, Elizabeth and Natalie (granddaughters)

Edmond Guay, Cindy, and Bill Beger sharing a 'little Sinatra'!

Fr. Eoin Murphy sings 'Danny Boy',
Cindy at the piano, Edmond Guay

Caption: Jim thanks Fr. Eoin for sharing his musical talents . . .

Jim toasts Family and Friends—Cindy at the piano

"Can you tell I have enjoyed myself"!

Thank you's from the podium; Julie Husak in the foreground

Jim and Christian

"Thanks for coming"

Cindy fussing with the "man of Honor" her Jim!

Ancestral Flags Centerpiece
Scotland, United States of America, and Ireland

Scottish tradition tables— Tartan plaid runners, "Irish" shamrocks, Heather, and eucalyptus with acanthus berries, and the 'deepest' red roses!

One More Birthday 'Encore' . . .

As a prelude to my March 8 birthday party, Cindy gifted me with a most memorable trip to Las Vegas.

She arranged for a flight and a lovely five-day stay at Steve Wynn's new hotel—appropriately called the "Encore." We had an exquisite suite at the top of the sixty-three-story hotel overlooking the entire city and valley.

The weather was beautiful—sunshine and clear skies—allowing us enjoyable pool time. Cindy treated us to the most fabulous shows in Las Vegas—i.e., the Jersey Boys (the life and career of Frankie Valli and the Four Seasons and the Danny Gans Show at the Wynn showroom. Both shows were equally outstanding. Sadly, a couple of weeks after we returned home, Danny Gans—age fifty-two—died at home in his sleep. This tragedy further underscores his great performances.

We were amazed at the growth of building on the strip and reminisced of trips taken years back. I have memories dating back to 1962. Unbelievable . . .

Cindy's brother Tim and wife Jeanne live in Las Vegas. They hosted us one evening at their home with birthday cake included—mmm!—making for a lovely get-together.

During our stay, we also had the opportunity to have dinner with my old pal's family—the late Tom Kummer a.k.a. Jay Sebring. The DiMaria family hosted an excellent Italian dinner just outside of Las Vegas. Peggy, Tom's sister, along with her husband, their daughters, and their son, our friend Anthony DiMaria, proudly showed us their hair salon where all are stylists. Another most pleasant evening.

One of the highlights toward the end of the trip was our visit to the Liberace Museum. Fortunately, with our connections—after signing the proper paperwork release—Cindy was permitted to play Liberace's original rhinestone piano used in many of his show appearances. Finally, the CEO asked again if I would donate my Liberace mink coat to the museum someday!

What an incredible trip and birthday gift! Kudos to Cindy for this thoughtful and memorable jaunt to Las Vegas. As I recount the trip in writing, it proves that everything that happens in Las Vegas doesn't necessarily stay in Las Vegas!

Beautiful 'Butterfly' mosaic and ceramic roses in a reflecting pool—the symbol of hospitality—at the Encore Hotel

A beautiful Birthday Dinner at the SINATRA
restaurant in the ENCORE

James Kenneth Patrick Graham J. D.

Room Features

- Approx. 700 - 745 square feet with floor-to-ceiling windows
- Offers three dazzling views: the Las Vegas Strip, Encore pool, or historic Downtown Las Vegas
- 42" flat panel HDTV on swivel and On-Demand movies
- L-shaped sofa, desk area with high-speed or wireless Internet capability
- Cordless phone and phone at desk, dual lines, speaker phone, fax machine
- In-room laptop safe, stocked mini-bar
- King-sized Sealy Posturpedic pillow-top bed with overstuffed pillows and shams
- Luxurious bedding, towels and amenities
- I-Home radio with alarm clock
- Signature Wynn Resorts robes and slippers, iron, ironing board, and hairdryer
- Bathroom with separate shower and soaking tub, dual sinks with night light, 19" flat screen LCD television
- Sitting area with lighted vanity mirrors, separate water closet with telephone
- Electronic drapes and sheers, one-touch climate control
- Connecting rooms are also available

Encore
WYNN LAS VEGAS

The view looking out our 62nd floor window

At leisure in our exquisite suite

Comfortable checking e-mails in our suite

Magnificent hallway to our suite—carpet patterns of flowers, butterflies, and leaves in magenta, scarlet, violet, black, and yellow; wall hangings with patterned mirrors and commissioned art work

JERSEY BOY
tickets and
Program—
March 1, 2009

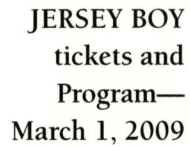

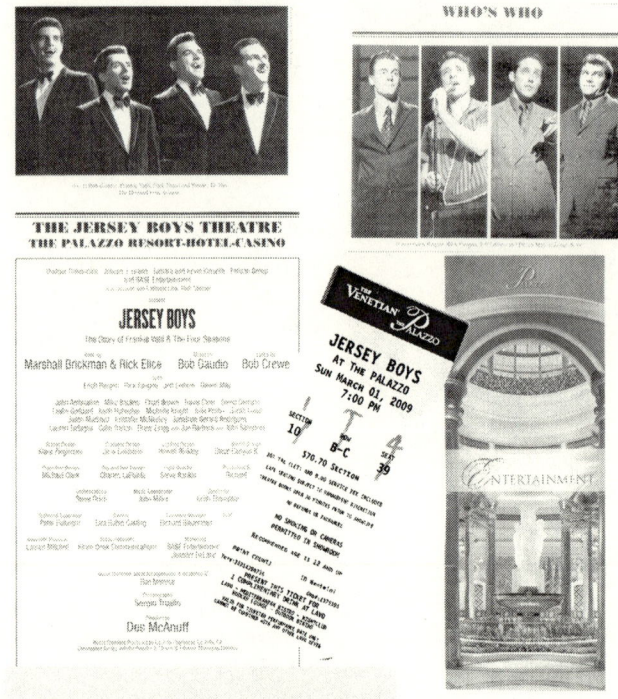

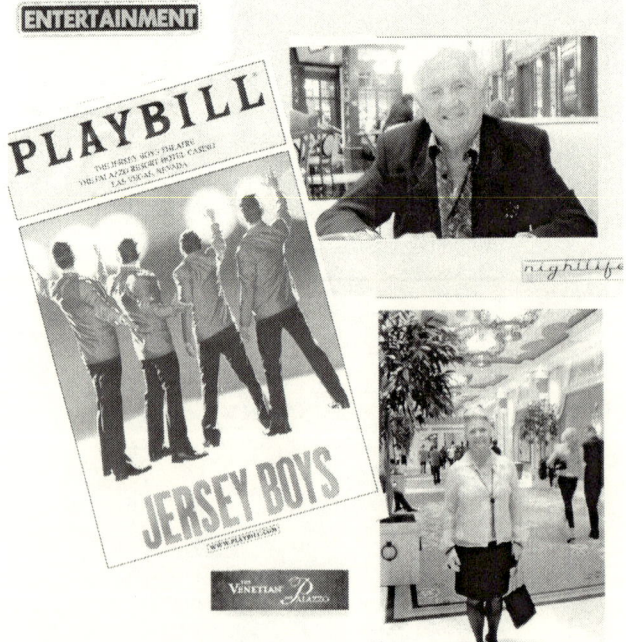

Wow! What
entertainment!
A wonderful
show—a
wonderful
evening!

Breathless Memories 445

March 4, 2009 . . .
Tickets, programs,
and memories of the
Danny Gans Show

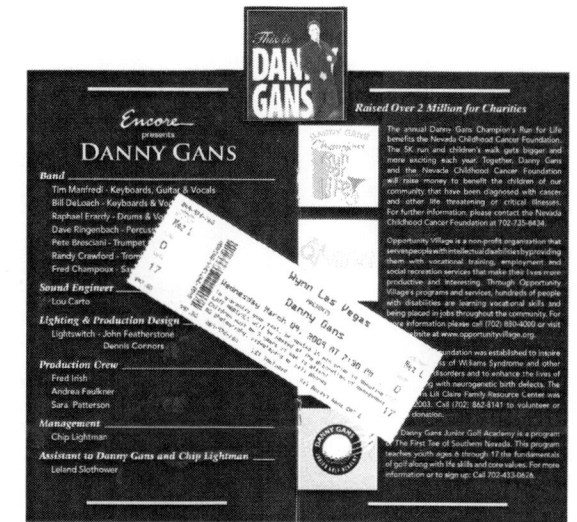

Jim in the lobby
of the ENCORE
theater before the
Danny Gans Show

Is there a new Hollywood Star in Las Vegas?
It must be handsome Jim in the spa pool . . .

Relaxing in the sunshine, poolside at the ENCORE . . .
More beautiful mosaics everywhere . . .

Breathless Memories 447

On the Strip . . . enjoying a classic 1963 red
Cadillac . . . really sleek!

. . . enjoying food and libation at the home of
Tim and Jeanne Hartmanszerbiec (Cindy's brother and
sister-in-law) in suburban Las Vegas . . .
Jeanne was born and raised in Las Vegas—her Dad was
one of the first bankers to come from California
to manage a bank in the 40's.

My favorite picture

"It is not the breaths in life you take that matter, but the moments that leave you breathless, that count"...

Cindy enjoying the privilege of playing
Liberace's famous 'Rhinestone Piano'—
this piano was used in most of his Vegas shows

. . . signed release

**Costumes and Memorabilia
In the Museum Galleries—
Wonderful displays of his jewelry, music, cars, pianos,
and the stories of those who created the
'splendiferous' costumes . . .**

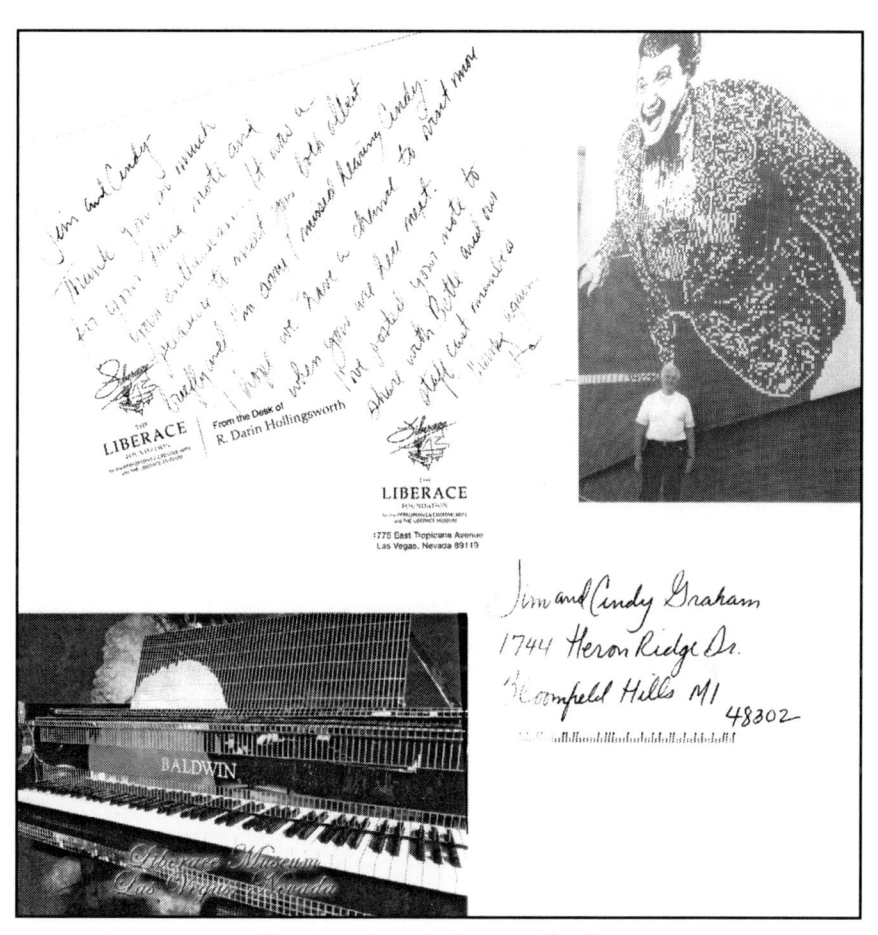

**Two-story mosaic outside the
Liberace Museum**

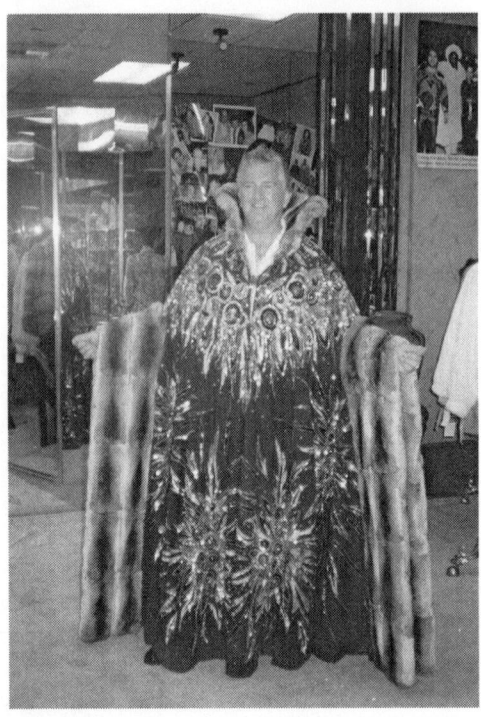

The "Furs by Anna" fur salon in the Dunes Hotel, Las Vegas Nevada.
Through the years, Betty and I had become friends
of Anna Nateece and Ray LaNoble who were
furriers located in Caesar's Palace,
the Riviera, the Dunes, and the Tropicana.
Anna created the show furs owned and used by
Liberace in his many stage shows.
Anna had often mentioned that I was the same fit
and build as Liberace and 'coaxed' me into trying
on several of his show pieces.
This particular one was spectacular and is on exhibit
at the Liberace Museum in Las Vegas where
Anna is now a Board Member.
I also own a full length black mink coat that had been
specifically designed, and on deposit for,
Liberace's personal use—
He died before it was completed—
Both his "Candelabra" signature and
my "James K. Graham" are on opposite inside panels
in the coat.

My personal "Liberace" mink coat
has an interesting lining.
The right front panel lining has Liberace's trademark
of piano and candelabra, while the left front panel lining
has my name embroidered in script.

SCINTILLATING CITY

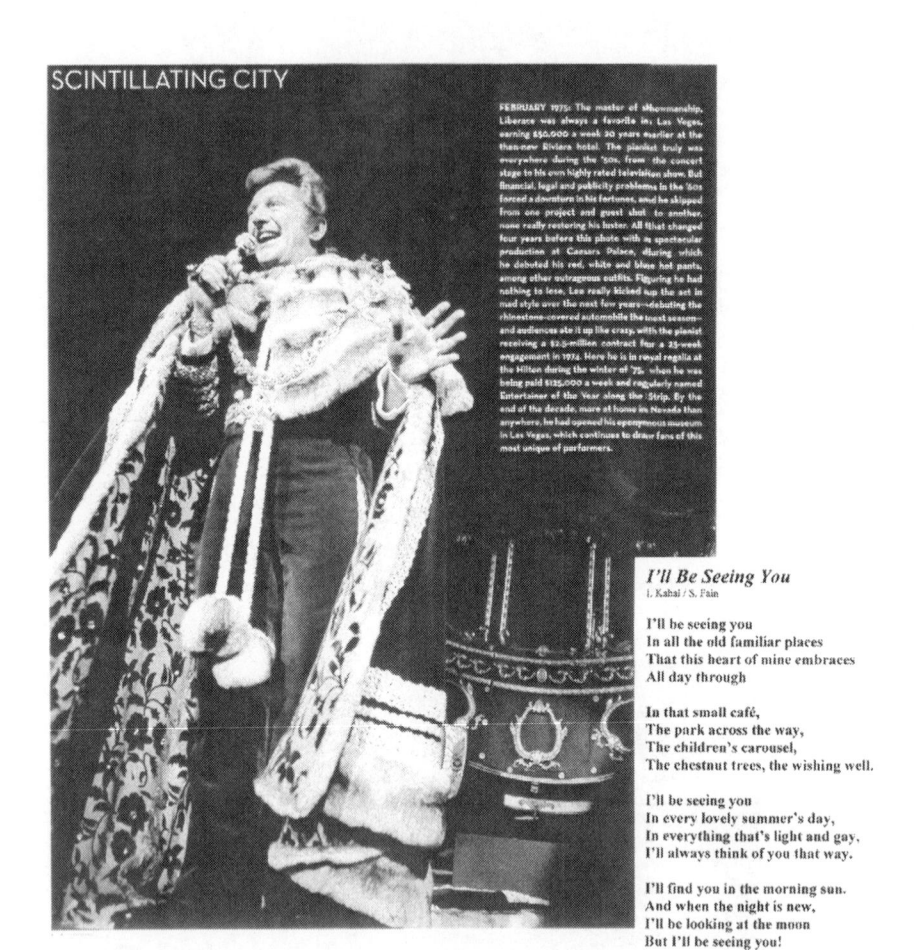

FEBRUARY 1975: The master of showmanship, Liberace was always a favorite in Las Vegas, earning $50,000 a week 20 years earlier at the then-new Riviera hotel. The pianist truly was everywhere during the '50s, from the concert stage to his own highly rated television show. But financial, legal and publicity problems in the '60s forced a downturn in his fortunes, and he slipped from one project and guest shot to another, none really restoring his luster. All that changed four years before this photo with a spectacular production at Caesars Palace, during which he debuted his red, white and blue hot pants, among other outrageous outfits. Figuring he had nothing to lose, Lee really kicked up the act in mad style over the next few years—debuting the rhinestone-covered automobile the next season—and audiences ate it up like crazy, with the pianist receiving a $2.5-million contract for a 25-week engagement in 1974. Here he is in royal regalia at the Hilton during the winter of '75, when he was being paid $125,000 a week and regularly named Entertainer of the Year along the Strip. By the end of the decade, more at home in Nevada than anywhere, he had opened his eponymous museum in Las Vegas, which continues to draw fans of this most unique of performers.

I'll Be Seeing You
I. Kahal / S. Fain

I'll be seeing you
In all the old familiar places
That this heart of mine embraces
All day through

In that small café,
The park across the way,
The children's carousel,
The chestnut trees, the wishing well.

I'll be seeing you
In every lovely summer's day,
In everything that's light and gay,
I'll always think of you that way.

I'll find you in the morning sun.
And when the night is new,
I'll be looking at the moon
But I'll be seeing you!

The "Showman" Liberace

Las Vegas dinner with Anthony DiMaria and his family—
Anthony DiMaria, Jim, Cindy, a sister of Anthony,
Peggy DiMaria (Tom Kummer's sister and Anthony's Mom), another sister, and
Anthony's dad—Tony Di Maria Sr.

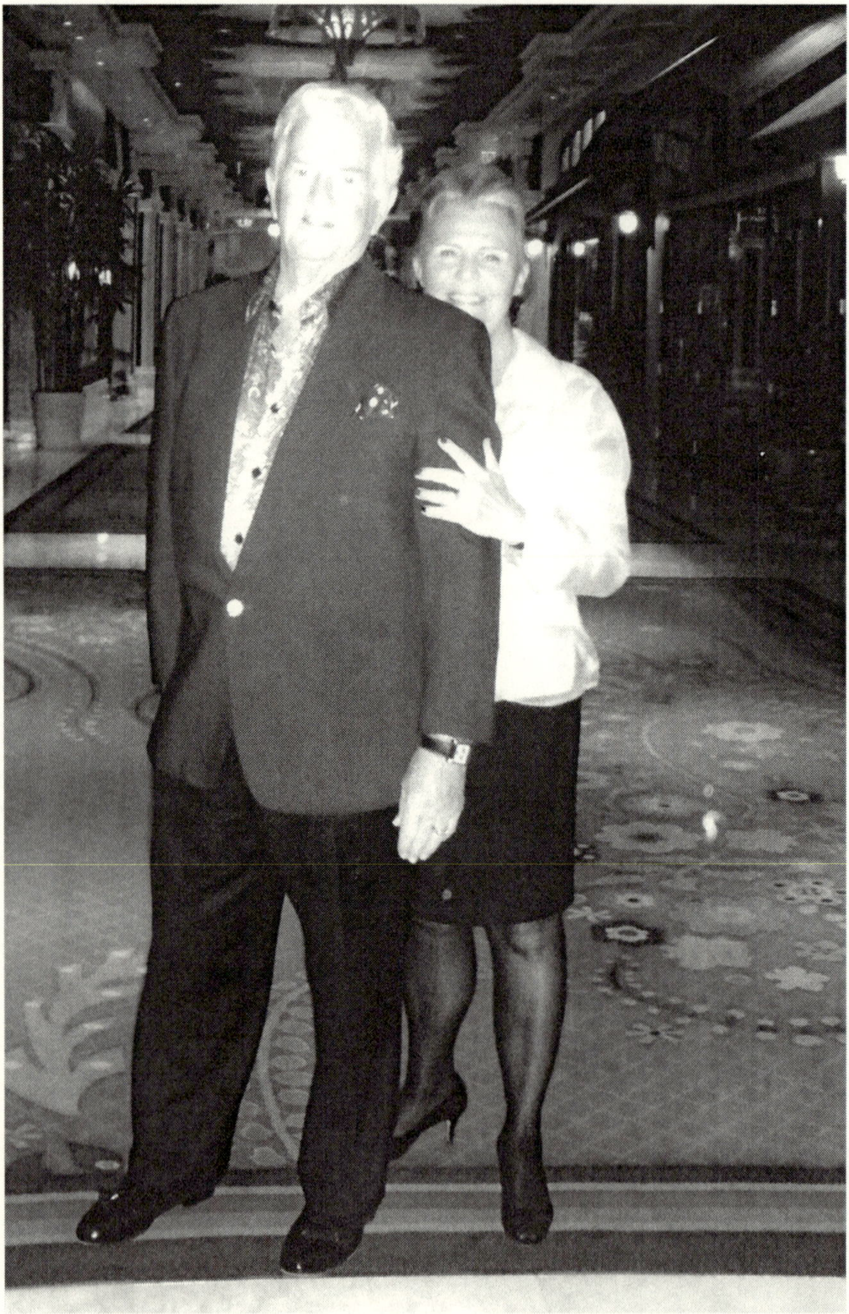

The Best of Gifts

(based on Romans 15:13 and Philippians 4:4-9 by Timothy Dudley-Smith)

May the God of hope fill you with all joy and peace
as you trust in Him
so that you may o'erflow with hope
by the power of the Holy Spirit.

The Best of Gifts is ours within our Father's hand,
with joy and peace beyond the powers
of mind to understand.

Bid ev'ry anxious care and wayward thought depart;
Make known your need to God in prayer,
and He will keep your heart.

Give love the highest place;
have all things good your goal.
Let truth and righteousness and grace
in peace possess your soul.

Become God's garden fair,
where virtue feely flow'rs;
And as the mind of Christ is there,
the God of peace is ours.

"Out Of The Mouths Of Babes . . ."

As a follow-up to my seventy-fifth birthday on March 8, 2009, Elizabeth (eight years old on June 20, 2009) was celebrating her first communion at St. Hugo of the Hills Church, our parish, on Sunday, April 26, 2009 . . . . Her celebration dinner was booked at the Iroquois Club, and we planned a gift for each attendee as a remembrance.

Just as with my birthday dinner, I ordered the same leatherette notepad calendars for each guest at the communion celebration dinner. Several days before the first communion, I gave Elizabeth a "preview" copy to review the appropriate wording commemorating her special occasion.

Elizabeth took it in her hands, carefully read the inscription, and, with a lovely, childlike, serious demeanor, looked up into my eyes and said," O Papa, thank you so much for ordering this diary, it will help me remember you after you are dead!"

"What!" I started to laugh and said, "Elizabeth, let's not go that far."

So much for the innocence and candor of youth. And, in the meantime, her twin sisters Keely and Natalie looked on in amusement.

Speaking of Keely and Natalie, the innocent humor of children is irreplaceable. For example, following a family outing to a Pistons' game, we stopped at the Moose Preserve Restaurant for dinner. Inside the restaurant with its wildlife décor, there is a unique mirrored display over the bar. On the ceiling area, are many wooden decoy ducks attached up-side down. While waiting to order, Rick said, "Look at the up-side down ducks on the ceiling, what would you call that?" All the adults and children looked to see . . . after a few seconds of non-answers, Keely spontaneously called out "I would call it **Duckorations**".

Not to be outdone, Natalie the studious thinker at only five—

(I'm sure this picked up from her Dad), occasionally says to me, "Papa, it's technically incorrect.

Another fun moment and hearty laugh . . . very clever, even if I am the grandfather, a/k/a Papa! Again, "Breathless Memories."

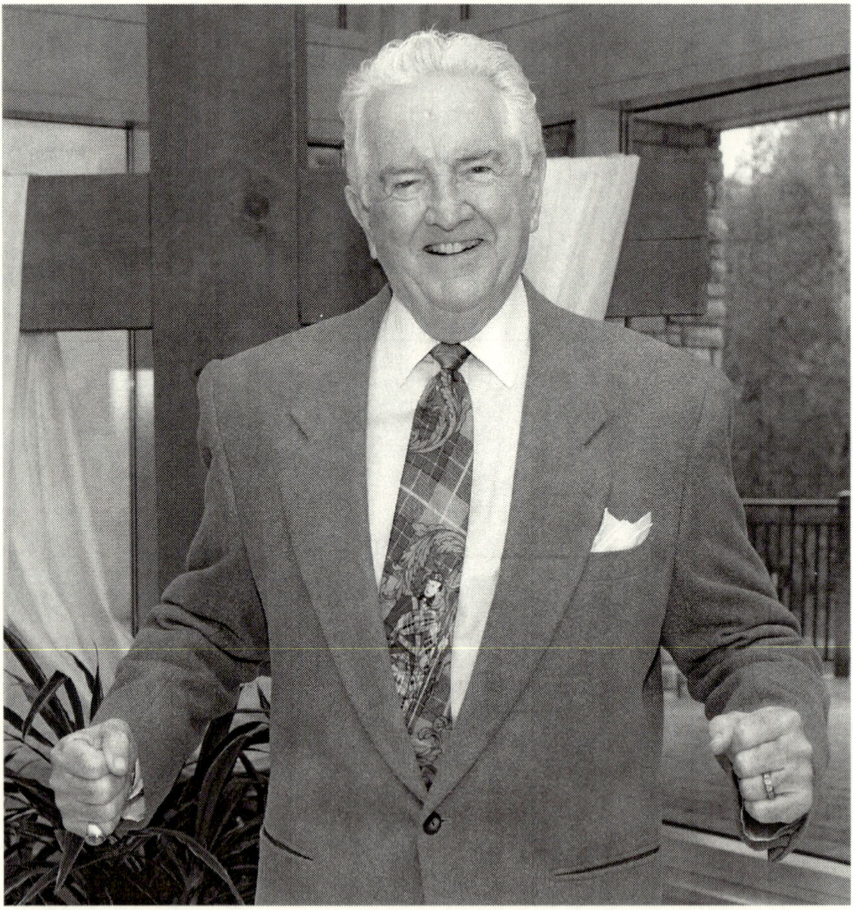

CHAPTER TWENTY-THREE

Summary and Conclusions

*T*he entertainer Dean Martin used to quip, "If I knew I would have lived this long, I would have taken better care of myself." Or as the Swedes say, "Old too soon, smart too late." Either way one verbalizes it, life's progress is the sum total of your experiences, how you deal with the people and experiences and what you learn from them, and how to improve and grow from the experience.

While you can't put an old head on young shoulders, good advice from those who have traveled the road can—if taken—help to smooth the bumps in life's road.

Life should be a quest for improvement. It makes for a happier journey. Observing a disciplined lifestyle is essential. This includes the positive exercise of good habits, regular medical checkups, practice of spirituality and values, proper dietary restraint, good eating habits, good physical-fitness regimen, positive thinking, a sensitive sense of humor, and good works in general.

Conversely, as you develop and nurture good habits (some would say good karma), you, by definition, avoid bad habits and destructive lifestyle. For example, smoking, drugs, and excessive alcohol are flat-out dumb. They are weaknesses in one's discipline and are counter-productive to a happy life. Weaknesses like the foregoing aversely affect the quality and longevity of your life.

Furthermore, bad traits, procrastination, and never seeing projects—big or small—to a continuous conclusion build frustration and snowball these bad habits. Seeing your endeavors to a conclusion is fulfilling and diminishes a cluttered lifestyle. Bad habits certainly send the wrong image about a person or their living environment.

Always try to foster a good commonsense approach to your life's undertakings. It matters less if a person is theoretically intelligent but cannot project an old-fashioned American "commonsense" approach to life's problems—large or small.

Case in point: When Henry Ford I—well-known inventor of the auto, mass-production methods, $5-a-day pay, and other innovations—was in his later years, chairing a meeting of his executives, and he made a tongue-in-cheek point.

Remember, he was a farm boy with little formal education before he grew up to be one of the great industrialists that helped build America. In any event, as he was calling the meeting to order, his executives were slow in quieting down. They were talking about their various colleges that they graduated from, i.e., Harvard, Yale, etc.

Impatient, Henry Ford I got their quick attention and silence by loudly saying, "It's good some of us never went to college, so we could hire those of you who did."

Rather pointed, but another way of looking at it, he was saying he fully developed his commonsense—in his case, genius—far beyond what his executives accomplished with their formal intellectual pursuits. We certainly would not diminish formal education credentials, but we can enhance education's values by innate commonsense.

In addition, developing good friendships/relationships with people of good habits and values is a positive impetus in life. While the average person only generally has no more really *good* friends than you can count on one hand, if they are a good influence, that can be enough.

In the extreme, some people really work at developing contacts for business or social success. This can be productive if one is so inclined. However, these superficially driven relationships are usually less dependable in the long run, even though useful.

As expressed earlier, a good life mission is to prioritize God, family, and country. This is a solid matrix for a stable, happy life. It is said, "Live each day as if it were your last."

While this adage is rather intense, it has some merit if you take it with a grain of salt. The intrinsic advice of a "last-day" approach to living is positive because it recommends that you motivate yourself to cultivate the good traits mentioned in this writing and to logically, then, avoid the debilitating actions. Keeping a positive, hopeful attitude is a good prescription for a good life.

We often hear the inquiry, "How would you like to be remembered?" This is a very insightful, but ponderous question.

Looking back on my life's journey, I would like to be remembered by values that I held dear and tried to live my life accordingly. These are precepts taught by my parents from the cradle and the way in which they lived their lives. All reinforced, of course, by the Christian Catholic faith that my ancestry and family baptized me into.

The following principals are vital to me, and these, I endeavored to emulate. A practical overview is as follows:

(1) *Honor God, family, and country.*
   I do not highly regard fair-weather people. People who give lip service and, ostensibly, support to the triad of God, family, and country when it pays off for them, but bash these values, i.e., country when they are unhappy, are not to be emulated.
(2) *Respect others and yourself.*
   Being sound of body and good character reflects well on your family and associates.
(3) *Loyalty flows from the foregoing.*
   A loyal friend (and/or family member) is a friend indeed—through thick and thin. Someone who practices convenient "situational ethics or loyalty" is not worthy of the name friend or associate.
(4) *"My word is my bond."*
   A powerful slogan . . . but diminishing in currency in the greed-driven, self-interest world. Your word (promise) is a reflection of one's essence as a human being.
(5) *A civilized demeanor should be a principal of your life*
   Stemming from these principals should be a manifestation of civility and common courtesy to others.
   Rudeness signifies an uncivilized disposition and begets more rudeness. Conversely, courteous behavior motivates reciprocal courtesy.

Finally, as I conclude this autobiography and think back to the time I began writing, I euphemistically asked myself, "What time is it?" I responded with this written autobiography, by building a watch! So much for the attorney in me . . .

In conclusion, I would like to be remembered as someone who strove to live up to the precepts that I admired and that I tried my best each and every day to live up to these aforementioned bedrock values.

Finally, *take time to smell the roses in life,* but be willing and careful to deal with the thorns on the stems of the roses.

Irish Lilt

Composed by (*"Himself"*) Jim Graham,
August 19, 2006, Killarney, Ireland

So when your life is all said and done
We pray we've had a very good run
Alas, remember what the Irish say
It will sustain you on your eternal way
"When St. Peter takes a break,"
"St. Patrick guards the heavenly gate."

CAVEAT: *"Breathless Memories" has been written over a period of five years . . . please excuse redundancies and anything that might be construed as braggadocio.*

Note: One of my good friends who lived through most of my career dismissed any merit to this possible critique by retorting, "Since it is the factual truth, it ain't bragging." Enough said!!!

Finally, when we depart this old earth, may it be said as our epitaph: "That person left this earth a better place because of their life-long presence in the world."

Appendix 1

My Whimsical Words—Sometimes in Rhyme

*All of the following poems
were penned by me, yours truly,
James K. Graham*

Christmas at Home—1940
193 E. Arizona St.
Mom, Dad, Billy, Cath, Bobby, and Jim in front

Mom and Dad

In recounting my "Breathless Memories", I would be remiss
If I failed to acknowledge my life's first loving kiss
As the second youngest of a family of five
It was my great Mom and Dad that caused us to thrive
They were loving, loyal and the best parents with no better peers
So on behalf of Catherine, Bill, Bob, Jim and Marianne
we persist in our eternal cheers
May the sacred blessings Mom and Dad bestowed on their descendants
Forever resound in heaven and enhance their souls so resplendent

We revere you, Nan and Bob Graham
From your loving family
January 10, 2009

James Kenneth Patrick Graham J. D.

1990

Lady

She was our regal pal
A royal, loyal gal.
A canine with a classic look
The gaze from her eyes was all it took.
We met her when she was just two
It was an instant love that stuck like glue.
The luxury of her coat of brown
Enhanced the beauty of a face of renown.
She raced daily to greet Kevin from school
And romped with Jennifer by the pool.
With lady to guide, dad retrieved the mail
Lady's needs were met by Betty without fail.
Our safety and home she always protected
The family love and affection Lady never neglected.
She loved to run and frolic with fun
But her respect for our home was always number one.
Lady grew old with grace
But her aging infirmities slowed her pace.
She was brave and strong to the end
But despite her will to win she could not mend.
So to family's great sorrow and pain
On March 29, 1989 our Lady passed from this domain.
Our love for Lady will always endure
The loss is great, but beautiful memories will forever reassure.

(April 1989)

Northern Michigan Tour

To Northern Michigan we did go
So we could join the tourist flow.
We covered all the highways and by-ways,
Always finding windshore (Windward Shore Inn) at the end of the day.
We caught all the scenic views,
Cindy even caught a sale or two . . .
The girls told Rick,
"Fill your tank,"
But he deferred, pulling Driver rank.
So when the needle hit empty
Rick had no choice, but to pay plenty . . .
In Charlevoix, we trudged to every shop in sight
To the point that our legs and feet became very tight . . .
In the Village of Alden, we recovered with ice cream,
The tasty varieties were nothing short of a dream.
For an end to a perfect day,
We shared a spectacular sunset at Torch Lake Bay.

(August 8, 2005)

**Old-time pals—Jim Graham and Bob Ortolan
Summer 2005**

Uncommon Roscommon

We took a side jaunt to Roscommon's Old School Road
To see our old pals—the Ortolan's—at their abode.
Bob and Judy were looking fine
But Bob had consumed all of his 100 gallons of wine . . .
With that news, we were disheartened and let down
But renewing old friendships wiped away the frown
Who could believe, it's been 35 years
Since we last raised a glass of good cheer . . .
So after discussing Bob's neighbors' right of prescription
We said adieu with this proscription,
"When you next brew your fine wine
Save a carafe or a twenty-five liter stein!"

(August 10, 2005)

Hollywood Trumps Foxwood

To Foxwood Lew Cohen did go
Hoping to see his fortune grow . . .
Dressed in his threads from Brioni
This man—for sure—was no phony!
He was praying to Ernie and Emory up above
When, from behind, he felt a gentle shove . . .
Stephie told him "just play it cool"
But the stacked chips made him drool.
He got Black Jack on his first hand
And Lew was feeling mighty grand.
They moved a new dealer in pronto,
He announced that his name was Tonto!
Lew's luck went from good to bad
The Indians sure felt glad.
The Indian from the ancient tribe muttered, "I'll take the Schmuck"
Unaware that Lew had the touch of Midas luck . . .
Since Lew's stack was not in danger
Tonto referred Lew to the cage with the "loan arranger"
Then when Lew returned with his marker stash
And his renewed luck turned into cash,
Tonto tried to call Lew's bluff,
But with a royal flush, Lew had the right stuff.
So, as Lew cashed out, a winner at Foxwood casino
The Indians learned not to mess with the shooter from
Hollywood and Reno!
As he rode off into the Sunday sunset, the Indian felt much
consternation,
Because they realized Lucky Lew now owned the reservation!

(August 2005)

Birthday Greetings To Our Pal Stephie

All the best, Stephie Dear
Lew says another Birthday is here . . .
So, for a gal in her sixties
You are really still quite the pixie and look nifty.
May you stay in good health!
For this is the real wealth . . .
So when you hit 101
Lew will still say, "Baby, you're the only one"
As for Cindy and Jim
We sing you a hymn . . .
Happy Birthday to You
And loads of Birthday kudos!

(July 15, 2005)

Best friends enjoying dinner . . .
Diplomat Resort Lounge—Hollywood, Florida
L to R: Lew Cohen, Jim, Cindy, and Stephie Winig

Time

If we could but dictate time
Who lives but does not die in Time
Each life is measured in meters of time
By One who knows no time
Time is a fragment falling from a cliff
It gathers momentum as it descends
We suffer by time and are relieved by time
Time never falters in its progression
But we, sooner or later cannot keep pace
And, as we hesitate
Time moves away with no regards
Continuing its un-relentless chase
So as we run life's race
Let's make each day a prayer of divine grace.

(October 24, 1992)

To Jennifer and Steve—Happy Anniversary

October 4th is your lucky day
So your family is here to say
From Elizabeth, Keely, Natalie, Christian, one and all
in Sunny Isles have a ball.
As you celebrate number "eight,"
"Eighty" more would be great!
So Happy Anniversary to you both now
Your love is just as new as the day of your 1st vows . . .

Love Always,
Dad, Cindy, Kevin, and Virginia

(October 4, 2005)

James Kenneth Patrick Graham J. D.

Jennifer
Forty Joyful Blessings

Where does one's life go?
Decades fly by like winter snow
So it is with our Jennifer's BIRTH DAY
It was a blessing that evoked many "Hurrays"
February 19, 1970 was the date
The afternoon time was 2:48 . . .
The place was North Detroit General Hospital
Our friends—the hospital staff—were all cordial
Mother Betty was once a young nurse here
Her Mom and Aunt were the delivery room nurses with no peer
It was truly a memorable day of blessing, joy and fun
Each day since then has enhanced our lifelong run
The finest daughter, sister, aunt, wife and Mom you are
A family could not have a brighter star
So, it is on this date of February 19, 2010
We celebrate the 40th anniversary of our "Jen"
May the blessings and joy that you have gifted your family and friends
Be returned to you, Jennifer, in multiples of tens!

Happy birthday to Jennifer
Love Always
Dad, Mom and Loving Family

Kevin and Jennifer

1960 and 1970 were very *good* years
Betty and I welcomed our two Baby Dears
It remains a cherished miracle to this very day
Our joy was brought to fruition in every way
We share the newborns' love that only parents can know
Celebrating the achievements as they grow
Working diligently to give them a good family life
Thanking your blessings and protecting them from strife
The quick passage of years brings them to adulthood
Always thanking God that our efforts succeeded,
Even if we did not achieve total sainthood
It is with great gratitude that we were blessed
with loving, loyal and caring daughter and son
but alas, we have only begun
because their children are a godsend
compounding again the bounty of another generational dividend

*Lovingly penned to the best son and daughter
by Dad and (Mom)—January 2009*

September 2003
Surprise "69 ½ Birthday Party"

Nifty Kevin Turns Fifty

Can Kevin be fifty?
No way! He looks too nifty.
November 6, 1960 was the special day that God selected
Happily, it was also the day JFK was elected.
Kevin's Mom and Dad were ecstatic
His blessed mark on our family was emphatic
North Detroit General was the family hospital
The medical staff of family and friends made the
birth all the more hospitable
Historic Vaughan School and Cranbrook Brookside
Constituted Kevin's early educational pride
On to Lahser High School and a Bachelor of Arts from
St. Mary's in hasty time
Then, achieving a Detroit College of Law Juris Doctor was so fine.
Then the rigors of the State of Michigan Bar exam
Kevin passed it with impressive élan
Soon a marriage with Virginia Caradonna M.D. and much more
Both gifted with a great son, Christian, on 7/15/94
The years fly by with amazing speed
But Kevin's life validates his quality and good deeds
Symbolizing the best son, brother, husband, dad,
uncle and man we all agree
We honor and praise our Kevin to the top degree
So raise Kevin's life flag with 50 stars and colors above
His family and friends sing his anthem of honor and love

With Love and respect

DAD and Your Entire Family

Glasgow—Relatives—McDevitt and Hathorne "Budget Airfares—2005"

Florida's golf in November sounded like a great treat
As the Hathorne's and McDevitt's were in golf heat
So a good fare would do just fine
They located Budget Air owned by Hamish McSwine
The price was just right
But the terms and conditions were rather tight . . .
Dick and Tommy were to be the flight crew
Margaret and Nancy handling luggage and be cabin stews
To Tommy, Dick did exclaim,
"How do we fly this big 747 plane?"
They jointly decided, just pull back on the stick to get it aloft
Just push forward for a landing so soft
So off to America, they did fly
And to their great delight they did not crash and die . . .
So having come so far
It would have been nice if anyone just broke par
But one out of two is not bad
Having a trip that was both glad and sad
But the "Gourock Four" had no last laugh at all
Because despite discounted fares, there was no money left to buy golf balls!

(August 15, 2006)

Cousin, Margaret McDevitt, Cindy, and Cousin, Myra Hanley

Jim, Cousin Dick McDevitt, and Cousin Andy Hanley

Edinburgh, Scotland
The Royal Mile

Ancestral Heritage: Exploring Ireland and Scotland with Cindy and Jim
(August 8-21, 2006)

It was again with great anticipation
That we journeyed toward our ancestral destination.
Detroit, Boston, Shannon, Dublin and a touch down in Glasgow town
All the great historic sites gave no cause to frown.
Our reunion with the cousins topped off with dinner
Remembrances of old and reminisces were a winner.
On the light side, Dick and Andy drove to Glasgow from Greenock
Unfortunately for Myra and Margaret,
they parked the car in Kilmarnoch!
Off to Loch Lomond we did go
To ride the ferryboat with the waters' flow
It's Inverness by afternoon
We may even shoot nine at Troon . . .
Bridging to the Isle of Skye was no hassle
Including a delightful visit to the Doonan Castle
Speeding onward to Loch Ness
Looking for "Nessie" more or less!

Then, an amazing demonstration of trained sheep dogs
Skillfully herding sheep by signal over the bogs
Stopping at Pitlocky to tour the Distillery Ednadour
Sampling their single malt scotch and then buying more
Thus lightening our mood as we hit historic St. Andrews and its renowned old course
Making this ancient city with ruins an educational source
Traveling west to Edinburgh with castles and Tattoo
It was an experience entitled to much ado
So flying from Scotland over the Irish Sea
We landed in Dublin with continued glee . . .
Off in the morning to Waterford's crystal works
Watching the artisans etch out the beauty that within lurks
Hurtling down the highways and by ways to County Cork
Enjoying the harbor and waterways until we reached the fork
To the traveled road to ancient Blarney Castle
Climbing the 129 steps to kiss the Blarney Stone
proved to be no hassle . . .
We came to the town of Gort, as we left County Cork
Then came the realization that our bus also contained some dorks
So as the sun was setting in the west with nature's golden harmony
It was our pleasure to arrive and disembark in bustling Killarney
So while our August 16th sojourn was busy and long
This day's memories of Mother Ireland were as a lilting song
August 17th found us departing Killarney with anticipation
It was our prayer the day would be spared precipitation
Our goal was to travel the sights of interest on the Ring of Kerry
We drove the road soaking in the sights, but did not tarry
Down the winding roads to Killarney's Lakes and Dells
Sur'n the sights and beauty were beyond swell
Stopping for pictures around the Bay of Dingle
The history and the sense of heritage surely made one tingle
Wasn't it from this Bay in the 6th Century sailed
St. Brendan the Navigator, to the new world of America to be hailed
From Waterdown down the scenic road and up
Admiring the Scellig C. C. where O'Meara and Woods
practiced for the Ryder Cup
Pausing again for awesome photos,
to buying a Ruth Fitzpatrick work of art

Then, a wee bit worse for wear, and back to our AM Killarney start
Off from Bunratty Castle on the 19th of August
After a good night's sleep and one Jameson the night before,
we were again robust
We journeyed to Connemara Marble and shopped with rejoice
As a bonus, we had a great geological treat from the owner himself,
Ambrose Joyce
Purchases aplenty we did make
Happy indeed, our credit card limits did take
Our transport hastily moved us to Claddagh home
Hither and yon through the Claddagh jewelry we did roam
Speeding along the coastland, we passed the beautiful Glen Lo Abbey
The club grounds and golf course so lovely, but undulating greens
making golfers crabby
We loved Galway City's beauty of boats and river
The Cathedral and gracious swans gave one a quiver
Returning through Irish countryside we feast at Dromoland Castle
Making the days long travel, well worth the hassle
As we prepare for tonight's Bunratty Castle Medieval Feast
We thank God for this days' safe journey at the very least
It is hard to believe it is August 20
We again begin this day with anticipation aplenty
Across Ireland's Midlands, narrow roads undulation on peat
But as Christian would say, "the countryside was sweet"
Through the fine City of Limerick
Best known for its history of limericks
Sure'n we came to the city of Rose of Tralee
It would only be right that we hummed it with glee
We stopped in Rosscraig's Racket Hall C. C. for a respite
A finer place you could not find for a spot o' tea and a biscuit
A touch of the hair o' the dog was on our mind
So our single purpose was a Irish distillery to find
It was our good fortune as we traveled in haste
To discover the 1757 John Locke Distillery for a taste
Nestled in Kilbeggen in County West Meath
We found Irish whiskey to shiver your teeth
Did you know Irish whiskey is spelled with an "E"
They say it stands for Excellent and that is the key

The Scots known for a spirit frugality
Spell the Scotch whisky without an "E"
Your whiskey education would be remiss
If some of the difference of Irish and Scotch whisky was amiss
The economical Scots distill scotch twice
Irish whiskey makers distill thrice
So with the extra distilling step for this brew
The Irish proudly feel they achieved a coup
We wound up our day at Cabra Castle in Cavan County
Although in Ulster, it had beautiful history in lavish bounty
Starting in 1699 with the O'Brien clan
It suffered the English Cromwell's killing plan
The beauteous castle and land were stolen
And so it was the native Irish were emboldened
So through decades of hard times the castle had passed
Until to this day that a purchaser had enough cash amassed
While Cabra Castle has returned to beauty
To recognize this elegant place is the tourist's duty
So spending our last night in an Irish Castle was a thrill
But our early morning departure was a pill!

Loch Lomand
2006

Father Eoin, "Are we goin?"

Sure'n it was St. Paddy's Day again
and our thoughts were of ancient Erin . . .
So we honor our Irish clans
by arrangin' an Ireland travel plan . . .
The answer was as plain as your Celtic face,
make a call to Fr. Murphy's place . . .
And, so it was on a Monday in March
with a taste of the hair of the dog to give me starch,
There was no beating around the bush
our 'green' plan needed a push . . .
For after all, the Irish were green
long before it was keen . . .
The question to Fr. Eoin was, "are we goin?"
Promptly, from the lad from Cork,
Cindy and I got a "no blarney" retort.
'We're off on the 19th of June
for a fortnight of the Emerald Isle and castle ruins.'
We will journey the valleys and vales
walking our ancestors' paths and trails.
The lure of the Emerald Isles
bringing nothing but happy smiles . . .
So thanks to Fr. Eoin's doin'
to the ancient isles we are a goin'.
SLAINTE to our priest pal
as we will fly home from Dublin with a fond farewell.

Erin Go Bragh

By
Jim Graham "himself"
With an assist from
Cindy "herself"
May 2010

Envy

We all know the evil word hate.
Did you know ENVY is its mate?
Is there something in the human condition
that drives some people to perdition?
It is wonderful to see success
but a personality warp causes some to obsess
Some politicians use envy to win elections.
Envy drives some to dereliction.
To envy someone who achieved what some person did not
is just a deficiency that causes their soul to rot.
So if someone has this mean inclination
they would be best served to say an Act of Contrition.
Then use the time spent on this prior negative trait
to treat others positively rather that act in hate
So as they emanate positive vibes
their own success will coincide.

(August 12, 2009)

The Neighborhood
Growing Up—Hanging Out

We grew up in the 1940s and 50's
Looking back it was pretty nifty
Thinking about our old neighborhood
Reminds me of good times just as it should
Our boundaries were Woodward, John R and 6 Mile
All the good memories bring back many smiles
Woodward was bordered by Palmer Park
Summer pony rides, winter ice-skating—always a lark
Six Mile had the PB Bar—the Palmer Park Bowling Alley
Woodward has the RKO and street car trolley
John R contained Leo's Texaco Service as a hang-out
Also, the Ambassador Theater and pool room for fighting bouts
Back then, you knew every neighbor on every street
So walking as we must, learning inter-personal feats
Sadly, some who had no long-term vision
Ultimately, paid the price and sentenced to prison
Fortunately, those who believed in good goals
Eventually, they achieved successful life-time roles
Alas, as we matured into adulthood
We must acknowledge we were educated by our neighborhood.

(2008)

2007—Christmas gathering of the "Old Neighborhood John R Gang" at our home in Bloomfield Hills

"Pop's Place" Sebawing, Michigan—
Annual reunion each year on the second Monday in August—
The St. Benedict 1952 Grade School Alumni, family,
and friends gather at Hank Arnoldi's Restaurant

St. Ben's Class Of 1952

Who are the class of 1952
They grew up near Church and Woodward Avenue.
We were children of the 1940's,
In a time when life was a tranquil sortie . . .
Our life revolved around sports, fun and teaching nuns-
Eternal summer meant, the beach, cruising, and sun.
Our rite of passage to high school came in the 1950's
When we felt growing up was pretty nifty.
Sad to say, we lost some pals along the way
Giving us an insight into life's future hard forays.
As Virg called the roll,
We again realize the toll.
It was August 1969 in the full bloom of summer
That we lost our childhood pal Tom Kummer.
His life was taken at age thirty-nine
Years and years before his full life's time . . .
As with all our friends who died and could not tarry
We cherish the fond memories that we carry.
So the Class of 1952 soldiered onto mid-life
Coping with kids, career and life's strife.
Years fly by, hurling us into senior status
Classmates still, we each appreciate the extra decades given gratis.
Therefore as we annually convene in reunion at Pop's Place,
For these childhood friendships we are thankful for this grace.
Continuing into the seventies of our life we slide
Let's count each year and our class friendships with great pride.
So Classmates of 1952, as we treasure our special bond
Let's always stay loyal, true, and most especially, fond.

Your Grade School Classmate
Jim (Jimmy) Graham

(At Pops' Place, August 15, 2005)

The Hair Studio

We all have our favorite places to go
Well! One of mine is the HAIR STUDIO . . .
I've been a customer since John opened 34 years ago
Still located in my former office building,
on Big Beaver—Suite # Seven-Five-O
The flavored cream with a little hot coffee
kicks my appointment off nifty
Preceded of course by a friendly "Welcome, Jim"
Then into Mary's den, to save my shirt by donning a smock
Then hot towels, creams and massaging fingers soothe my face
Are the aging wrinkles winning the time race?
Mary peeks out the "Drive-in window" to check the timer
Go! It's time to move to Chris' chair (#1 recliner)
My head descends into the hot water basin
The sudsy shampoo has the fragrant scent of warm raisins
Then Mary attacks my nails
The clippings of 10 fingers and a head of hair fill a pail
As my hair cutting has reduced my mop
The razor is about to shave my neck, we beg Mary that her clippings stop
And, so it goes on another fun bi-weekly visit to the hair shop
After 850 visits, thank God I still have hair to trim
Even if I didn't, I would still go to enjoy the vigor and vim
So when you need an all-around lift
You can't beat Chris, Mary, Char, and Christine for their friendship's gift
In addition, Mary and I discovered a therapy to relieve gloom
Just hit your forehead with the palm of your hand and sing
BA-DA-BOOM!

Happy Facials and Trims
June 27, 2009

Monsignor Tony—"70" on July 11, 2009

From bambino to Monsignor
From Altar Boy to Pastor
From St. Margaret of Scotland to St. Hugo of the Hills
Baptisms, weddings, funerals, requiring priestly skills
Counseling Popes, Cardinals, Archbishops, over five decades
Reliving their liturgical duties with respectful accolades
So as we celebrate our good friend's birthday with
the toss of a bocce ball
Best wishes for 70 more with health and happy incense from one an all

Ciao!
Jim and Cindy Graham
St. Hugo Parishioners in Perpetuity

Jim and Cindy celebrating at Palazzo de Bocce with Fr. Tony on his 70th Birthday

Friends for 25 years!
Jim, Cindy and Msgr. Tony

Msgr. Tony's Blessed Numbers

"Numbers" is a popular secular TV Show
Well, when it comes to blessed numbers, Msgr. Tony is the real pro
His life's journey began on 7/11
Can you believe it was 1939 when he came from heaven . . .
Onward to grade school in '45
At St. Catherine's, young Tony Tocco began to thrive
On the DSR bus in 1954,
to Sacred Heart Seminary he traveled many miles and more.
As a seminarian, Fr. Tony made the gospel come alive
Successful again, he completed his priestly academics in 1965.
Blessed numbers, Tony was only 25 at ordination
For the first time and thereafter, "FATHER" Tony was the exclamation!
Now, 2010, 45 years as a priest and 25 years as St. Hugo Pastor
Could the decades have gone by any faster?
Wow, 45 plus 25 equals seventy
This number matching Msgr. Tony's birthday year a plenty
So June 5th and 6th, 2010 are days of love
As we pray thanks for Fr. Tony to our God above.
And just so you know, Fr. Tony,
Our sincere prayer is no Sicilian Baloney!

Prayerful Blessings Always,
Your friends,
Jim & Cindy Graham
(on the occasion of your "Special" anniversaries)

August 1966

"Hi, I'm Director of Marketing—Bob
How about a new job?
You are a young attorney
We can pioneer a new career journey . . .
We are creating a unique product and company
Your position is to manage and protect me from home-office acrimony
You will take a cut in pay
But the potential is great if you stay
Our corporate logo is 'VALIC'
We must outsell our competitor 'PALIC'"
So Bob and Jim started our corporate team
Sales became great and we kept our overhead lean
It was that Bob was my mentor,
Together we achieved our goals right in the targeted center
So after 33 years of VALIC trips
On 12/31/99, I called it a career and cashed in some of my chips
It could only have happened by partnering with a friend who had
the chutzpah to be born on Bastille Day
Therefore, for Bob a chorus of big hoorays.
More importantly our friendship has grown for 43 years
So, to my good pal Bob, nothing but the best of cheers.

Yes, Bob and I shared the U.S. military experience,
we partnered as business warriors
and have mutually run a winning life's marathon.

All the Best,

Your lifelong friend

James K. Graham

Penned on July 14, 2009

Good Friends
Bob Phillips and Jim Graham

John Graf and Jim Graham

Top of the Day, John

. . . this is Himself, Jim Graham and Herself, Wife—Cindy,
(playing background piano music)!
We are commemorating the 2nd Anniversary of your 25th Birthday
from our Living Room in Heron Bay, Bloomfield Hills, Michigan.
. . . this brings back the enjoyable memory of you John, on a
previous visit to Michigan with Bob Condon—
God rest his soul—sharing a Jamieson and each others' company in
about 1977, in this very room.
Cindy is playing on the Schimmel crystal grand, one of our favorite
songs entitles "The Best of Gifts."
The piece is so appropriate because it signifies what you are to your
family and friends.
However, before I get too gushy,
I will recite a lyrical verse I penned for this special occasions for you
and Maureen.
The verse is entitles: "John Achieves the Big Five-O"

JOHN ACHIEVES THE BIG "FIVE-O"

Devlin to Poulous, "Graf can't be Fifty,"
Poulous to Devlin, "Right! He looks too nifty."
But just as sure as birds fly
The aging calendar does not lie . . .
Yes, September 14, 1959 was recorded as a special day
Because, our pal John Graf began to mark
His impressive earthly way.
So, a big "Happy Birthday John" from all your fans
Another fifty years is the big plan
"All the Best Regards" is our "Forethought"
Health, Wealth, and Happiness is our "Afterthought".

Jim and Cindy Graham & Family

Elizabeth Elaine Graham
"Betty"
April 2, 1932-April 8, 2000

Betty was only 67
Too soon to be on her way to heaven
Betty (given name Elizabeth) lead a great life
From childhood, academy, head nurse to a wonderful wife
From looks to personality she had it all
To repeat a cliche, just like Bogie and Bacall,
She exhibited a warm personality
Those who knew and love her considered her Miss Congeniality
A better daughter, mother, wife and Gannie you could not find
Betty was, in truth, one of a kind
She died in a hospital of a malpractice error
Taken too soon, like the 9/11 terror
However, we are left with a beautiful legacy
Which is a blessing in perpetuity.

With Love
Jim

Betty

Betty was her name
Pretty was her fame
Nursing was her skill
Helping people was her thrill
Marriage was her vow
To all its holy tenets she did bow
Motherhood was her love
Her children were her passion from above
Good cooking was her fun
Without discipline, you could gain a ton
Loyal friendship was her demeanor
No one could have a friend more keener
Tennis was her special sport
Just turn her loose on any court
So live a life so fine
And your legacy will live an infinite time.

*In Memory of Elizabeth "Betty" Graham
August 15, 2009*

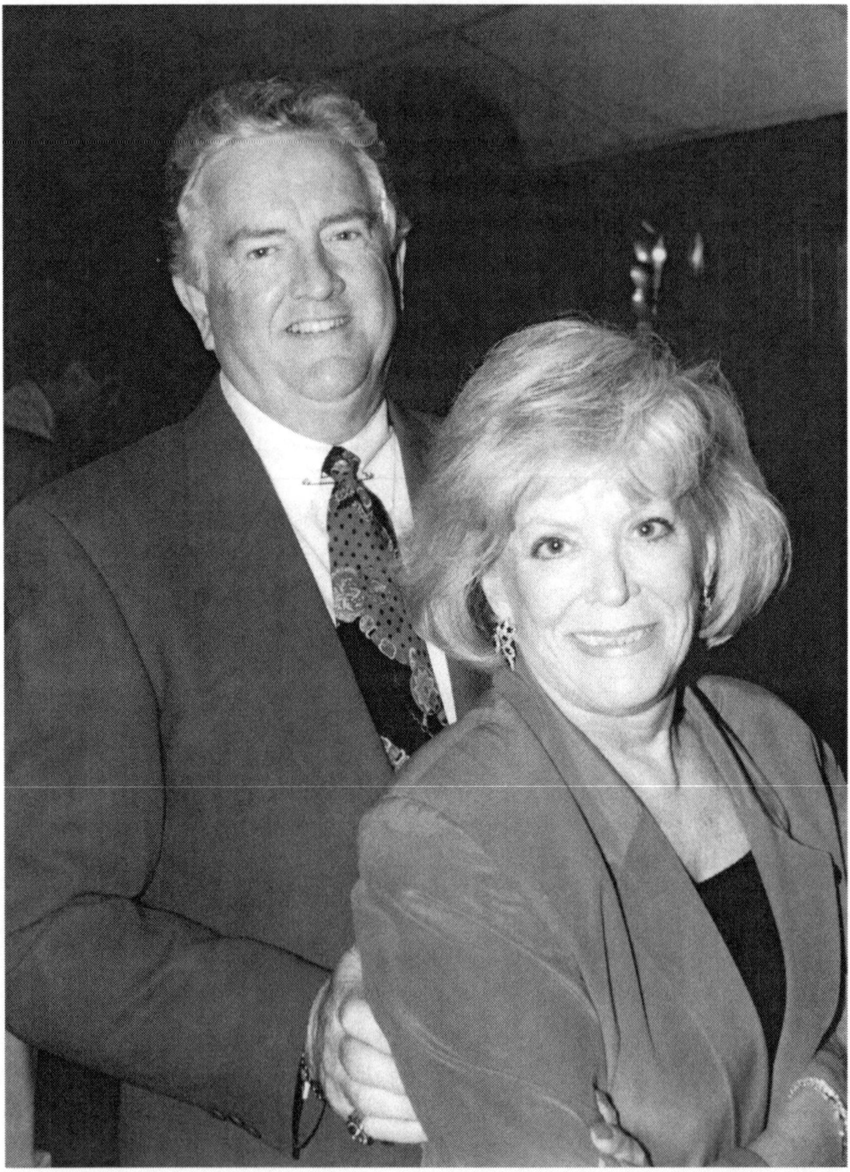

February 2000
Jim and Betty celebrating Jennifer's
30th birthday

In Memoriam
Elizabeth (Betty) Graham
(April 2, 1932-April 8, 2000)

Though it has been ten years,
Your loving memory still brings a tear.
Charitable woman, nurse, mother
Gannie, and wonderful wife,
Thank God for Betty's life.

*With much love and respect
Jim, Kevin, Jennifer, Virginia, Steve
Christian, Elizabeth, Keely, and Natalie*
April 8, 2010

An Anniversary Ode To Cindy

A Scottish (no cost) anniversary card for my pard'
As you can readily see,
no routine store bought card for me
It is not by mere chance,
that we share such a beautiful romance
You say I am your "one and only Jim,"
may I be your one and only hymn!
In the long view, if—God forbid—we both get dementia,
We will always love in absentia . . .
So as we shared the loveliness of Bellagio,
Always know you also make me feel fantastico
May you always quench my thirst,
Knowing this forever on our memorable first
So as our childhood hero Roy sang to Trigger and Gabby Hayes,
May we eternally have happy trails all our days.
Alas! we cruised Lake Como's shore,
now as we sail the Greek Isles,
may our affection grow all the more

Penned on Lake Como and Writ by hand on the Mediterranean
October 18, 2003
P. S. Shakespeare I may not be
But this ode from the heart is just for thee!

Villa D'Este—overlooking Lake Como
Jim and Cindy—1ˢᵗ Anniversary

Streets of Bellagio, Italy

James Kenneth Patrick Graham J. D.

A Love Ode To Cindy

Here's my anniversary wish for you
May you always stay so true
You are my Cindy Doll for all seasons
Which is why I love you for a myriad of reasons
So when we say our prayers at night
Know always your love makes all things right!

Forever and Always, "Your Jim"
October 18, 2005

**In Rome outside the Vatican at night
Anniversary Dinner in Rome, Italy**

'Cindy Doll' and her 'Precious Jim'

Cindy's Devotion

We admire Cindy who exhibits such energy and drive
It is the characteristic that makes her thrive
Up in the AM to give Rick a hand
Covering Somerset Mall like a swift marching band
Buying Jim some shoes and socks
Always working against the typical Saturday ticking clock
Then, due to winter weather and heavy snow
Cindy must postpone her Mom's visit and bid a sad no-show . . .
Not to be undone, she picks up grandson Thomas
for a visit and a treat
then Cindy dismantles the Christmas décor,
including giving the carpet a clean beat
Followed by polishing the vases and artwork décor
With a piano finale by Cole Porter and much more
So it's off to bed with prayers as night shadows fall
Already planning her next day's agenda so tall
But that is why I call this poem "Cindy's Devotion"
She approaches all with energy and emotion
So if you experience passion in life
You know Cindy is your motivated wife

Devoted husband—Jim Graham
January 2009

February 2007
Sunny Isles Beach Florida

Cindy Segues Into Her Sixties
February 6, 2007

You say, "It cannot possibly be
That our Cindy has just turned a mere "Sixty"
She always looks so perky and nifty
No one would believe she is not just fifty . . .
But alas, Father Time has no favorite pets
With each passing year, we "gets what we gets"
As we say, "Aging is not for wimps"
So we deal, as best we can, with the cramps and crimps
But in our Cindy's case
She has outrun the aging chase
Her beauty and looks are still so great,
So too, her energy, musicianship and talent remain first-rate
Yes, Cindy Dear, we are singing to you
May the passing years continue to bless all you do
It was suggested, we surprise you with "60" spanks
But your derriere anticipated with a definite, "no thanks"
So with our deepest love and affection
Keep living life to perfection
Do you believe aging is still only a "state of mind"?
Well, may the ensuing years continue to be very kind
We raise a toast to Cindy so "Dear"
Wishing you health, happiness, and love
Throughout your next 60 years!

Christian Becomes a Teen

July 15, 1992, was a very special day
because Christian James Graham's birth came into play.
We all gathered at Providence Hospital in joy
as we came to see the beautiful blond baby boy . . .
Even this week as Michelle Rodriguez traveled from Palm Springs
She cried seeing Christian these 13 years later,
As she recalled the joy that day of birth brings.
Just as his birth experience brought his Gannie to joyful tears
She's still remembered, though she is gone seven years . . .
Christian remains a source of joy to all who know him
Whether in school, family or sports, filled with vigor and vim
Elizabeth, Keely, and Natalie think he is the BEST
That's because he treats them with love and patient zest.
Yes, our fine Christian is one of a kind
Of that, we are all of one unanimous mind.
So look out teens
Christian will enjoy even more esteem.
So a big "Happy Birthday, Christian" on this July 15
As we happily celebrate our love on your Thirteenth!

Papa
(July 15, 2007)

July 15, 2007
Christian reaches the magic number of "13"!

"Sweetness" At The Plate

The Sea Dogs were down to their last out
That the game was on the line there was not doubt . . .

Larry, the manager muttered, "IT is now or never"
He had to come up with something very clever . . .

The "Dogs" had a runner at third
To lose this tied game would be absurd . . .

So as Christian Graham stepped up to the plate
The manager firmly decided, that caution would not dictate.

He flashed Christian the signal for a squeeze bunt
The anticipation in the spectators was truly no funk . . .

The pitcher would up and let the ball fly,
The runner at third was making his try . . .

Christian squared round to drop the squeeze bunt
He made contact just right as the ball started its run . . .

The opponents' infield was caught by surprise
As the catcher, 3rd and 1st basemen all over-surmised,

The "Dogs" runner crossed the plate with the winning run
Christian crossed 1st base running into the setting sun.

All in attendance broke into wild cheers
Christian was celebrated so that all could hear . . .

On their shoulders, Christian was proudly carried by his team
And Christian's face broke into a radiant beam . . .

And so it was, Christian's fine play was a great treat
All will always look back and say Christian's bunt was "sweet!"

Remembering Christian J. Graham (second base) and his Traveling Team
Sea Dog Game at Allen Field, Rochester, Michigan
July 10, 2006

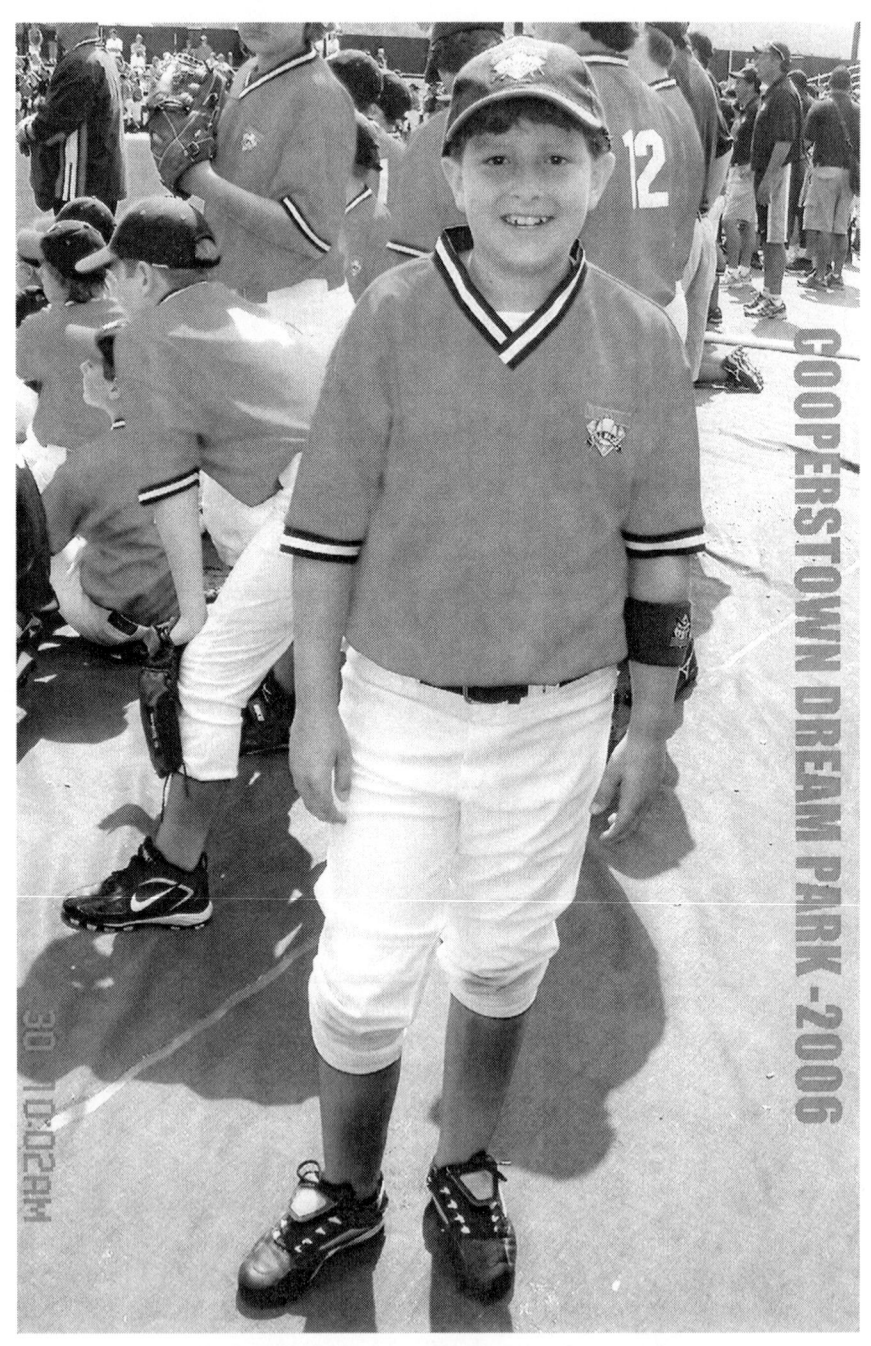

Christian at Cooperstown—Summer 2006

Cooperstown Remembered

Finally, it was the much-awaited Baseball Hall of Fame Date
In Christian's priorities, this trip had a high rate . . .

So Christian, Mom and Dad did travel
To personally see the Cooperstown mystique unravel.

Saturday, July 26 was the formal induction
To recognize up close Bench and Feller was no big deduction

On to the barracks where the Sea Dogs slept
Dreaming—if you will—of not being swept . . .

Teams came from all across the good old USA
To put their varied baseball skills into play.

They took in all the Cooperstown sights
Enjoying the Hall of Fame scene well into the nights

In keeping with the spirit of Cooperstown 2006
Christian exchanged 84 Sea Dog pins for a fine mix!

The Sea Dogs played many teams, giving no yield
Across the 26 Cooperstown Dream fields . . .

So it was from the opening to closing ceremonies
Christian came away with life-long memories.

It is recorded, on the summer Field of Dreams
That Christian J. Graham fulfilled one of his baseball dreams!

Yeah Christian!

Lovingly written on August 5, 2006, by Christian's "Papa"

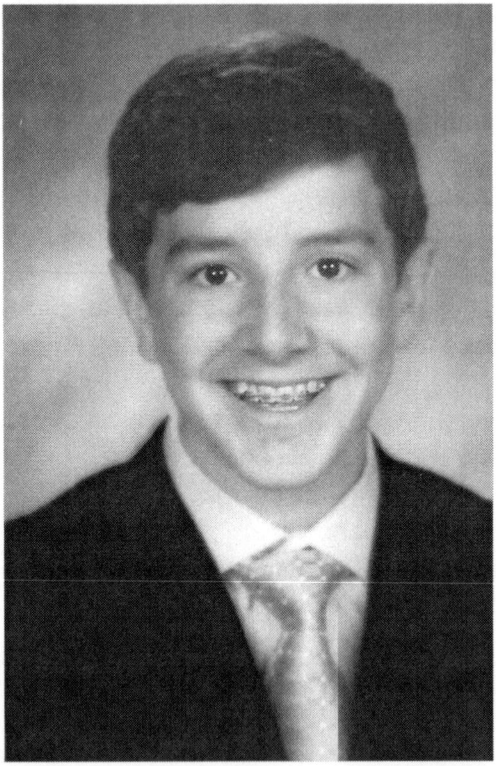

Christian Celebrating 15 on the 15th

Could there be a better way
To cheer a big "Hooray!"
Our #1 guy is celebrating birthday 15
And on what better day than July 15
It was the best day in 1994
That Christian entered the family lore
Virginia and Kevin couldn't be prouder
And Christian's first yell could not have been much louder
And we grandparents were so happy one and all
We could not be more loving and enthralled
Watching him grow from infant to childhood
Then into Christian's teen and beginning adulthood
Prospering in academics at St. Hugo of the Hills
In addition, his athletics gave us thrills
Qualifying for U of D Jesuit High admittance
Alas, the scholastic tuition is not a pittance
In the 1950's my parents paid $300 per year
Now in 2009, the annual stipend of $10,000 generates fear
However, Christian is maximizing his opportunity
By achieving First Honors both semesters with fluidity
This notwithstanding the fact that he took the more difficult
course curriculum
Even with baseball and soccer, his freshmen year
was a winning 'valedictum'
So as we mark July 15, 2009 as a special commemoration
We pray for Christian's ongoing health, happiness, and
perpetual celebration.

*With much love,
James "Papa" Graham and Cindy
July 15, 2009*

**Elizabeth, Natalie, PAPA, Keely, and Christian
Christmas morning 2009**

Grandchildren

It is jokingly said that our grandchildren
Are the payback grandparents bequeath their own children
However, I can tell you nothing could be so obtuse
Grandkids are the ultimate best—that is the truth
The beauty of their flowering maturation
Evokes enduring emotions of love and devotion
Christian has grown into a fine young man
His parents' legacy of refined characteristics and respect
make me his Number One fan
Elizabeth is an excellent embodiment of her namesake—Betty
Her enjoyment of school and performance is always pretty
Twin Keely—like her Mom—always charms and dances
One must smile as she sings, and in her costume, prances
Finally, twin Natalie tends to be intellectually critical
Like her engineer Dad, she is constantly precisely analytical
So, let's hear a big cheer for grandchildren one and all
You give us new love for life and continually enthrall.

*Deep affection, Papa Graham
January 2009*

PAPA and Christian (1) 1995

2004—Christmas
the "Girls"
Natalie, Elizabeth, and Keely Nykerk

Christmas Portrait 2005
Thomas Dailey, PAPA Jim with Keely Nykerk,
Emily Dailey, Christian Graham, Cindy with Theresa Dailey,
Elizabeth Nykerk, and Natalie Nykerk

2006
Christian and PAPA

Newly Christened Twins
Keely Noelle and Natalie Elaine
in the arms of Jennifer and Cindy
with PAPA and Steve
July 25, 2004

2009
Ventura, California Harbor

Halloween 2007
Keely, PAPA, Natalie, Cindy, Elizabeth, Aunt Virginia

Precious Elizabeth about 18 months old

Keeley and Natalie enjoying a bath a year old

The joys of a Granddaughter
Elizabeth—age 4

2007
Christian (age 13) with PAPA

"Three 'Big' Nykerk Sisters"
Natalie, Keely, and Elizabeth
in awe of their baby sister Delaney, only 3 hours old . . .
September 27, 2010

Papa with his newest granddaughter—
Delaney Renee Nykerk on October 5, 2010

Christmas Eve 2005
St. Hugo of the Hills Church
PAPA, Keely, Natalie Cindy, Theresa (front),
Thomas, Emily, Elizabeth

Comerica Park—Tigers' Game
Summer 2001

St Patrick's Day—March 17, 2005
Hats are the style with the Twins
Keely and Natalie

First Communion Day
May 2002
Christian James Graham
with Papa and Cindy

A very special '4th' Birthday
PAPA, Natalie, Cindy, and Keely
May 2008

VALIC Regional office in Troy
Christian Graham (2 years old) making
Corporate decisions with PAPA listening

Fall 2004
Special credentials for a Detroit Lion's game
PAPA and Christian on the sidelines

Elizabeth's First Dance Recital
2004
with Cindy and PAPA
. . . the joys of little one's smiles . . .

Summer 2009
Elizabeth, Natalie, and Keely with their cousin
Christian on the beach at Sunny Isles

Summer is Goin'

The late August night has fallen
Nocturnal owls and crickets are callin'
The soft summer breeze is blowin'
Sorry! Another summer is goin'
But no more lawns to be mowin'
Conversely, more shovels of snow we'll be throwin'
Spring's anticipation of summer is fleetin'
We are coming to the end of song birds tweetin'
The lazy, hazy days of our summer funnin'
We'll soon see our hours of daylight runnin'
And so we start to see autumn colors showin'
As we begin to enjoy the days of Indian summer
We realize we are heading to another winter bummer
So as autumn leaves start fallin'
It's to Sunny shores we'll be haulin'.

August 21, 2010

Elizabeth Anne Nykerk
A Very Special First Holy Communion

Darling Elizabeth,
This is your special day
Jesus has blessed you in a divine way
You are so beautiful in your gown of white
Your soul is glowing with a spiritual light
Your loving family shares your joy and love
As the consecrated host embraces you from above
Remember, April 26, 2009 forever
As a milestone in your life,
And celebrate with us our hope that the sacred
Host will elevate you above all strife.
So, as you journey through life in God's
Almighty bright light,
Always know we also love you with all our might.
With our blessings and affectionate love,

James "Papa" Graham and Cindy
April 26, 2009
St. Hugo of the Hills Church

Precious Elizabeth on her First Communion Day

March 6, 2010
Celebrating my 76th Birthday at Loccino's

A Loving Family

When life is all said and done
A "Loving Family" is number ONE
There is no better support that anyone can conceive
Which, happy to say, I have been blessed to receive
Kevin's my best and trusted pal
Likewise, Jennifer is my finest, loving gal
We share a beautiful caring respect
What more could a Dad expect
They gave me grandchildren so fine
They render Papa feelings totally sublime
So, thanksgiving for a marvelous clan
You could not construct a better family plan
Therefore, at the end of the day, Kevin and Jennifer's loving loyalty
Makes the "old man" feel like paternal royalty

God Bless Our Family
Jim (Dad & Papa) Graham
July 22, 2010

Christmas 2006

August 2009—Ventura, California
Jim, Jennifer, and Kevin
attending the beach wedding of Jim's niece
and their cousin—Lisa Nowakowski

Dad

What is a good Father?
He's the one who says "It's no bother"
Dad is your role model
From the time you begin to toddle
When you start to school
Does he still qualify as cool?
Into High School and growing up glad
Tutor, coach, supporter, anchor—all in one—that's Mom and Dad
So, it's off to college to enhance your brain
Suddenly you realize good ol' Dad is smart again
Mark Twain said it best
You—and not Dad—are failing the life's consistency test
So, as one becomes a parent
You realize being a good Dad is not for the errant
It is certainly not for wimps or is not a lark
Well, being a good Dad demands the tenacity of a shark
So, having a good Mom and Dad is what a family is all about
This is what the bedrock of civilization is—out and out
So, as life's journey moves you along
There is no better song
Than to be greeted each day anew with a melodious exclamation,
My Dad, "I love You."

Dedicated to my dad—Bob and Bill Graham and all good dads—
(Kevin and Steve for sure)
(Phil and Rick—Cindy's sons, too)
Lovingly subscribed October 3, 2008,
Sunny Isles Beach
Jim Graham

Hannah "Nan" Graham
1898-1963

Our Loving Mom

From my first childhood precious memories
I fondly recall my Mom as a bountiful treasury
Mom was our family treasury of beauty, charity, and love
A true treasure trove from heaven above
Her beauteous smile was tender and sweet
Mom's matching personality was a marvelous treat
Family, friends, and neighbors, she willingly answered their needs
Her unsolicited testimonials were truly saintly, both in word and deed
She was lovingly known as wife, Mom, Grandma, and Nan
Her lifelong acts of charity were a short 65 year span
I, my sister Catherine, and brothers Bill and Bob loved and
cherished her very sweetly
As a result, we adored this person of beauty completely
So, to our beautiful, unique, Grandmother, Mom and Wife
We daily pray that you remember your loving family in your eternal life.

Revered Love Always,

Catherine, Bill, Bob and Jim
August 20, 2010

James Kenneth Patrick Graham J. D.

In Appreciation of Cath, Bill, and Bob

It was my good fortune to have siblings so swell
As the youngest brother, they guided me well
They nurtured me as well as being great pals
The bounty of their love is too great to try and tell
Cath instilled her skill and love of music in me
Her piano scores always struck the right key
Bill's mild, Boy Scout manner and nice demeanor
Motivated yours truly to try to replicate the personality so keener
Bobby's carefree and adventurous nature
Leaves me with memories of his youthful stature
So in my daily prayers of thanksgiving
I reverently acknowledge their impact of my life's upbringing

Thanks always—Catherine, Bill, and Bob
From your younger brother—Jim
January 10, 2009

October 1993—
Jim, Catherine, Bob, and Bill

Life

So they say "This is the life?"
Filled with sun, rain and at times, strife . . .
You are born and then you die
What happens in between, should I lie?
Daily life giving you highs and lows
Confronting situations, you never know
Blessed to live in the good old USA
Eases our life in many ways
Getting an education, getting a job
Dealing with good people, dealing with slobs
Striving to maintain good health
Endeavoring to build and sustain your wealth
So life comes and so life goes
From youth to old age, it quickly flows
We lose good, old friends
Sometimes before we can say our "Amen"
So pray you enjoy a lengthy and healthy life
And leave a legacy of family, love, loyalty and not strife.

Family Memories

Our earthly life is over all too soon
So it is wise to memorialize the special memory balloons
My loving family of four siblings, Cath, Bill, Bob and Jim
A wonderful Mom and Dad to grow us fit and trim
As the youngest—and last married—I had the best view from life's back seat
So—as the last survivor—I must record special occasions for future repeat
Catherine and Bill Jordan were wed at St. Benedict's in Highland Park
A wonderful marriage with 6 children set the family mark
Next came Bill and Pat Wriggle who exchanged vows in Louisiana at Bill's U.S. Army post
A fine relationship, with 5 boys, one short of the family most
Then Army Vet Bob and Lorene Bolanger shared nuptials at
St. Gemma Church by Passionist Fr. Mel
Another swell match, but with 3 siblings, 3 short of the record, they fell
Jim and Elizabeth (Betty) Opalewski consummated marriage on
November 30, 1957 at St. Raymond's parish
However, even with 43 years of bliss, our 2 kids would not make the family record of six vanish
So, as they say, what's in a name or number
Do we whimsically view their numerical regression as one would view an encumber?
Is it attributable to the natural law of diminishing returns?
Or were succeeding generations simply more taciturn?
No! just think of the marketing adage "Keep it Simple Stupid" or simply KISS
No Member of the Graham Clan would be so remiss
The answer is staring you right in the face
Each respectful younger family member would never exceed their senior sibling birth in the family race!
So there! On behalf of Cath, Bill Bob and Jim—
Stuff that in your genealogical bagpipe and play it!
Finally, the sweet music of our family memories linger still
Forever memorializing these family siblings that have lovingly bequeathed the Graham Family
Its Last Testament and Will!

Family Christmas 1965 at Jim and Betty's Home, 13351 Iowa, Warren, Michigan

June 30, 2010
Kinsale, Ireland
'Drambuie"
the favorite of two friends—
Jim and Fr. Eoin Murphy—
Scotch whisky in an Irish pub!

Appendix 2

Little Pleasures I Enjoy!

1. An occasional sip of Drambuie—an excellent Scottish Liqueur distilled from a special recipe in the year—1750
2. Good chocolate—Hershey's (Is there any that is bad?)
3. Hot fudge sundaes (Who doesn't?)
4. Quality clothing (Clothes help make the man?), ties, and shirts . . .
5. Fine jewelry (watches, pens, cuff links)
6. Artworks (oil paintings, sculpture works, mosaics, lithographs)
7. Clean well-detailed automobiles
8. Relaxing in a steam room or sauna or a hot bath while reading a good book
9. Again, reading good books or listening to good music
10. Listening to the forlorn late-night whistle of a train
11. A mesmerizing, stratospheric contrail of a USA Strategic Air Command jet
12. An American Flag on display—especially unfurled in the wind
13. The relaxing sound of a "soft" rainfall
14. Patriotic music and inspiring spiritual hymns
15. Beautiful gardens and water views

Big Pleasures I Cherish

1. Loyal family loved ones and "great" grandchildren
2. Holidays celebrated—past and present—with family and friends
3. Good Catholic faith, family, parents and siblings, ancestors, and the good-old USA
4. True friendships, especially lifelong ones
5. A job well done
6. Financial security—giving ability to have choices and flexibility to more fully enjoy life
7. Charity and helping others
8. Good health (good nutrition and physical fitness)
9. Nice home, well decorated, nicely landscaped, well kept, and tidy
10. Blessings in life (or in the lay vernacular, "Good Luck")
11. Travel so as to "see the world"
12. Enjoying a good show and the sights in Las Vegas
13. Vacationing at the condo at Sunny Isles Beach . . . fabulous sunrises (occasionally), sunsets (frequently), full moons with the silver ribbon on the ocean in the nighttime, ocean swimming, and beach/surf walking. Whew!

Appendix 3

Bibliography of Life

Born: Detroit, Michigan—March 8, 1934
    Parents—Hannah (Nan) Boyle Graham and Robert Graham

Siblings: Catherine, William, Robert, and Marianne

St. Benedict (1940-1948)
    Baptized, First Communion, Confirmation, "All-A" Student, Altar Server, Boys Choir, Football, Basketball, Baseball, Representative to Blessed Sacrament Cathedral for the Installation of Cardinal Mooney (1948)

U of D Jesuit High School (1948-1952)
    Academic Program—College Prep Degree
    Athletics—Football (Quarterback), Basketball, Baseball
    Class President—Sophomore and Junior Years

University of Detroit (1952-1956)
    Economics Major and Finance Minor
    Bachelor of Science Degree
    Economics Club, Air Force ROTC
    Worked during College

Detroit College of Law (1956-1959)
    Law Studies—graduated with Juris Doctor degree

Worked during Law School
Passed Law Boards and admitted to State Bar (1960)

U.S. Army (1959-1960)
Ft. Leonard Wood, Missouri and Ft. Knox, Kentucky, High Honor Graduate
Training Platoon Sergeant, Tank Commander, Selected Best Regimental Soldier
(Award presented by Post Commanding General Butcher)

State Farm Insurance Company (1960-1961)
Bodily Injury Claims Specialist

Chrysler Corporation (1961-1962)
Defense Engineering Attorney

Citizens Mutual Insurance Company (1962-1966)
House Trial Counsel Attorney

Variable Annuity Life Insurance Company (VALIC) (1966-1999)
Regional Manager 1974: Regional Vice President
National Market Ratio Winner many years
National Manager of the Year winner record five times

Law Practice: Negligence and Probate Practice
First Attorney to video a Last Will and Testament in America for Probate filing—covered by national media and on national TV

Marriage: James Kenneth Patrick Graham married
November 30, 1957, at 10:00 AM,
St. Raymond Catholic Church
Elizabeth Elaine Opalewski (Betty)
Betty was a nurse at North Detroit General Hospital and later head nurse for Dr. Barney Leiberman, MD (Pioneer Obesity Specialist)

Children: Kevin James Graham born November 6, 1960,
North Detroit General Hospital, Detroit, Michigan
Kevin married *Virginia Mary Caradonna, MD*,

St. Hugo of the Hills Church on October 23, 1993,
Bloomfield Hills, Michigan
Jennifer Elaine Graham born February 19, 1970,
North Detroit General Hospital, Detroit, Michigan
Jennifer married *Steven James Nykerk*,
St. Hugo of the Hills Church on October 4, 1997,
Bloomfield Hills, Michigan

Grandchildren
    Christian James Graham born July 15, 1994
    (Beaumont Hospital, Royal Oak)

    Elizabeth Anne Nykerk born June 20, 2001
    (Beaumont Hospital, Royal Oak)
    Keely Noelle Nykerk and *Natalie Elaine Nykerk* (twins) born May 18, 2004
    (Beaumont Hospital, Royal Oak)
    Delaney Renee Nykerk, born September 27, 2010
    (Beaumont Hospital, Royal Oak)

Spousal Death
    Elizabeth E. Graham (Betty) died April 8, 2000,
    Aventura Hospital (Aventura, Florida)

Remarriage
    James Kenneth Patrick Graham and
    Cynthia Elaine Zerbiec Dailey (Cindy)

Our marriage took place on October 18, 2002, at St. Ninian Church in Gourock, Scotland, with Msgr. Tom Monaghan officiating. Our children and immediate family were in attendance—all in kilts, if you please! Upon returning home, Msgr Anthony Tocco blessed our marriage again at St. Hugo of the Hills Chapel o November 1, 2002! Both Cindy (March 6, 1998—Thomas Dailey, and I (April 8, 2000—Betty), were widowed. We (as well as our departed spouses (Tom and Betty) had known each other for many years through our Parish Church—St Hugo of the Hills in Bloomfield Hills, Michigan.

James K. Graham
30th VALIC Anniversary

1956 Bachelor of Science Degree

1959 Juris Doctor

Hired: September 21, 1966. Regional Manager

1974: VAMCO Vice President/VALIC Regional Manager

1974, 76, 77, 78: VALIC Manager of the Year

1976, 77, 80, 81: VALIC Manager Association President

1975, 76, 78, 81, 83: Market Ration #1 Michigan Region

1975, 76, 77, 78, 79, 80, 81, 82, 87, 90, 93, 95: Gold Circle Winner

1978: Michigan First VALIC Office to exceed 10 Million in annual sales

Sept 21, 1996: First VALIC employee to achieve 30 years of service

1997: Detroit Regional Office signs the One Millionth Client

Certificate of Award

Appendix 4

Scottish Clans and Tartans

The Clan Graham

Graham as a Family Name

The Graham surname has a likely origin from a Gaelic adjective, "Gruaim" meaning dark, fierce, or courageous, and was probably the first used as a nickname for a warrior. Such qualities could also be attributed to a god. A translation among the Anglo-Saxon tribes suggested dark and angry.

In Scotland, the Graham surname became known as a Highland subclan name. Several origins have circulated. Research indicates that genealogists attribute Graham to a Scottish form of "Grantham," which was the name of a Norman aristocrat "William de Grantham," who was believed to have come from the city of Grantham in Lincolnshire, England, to Scotland in the middle of the twelfth century.

The second-most popular lineage considered Graham the name of a subchieftain. Blood relatives and loyal followers of this chief would have called themselves "Clan Graham."

Tartan

Tartans of the Grahams include deep bluish purple and dark green squares with alternating black, double black, and white lines throughout.

The Coat of Arms

During the Middle Ages battle armor was essential. Supporters of warring noblemen distinguished themselves by adopting matching symbols, patterns and colors which were emblazoned onto their clothing and horse trappings.
This clothing gave rise to the term
"Coat of Arms".

Graham

The Shield

The shield of the Arms most frequently referred to
In association with the GRAHAM name
Is described in heraldic language as:

D'or on a chief sable three scallops or the first.

This translated into modern language is:
A gold shield with a black band at the top
On which are three scallop shells.
Or is gold, one of the metals of a shield
Usually painted yellow.
It represents Generosity and Improvement of the mind.
The Escallop is a scallop shell.
It represents Venture and Travel.

Motto

Ne oublie
"Do not forget"

The Crest

A Crest, made of wood or boiled leather, was worn as an attachment
To the helmet at tournaments
When horsemen jousted with lances to prove
Their valor and courage.
The Crest most often associated with the GRAHAM name is:

*A falcon proper beaked and armed or killing
a stork argent armed gules.*

Translated into modern language this is:
A falcon with a gold beak and talons, killing a stork of silver.
Argent is silver, one of the metals of a shield usually painted white.
It represents Peace and Sincerity.

Appendix 5

Graham Family History

by

Your Ancestral Family

Graham

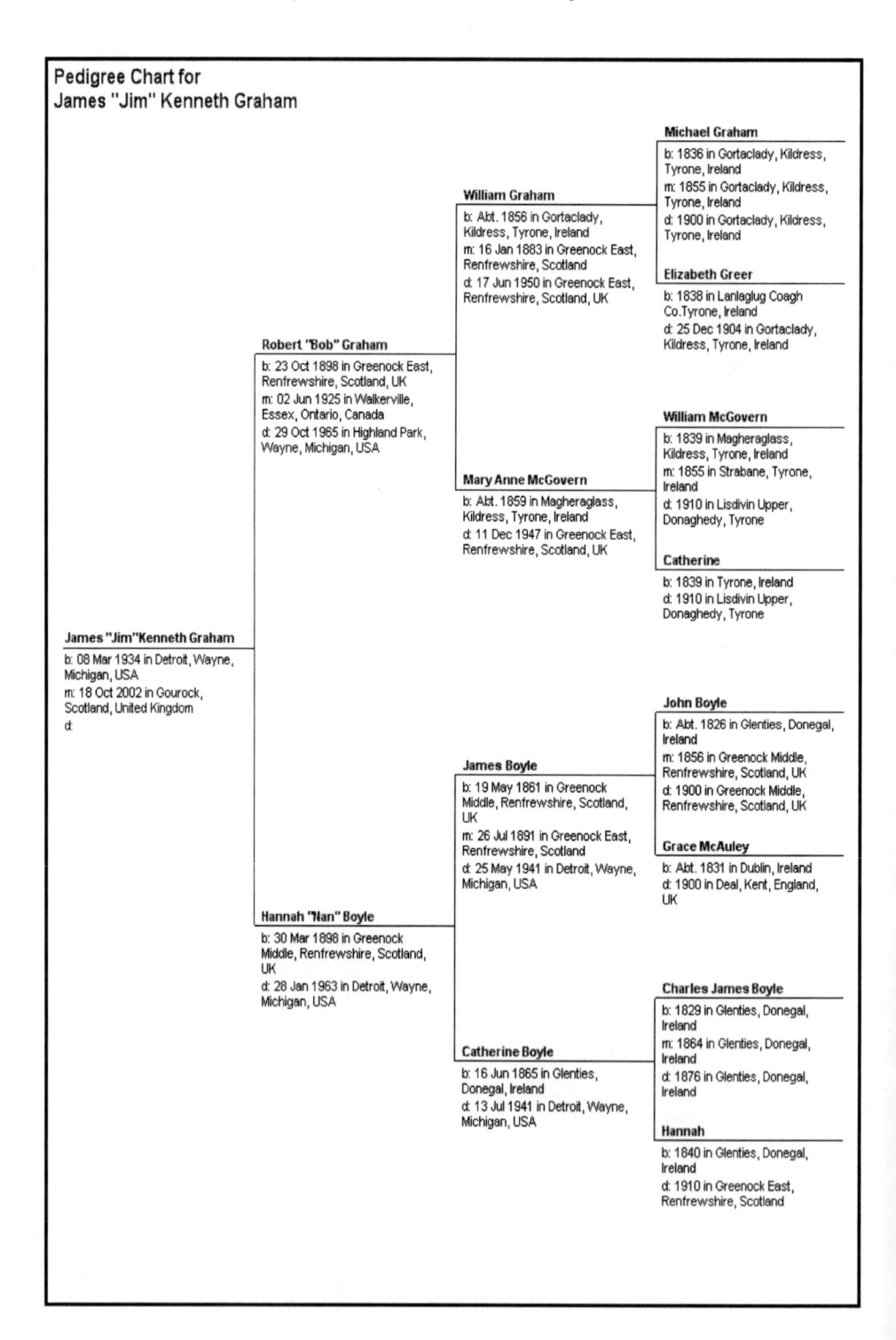

Pedigree Chart for James "Jim" Kenneth Graham

James "Jim" Kenneth Graham
b: 08 Mar 1934 in Detroit, Wayne, Michigan, USA
m: 18 Oct 2002 in Gourock, Scotland, United Kingdom
d:

- **Robert "Bob" Graham**
  b: 23 Oct 1898 in Greenock East, Renfrewshire, Scotland, UK
  m: 02 Jun 1925 in Walkerville, Essex, Ontario, Canada
  d: 29 Oct 1965 in Highland Park, Wayne, Michigan, USA

  - **William Graham**
    b: Abt. 1856 in Gortaclady, Kildress, Tyrone, Ireland
    m: 16 Jan 1883 in Greenock East, Renfrewshire, Scotland
    d: 17 Jun 1950 in Greenock East, Renfrewshire, Scotland, UK

    - **Michael Graham**
      b: 1836 in Gortaclady, Kildress, Tyrone, Ireland
      m: 1855 in Gortaclady, Kildress, Tyrone, Ireland
      d: 1900 in Gortaclady, Kildress, Tyrone, Ireland

    - **Elizabeth Greer**
      b: 1838 in Lanlaglug Coagh Co.Tyrone, Ireland
      d: 25 Dec 1904 in Gortaclady, Kildress, Tyrone, Ireland

  - **Mary Anne McGovern**
    b: Abt. 1859 in Magheraglass, Kildress, Tyrone, Ireland
    d: 11 Dec 1947 in Greenock East, Renfrewshire, Scotland, UK

    - **William McGovern**
      b: 1839 in Magheraglass, Kildress, Tyrone, Ireland
      m: 1855 in Strabane, Tyrone, Ireland
      d: 1910 in Lisdivin Upper, Donaghedy, Tyrone

    - **Catherine**
      b: 1839 in Tyrone, Ireland
      d: 1910 in Lisdivin Upper, Donaghedy, Tyrone

- **Hannah "Nan" Boyle**
  b: 30 Mar 1898 in Greenock Middle, Renfrewshire, Scotland, UK
  d: 28 Jan 1963 in Detroit, Wayne, Michigan, USA

  - **James Boyle**
    b: 19 May 1861 in Greenock Middle, Renfrewshire, Scotland, UK
    m: 26 Jul 1891 in Greenock East, Renfrewshire, Scotland
    d: 25 May 1941 in Detroit, Wayne, Michigan, USA

    - **John Boyle**
      b: Abt. 1826 in Glenties, Donegal, Ireland
      m: 1856 in Greenock Middle, Renfrewshire, Scotland, UK
      d: 1900 in Greenock Middle, Renfrewshire, Scotland, UK

    - **Grace McAuley**
      b: Abt. 1831 in Dublin, Ireland
      d: 1900 in Deal, Kent, England, UK

  - **Catherine Boyle**
    b: 16 Jun 1865 in Glenties, Donegal, Ireland
    d: 13 Jul 1941 in Detroit, Wayne, Michigan, USA

    - **Charles James Boyle**
      b: 1829 in Glenties, Donegal, Ireland
      m: 1864 in Glenties, Donegal, Ireland
      d: 1876 in Glenties, Donegal, Ireland

    - **Hannah**
      b: 1840 in Glenties, Donegal, Ireland
      d: 1910 in Greenock East, Renfrewshire, Scotland

Ancestors of James "Jim" Kenneth Graham

Generation 1

1. **James "Jim" Kenneth Graham** son of Robert "Bob" Graham and Hannah "Nan" Boyle was born on 08 Mar 1934 in Detroit, Wayne, Michigan, USA.

   Cynthia "Cindy" Elaine Zerbiec Dailey daughter of John Joseph Zerbiec and Wanda Mary Karpinski was born on 06 Feb 1947.

   James "Jim" Kenneth Graham and Cynthia "Cindy" Elaine Zerbiec Dailey were married on 18 Oct 2002 in Gourock, Scotland, United Kingdom (St. Ninian Church - Msgr - Tom Monaghan). They had no children.

   Elizabeth "Betty" Elaine Opalewski daughter of Bruno Opalewski and Emily Lyczynski was born on 02 Apr 1932 in Detroit, Wayne, Michigan, USA. She died on 08 Apr 2000 in Aventura, Florida, USA.

   James "Jim" Kenneth Graham and Elizabeth "Betty" Elaine Opalewski were married on 30 Nov 1957 in Detroit, Wayne, Michigan, USA (St. Raymond Catholic Church - Father Hogan). They had 2 children.

Generation 2

2. **Robert "Bob" Graham** son of William Graham and Mary Anne McGovern[1, 2, 3, 4, 5, 6] was born on 23 Oct 1898 in Greenock East, Renfrewshire, Scotland, UK[1, 2, 3, 4, 5, 6]. He died on 29 Oct 1965 in Highland Park, Wayne, Michigan, USA[5].

3. **Hannah "Nan" Boyle** daughter of James Boyle and Catherine Boyle[2, 7, 8, 9, 10] was born on 30 Mar 1898 in Greenock Middle, Renfrewshire, Scotland, UK[2, 7, 8, 9, 10]. She died on 28 Jan 1963 in Detroit, Wayne, Michigan, USA.

Generation 2 (con't)

Robert "Bob" Graham and Hannah "Nan" Boyle were married on 02 Jun 1925 in Walkerville, Essex, Ontario, Canada (Reverend James B. Neville, Catholic Priest). They had the following children:

    i. **Catherine Francis Graham** was born in 1926 in Detroit, Wayne, Michigan, USA. She married William "Bill" Jordon in 1948 in Detroit, Wayne, Michigan, USA. She died in 2001 in Detroit, Wayne, Michigan, USA.

    ii. **William Robert Graham** was born in 1928 in Detroit, Wayne, Michigan, USA. He married Pat Wriggle on 23 Dec 1950 in Detroit, Wayne, Michigan, USA. He died in Apr 1995 in Royal Oak, Oakland, Michigan, USA.

    iii. **Robert James Graham** was born in 1930 in Detroit, Wayne, Michigan, USA. He married Lorene Bolanger in 1950 in Detroit, Wayne, Michigan, USA. He died in 1995 in Detroit, Wayne, Michigan, USA.

+ 1. iv. **James "Jim" Kenneth Graham** was born on 08 Mar 1934 in Detroit, Wayne, Michigan, USA. He married Cynthia "Cindy" Elaine Zerbiec Dailey on 18 Oct 2002 in Gourock, Scotland, United Kingdom (St. Ninian Church - Msgr - Tom Monaghan).

    iv. **Marianne Graham** was born in 1939 in Detroit, Wayne, Michigan, USA. She died in 1939 in Detroit, Wayne, Michigan, USA.

Generation 3

4. **William Graham** son of Michael Graham and Elizabeth Greer[11] was born about 1856 in Gortaclady, Kildress, Tyrone, Ireland[11]. He died on 17 Jun 1950 in Greenock East, Renfrewshire, Scotland, UK.

5. **Mary Anne McGovern** daughter of William McGovern and Catherine[12] was born about 1859 in Magheraglass, Kildress,

Generation 3 (con't)

Tyrone, Ireland[12]. She died on 11 Dec 1947 in Greenock East, Renfrewshire, Scotland, UK.

William Graham and Mary Anne McGovern were married on 16 Jan 1883 in Greenock East, Renfrewshire, Scotland. They had the following children:

- i. **William Graham** was born in 1883 in Ballymoile Moneymore, Derry, Ireland. He died in Greenock East, Renfrewshire, Scotland, UK.

- ii. **Catherine Graham** was born in 1888 in Greenock East, Renfrewshire, Scotland, UK. She died in Greenock East, Renfrewshire, Scotland, UK.

- iii. **George Graham** was born in 1891 in Greenock East, Renfrewshire, Scotland, UK. He died in Greenock East, Renfrewshire, Scotland, UK.

- iv. **Margaret Graham** was born in 1893 in Greenock East, Renfrewshire, Scotland, UK. She died in Greenock East, Renfrewshire, Scotland, UK.

- v. **Matilda Graham** was born in 1895 in Greenock East, Renfrewshire, Scotland, UK. She died in Greenock East, Renfrewshire, Scotland, UK.

- vi. **Sarah Graham** was born in 1896 in Greenock East, Renfrewshire, Scotland, UK. She died in Greenock East, Renfrewshire, Scotland, UK.

+ 2. vii. **Robert "Bob" Graham**[1, 2, 3, 4, 5, 6] was born on 23 Oct 1898 in Greenock East, Renfrewshire, Scotland, UK[1, 2, 3, 4, 5, 6]. He married Hannah "Nan" Boyle on 02 Jun 1925 in Walkerville, Essex, Ontario, Canada (Reverend James B. Neville, Catholic Priest). He died on 29 Oct 1965 in Highland Park, Wayne, Michigan, USA[5].

Generation 3 (con't)

    viii. **Rosina Graham** was born in 1901 in Greenock East, Renfrewshire, Scotland, UK. She died in Greenock East, Renfrewshire, Scotland, UK.

    ix. **James Graham** was born in 1903 in Greenock East, Renfrewshire, Scotland, UK. He died in 1940 in Greenock East, Renfrewshire, Scotland, UK.

    x. **Sammy Graham** was born in 1905 in Greenock East, Renfrewshire, Scotland, UK. He died in 1939 in Detroit, Wayne, Michigan, USA.

6. **James Boyle** son of John Boyle and Grace McAuley[13, 14, 15, 16, 17, 18] was born on 19 May 1861 in Greenock Middle, Renfrewshire, Scotland, UK[13, 14, 15, 16, 17, 18]. He died on 25 May 1941 in Detroit, Wayne, Michigan, USA.

7. **Catherine Boyle** daughter of Charles James Boyle and Hannah[2, 13, 19, 20] was born on 16 Jun 1865 in Glenties, Donegal, Ireland[2, 13, 19, 20]. She died on 13 Jul 1941 in Detroit, Wayne, Michigan, USA.

James Boyle and Catherine Boyle were married on 26 Jul 1891 in Greenock East, Renfrewshire, Scotland. They had the following children:

    i. **John Boyle** was born in 1892 in Greenock East, Renfrewshire, Scotland, UK. He died in 1900 in Greenock East, Renfrewshire, Scotland, UK.

    ii. **Jeanie Boyle** was born in 1893 in Greenock East, Renfrewshire, Scotland, UK. She died in Detroit, Wayne, Michigan, USA.

    iii. **James "Jim" aka "Steve" Boyle** was born in 1895 in Greenock East, Renfrewshire, Scotland, UK. He died on 21 Jul 1968 in Brooklyn, New York, USA.

Generation 3 (con't)

iv. **Catherine "Kitty" Boyle** was born on 11 Nov 1896 in Greenock East, Renfrewshire, Scotland, UK. She died on 05 May 1971 in Detroit, Wayne, Michigan, USA.

+ 3. v. **Hannah "Nan" Boyle**[2, 7, 8, 9, 10] was born on 30 Mar 1898 in Greenock Middle, Renfrewshire, Scotland, UK[2, 7, 8, 9, 10]. She married Robert "Bob" Graham on 02 Jun 1925 in Walkerville, Essex, Ontario, Canada (Reverend James B. Neville, Catholic Priest). She died on 28 Jan 1963 in Detroit, Wayne, Michigan, USA.

vi. **John Boyle** was born in 1901 in Greenock East, Renfrewshire, Scotland, UK. He died on 26 Jul 1966 in Boston, Suffolk, Massachusetts, USA.

vii. **Frank Boyle** was born on 17 Jan 1903 in Greenock East, Renfrewshire, Scotland, UK. He died on 28 Sep 1964 in Detroit, Wayne, Michigan, USA.

viii. **Charles "Charlie" Boyle** was born in 1905 in Greenock East, Renfrewshire, Scotland, UK. He died in Detroit, Wayne, Michigan, USA.

Generation 4

8. **Michael Graham**[21] was born in 1836 in Gortaclady, Kildress, Tyrone, Ireland. He died in 1900 in Gortaclady, Kildress, Tyrone, Ireland.

9. **Elizabeth Greer**[22] was born in 1838 in Lanlaglug Coagh Co.Tyrone, Ireland. She died on 25 Dec 1904 in Gortaclady, Kildress, Tyrone, Ireland.

Michael Graham and Elizabeth Greer were married in 1855 in Gortaclady, Kildress, Tyrone, Ireland. They had the following children:

Generation 4 (con't)

+ 4. i. **William Graham**[11] was born about 1856 in Gortaclady, Kildress, Tyrone, Ireland[11]. He married Mary Anne McGovern on 16 Jan 1883 in Greenock East, Renfrewshire, Scotland. He died on 17 Jun 1950 in Greenock East, Renfrewshire, Scotland, UK.

10. **William McGovern**[23] was born in 1839 in Magheraglass, Kildress, Tyrone, Ireland. He died in 1910 in Lisdivin Upper, Donaghedy, Tyrone.

11. **Catherine** was born in 1839 in Tyrone, Ireland. She died in 1910 in Lisdivin Upper, Donaghedy, Tyrone.

William McGovern and Catherine were married in 1855 in Strabane, Tyrone, Ireland. They had the following children:

+ 5. i. **Mary Anne McGovern**[12] was born about 1859 in Magheraglass, Kildress, Tyrone, Ireland[12]. She married William Graham on 16 Jan 1883 in Greenock East, Renfrewshire, Scotland. She died on 11 Dec 1947 in Greenock East, Renfrewshire, Scotland, UK.

12. **John Boyle**[24, 25] was born about 1826 in Glenties, Donegal, Ireland[24, 25]. He died in 1900 in Greenock Middle, Renfrewshire, Scotland, UK.

13. **Grace McAuley**[26, 27, 28] was born about 1831 in Dublin, Ireland[26, 27, 28]. She died in 1900 in Deal, Kent, England, UK.

John Boyle and Grace McAuley were married in 1856 in Greenock Middle, Renfrewshire, Scotland, UK. They had the following children:

i. **John Boyle** was born in 1857 in Greenock Middle, Renfrewshire, Scotland.

Generation 4 (con't)

    ii. **Francis "Frank" Boyle** was born in 1859 in Greenock Middle, Renfrewshire, Scotland, UK.

+ 6. iii. **James Boyle**[13, 14, 15, 16, 17, 18] was born on 19 May 1861 in Greenock Middle, Renfrewshire, Scotland, UK[13, 14, 15, 16, 17, 18]. He married Catherine Boyle on 26 Jul 1891 in Greenock East, Renfrewshire, Scotland. He died on 25 May 1941 in Detroit, Wayne, Michigan, USA.

    iv. **Daniel Boyle** was born in 1863 in Greenock Middle, Renfrewshire, Scotland, UK.

    v. **Mary Boyle** was born in 1864 in Greenock Middle, Renfrewshire, Scotland, UK.

    vi. **Eder Boyle** was born in 1868 in Greenock Middle, Renfrewshire, Scotland, UK.

    vii. **Grace Boyle** was born in 1869 in Greenock Middle, Renfrewshire, Scotland, UK.

    viii. **Rose E. Boyle** was born in 1870 in Greenock Middle, Renfrewshire, Scotland, UK.

14. **Charles James Boyle** was born in 1829 in Glenties, Donegal, Ireland. He died in 1876 in Glenties, Donegal, Ireland.

15. **Hannah** was born in 1840 in Glenties, Donegal, Ireland. She died in 1910 in Greenock East, Renfrewshire, Scotland.

Charles James Boyle and Hannah were married in 1864 in Glenties, Donegal, Ireland. They had the following children:

+ 7. i. **Catherine Boyle**[2, 13, 19, 20] was born on 16 Jun 1865 in Glenties, Donegal, Ireland[2, 13, 19, 20]. She married James Boyle on 26 Jul 1891 in Greenock East, Renfrewshire, Scotland. She died on 13 Jul 1941 in Detroit, Wayne, Michigan, USA.

Sources

1 Ancestry.com, Canadian Passenger Lists, 1865-1935 (Online publication - Provo, UT, USA: The Generations Network, Inc., 2008.Original data - Library and Archives Canada. Passenger Lists, 1865-1935. Ottawa, Canada: Library and Archives Canada. RG76, T-479 to T-520, T-4689 to T-4874, T-14700 to T-14939, C-451), Birth date: abt 1899Birth place: ScotlandArrival date: 16 Jan 1928Arrival place: St.John, New BrunswickDeparture date: Departure place: Greenock, Scotland.

2 Ancestry.com, Detroit Border Crossings and Passenger and Crew Lists, 1905-1957 (Online publication - Provo, UT, USA: The Generations Network, Inc., 2006.Original data - Detroit, Michigan. Card Manifests (Alphabetical) of Individuals Entering through the Port of Detroit, Michigan, 1906-1954. Micropublication M1478. RG085. 117 rolls. Na), Birth date: abt 1897Birth place: GreenorkArrival date: 1 Feb 1928Arrival place: Detroit, Michigan.

3 Ancestry.com, 1930 United States Federal Census (Online publication - Provo, UT, USA: Ancestry.com Operations Inc, 2002. Original data - United States of America, Bureau of the Census. Fifteenth Census of the United States, 1930. Washington, D.C.: National Archives and Records Administration, 1930. T626,), Year: 1930; Census Place: Detroit, Wayne, Michigan; Roll: 1040; Page: 3B; Enumeration District: 224; Image: 238.0. Birth date: abt 1898Birth place: ScotlandResidence date: 1930Residence place: Detroit, Wayne, Michigan.

4 Ancestry.com, 1901 Scotland Census (Online publication - Provo, UT, USA: Ancestry.com Operations Inc, 2007.Original data - Scotland. 1901 Scotland Census. Reels 1-446. General Register Office for Scotland, Edinburgh, Scotland.Original data: Scotland. 1901 Scotland Census. Reels 1-446. Genera), Birth date: abt 1899Birth place: Greenock, RenfrewshResidence date: 1901Residence place: Greenock East, Renfrewshire, Scotland.

5 Ancestry.com, Social Security Death Index (Online publication - Provo, UT, USA: Ancestry.com Operations Inc, 2009.Original

Sources (con't)

data - Social Security Administration. Social Security Death Index, Master File. Social Security Administration.Original data: Social Security Administration. Social Security D), Number: 376-10-3884; Issue State: Michigan; Issue Date: Before 1951. Birth date: 21 Oct 1898Birth place: Death date: Oct 1965Death place:.

6   Ancestry.com, New York Passenger Lists, 1820-1957 (Online publication - Provo, UT, USA: The Generations Network, Inc., 2006.Original data - Passenger Lists of Vessels Arriving at New York, New York, 1820-1897; (National Archives Microfilm Publication M237, 675 rolls); Records of the U.S. Customs Service, R), Year: 1922; Arrival: ;, ;; Microfilm serial: T715; Microfilm roll: T715_3154; Line: 18; List number:. Birth date: abt 1899Birth place: ScotlandArrival date: 6 Aug 1922Arrival place: New York, New YorkDeparture date: Departure place: Glasgow, Scotland.

7   Ancestry.com, Canadian Passenger Lists, 1865-1935 (Online publication - Provo, UT, USA: The Generations Network, Inc., 2008.Original data - Library and Archives Canada. Passenger Lists, 1865-1935. Ottawa, Canada: Library and Archives Canada. RG76, T-479 to T-520, T-4689 to T-4874, T-14700 to T-14939, C-451), Birth date: abt 1899Birth place: ScotlandArrival date: 16 Jan 1928Arrival place: St.John, New BrunswickDeparture date: Departure place: Greenock, Scotland.

8   Ancestry.com, 1930 United States Federal Census (Online publication - Provo, UT, USA: Ancestry.com Operations Inc, 2002. Original data - United States of America, Bureau of the Census. Fifteenth Census of the United States, 1930. Washington, D.C.: National Archives and Records Administration, 1930. T626,), Year: 1930; Census Place: Detroit, Wayne, Michigan; Roll: 1040; Page: 3B; Enumeration District: 224; Image: 238.0. Birth date: abt 1898Birth place: Residence date: 1930Residence place: Detroit, Wayne, Michigan.

9   Ancestry.com, 1901 Scotland Census (Online publication - Provo, UT, USA: Ancestry.com Operations Inc, 2007.Original

Sources (con't)

data - Scotland. 1901 Scotland Census. Reels 1-446. General Register Office for Scotland, Edinburgh, Scotland.Original data: Scotland. 1901 Scotland Census. Reels 1-446. Genera), Birth date: abt 1898Birth place: Greenock, RenfrewshireResidence date: 1901Residence place: Greenock West, Renfrewshire, Scotland.

10 Ancestry.com, Detroit Border Crossings and Passenger and Crew Lists, 1905-1957 (Online publication - Provo, UT, USA: The Generations Network, Inc., 2006.Original data - Detroit, Michigan. Card Manifests (Alphabetical) of Individuals Entering through the Port of Detroit, Michigan, 1906-1954. Micropublication M1478. RG085. 117 rolls. Na), Birth date: abt 1898Birth place: GreenockArrival date: 7 Oct 1933Arrival place: Detroit, Michigan.

11 Ancestry.com, 1901 Scotland Census (Online publication - Provo, UT, USA: Ancestry.com Operations Inc, 2007.Original data - Scotland. 1901 Scotland Census. Reels 1-446. General Register Office for Scotland, Edinburgh, Scotland.Original data: Scotland. 1901 Scotland Census. Reels 1-446. Genera), Birth date: abt 1860Birth place: IrelandResidence date: 1901Residence place: Greenock East, Renfrewshire, Scotland.

12 Ancestry.com, 1901 Scotland Census (Online publication - Provo, UT, USA: Ancestry.com Operations Inc, 2007.Original data - Scotland. 1901 Scotland Census. Reels 1-446. General Register Office for Scotland, Edinburgh, Scotland.Original data: Scotland. 1901 Scotland Census. Reels 1-446. Genera), Birth date: abt 1867Birth place: IrelandResidence date: 1901Residence place: Greenock East, Renfrewshire, Scotland.

INDEX

A

Abercrombie, Bella, 63
Abercrombie, Bill, Jr., 63, 93-94, 224, 305, 321
Adams, Todd, 288, 399
Air Tech Screen, 166
Alexander, Catherine Boyle, 27-28
Alexander, Catherine Boyle. *See* Boyle, Catherine
Amata, Mother (principal at St. Benedict Grade School), 74
"'Ancestral Heritage: Exploring Ireland and Scotland with Cindy and Jim,'" 484
Anita (teacher at St. Benedict Grade School), 74
"An Anniversary Ode to Cindy," 506
Armstrong, Jones, Lawson, and White (law firm), 169
"August 1966," 169, 498

B

Bailey, Maureen, 74
Barnett, Larry, 224
Bateman, Archie, 65
Bateman, Ivy, 65
Bateman, Kenny, 65
Becker, Rene, 65
Beeckman, Al, 169
Beger, Bill, 425, 435
Belleperche (philosophy professor), 389
Bendall, Bob, 240, 247
Benedict XVI (pope), 203, 329
"Birthday Greetings to Our Pal Stephie," 475
Blanda, George, 383
Bobbie (Willie Nelson's sister and pianist), 224
Bolanger, Lorene (Mrs. Lorene Graham), 55, 246, 322

Boyle, Charles James (father of Catherine Boyle Alexander), 28
Boyle, Charlie (son of Catherine Boyle Alexander and Charles James Boyle), 28, 386, 559
Boyle, Frank, 28
Boyle, Grace McAuley, 28
Boyle, Hannah (mother of Catherine Boyle), 28, 39
Boyle, Hannah "Nan" (Mrs. Hannah Graham), 28, 63, 73
  birth, 38, 246
  death, 245, 247
  marriage to Robert Graham, 38
  as a mother, 63, 157, 223, 245, 405, 415, 469, 538
Boyle, James, 27-28
Boyle, Jean, 38, 45
Boyle, John (elder son of Catherine Boyle Alexander and Charles James Boyle), 28
Boyle, John (father of Charles James Boyle), 28, 558-60
Boyle, John (younger son of Catherine Boyle Alexander and Charles James Boyle), 28
Bradley, Ed, 198
Brobyn, Laura, 258-59, 273
Brobyn, Tom, 224, 238, 240, 247, 273, 282, 286
Burke, Charlie, 157
Butcher (post commander), 161

C

Campbell, Herman, 224
Campbell, Jack, 74, 79, 223
Camp Cooke, 65
Caradonna, Virginia Marie (Mrs. Kevin James Graham), 60, 141, 477, 517
Carling Beer Distributor, 166, 303
Carrier, Paul, 157, 224
Catholic Central High School, 83
Chesterton, G. K., 391
Chisholm, Tom, 87, 218, 224, 233
"Christian Becomes a Teen," 512
"Christian Celebrating 15 on the 15th," 517
Chrysler Defense Engineering, 167
"Cindy's Devotion," 509
Cindy's Ensemble, 425
Citizens Mutual Insurance, 167-68, 224, 304
Clinton, Bernardine, 106
Condon, Bob, 247, 501
Conklin, Tom, 168
Conklin and Maloney (law firm), 168
"Cooperstown Remembered," 515
Costello, Jim, 198, 224-25, 247, 273, 277, 282, 286, 288
County Tyrone, Ireland, 19-20, 27
Coyne, Jerry, 224
Cremen, Larry, 224
Cromwell, Oliver, 20
Cub 75th Anniversary 1952, 87

D

"Dad," 534
Dailey, Cynthia Elaine "Cindy" Zerbiec, 7, 203, 328, 407, 425-27, 472, 475, 477
  as grandmother, 517, 530
  marriage to James Kenneth Graham, 60, 223, 288, 295,

323, 405, 439, 506, 509
musical talent, 247, 288, 386, 425, 439
as St. Hugo parishioner, 206, 326, 329, 495
travels, 94, 328-29, 407, 484
Dailey, Tom, 200, 202, 288
Davidson, Gotschall, et al. (law firm), 168
Davis, Paige, 247, 406
Dearborn Beer Distributor, 93
Desmond, Al, 166
Detroit College of Law, 91, 140
Detroit Free Press, 165, 305, 311
Devlin, Bob, 224
Dodge Forge Plant, 93, 166
Donneley, John, 63

E

Eisermann (regular army master), 161

F

Fahoome, Bobby, 73
"Family Memories," 538
Feliciano, Jose, 203
Finsterwald, Dow, 224
Ford, Henry, I, 462
Fort Knox, 161
Fort Leonard Wood, 157-58, 161
Francesca (teacher at St. Benedict Grade School), 73-74
Frankie Valli and the Four Seasons, 328, 439
Fr. Cotter Knights of Columbus Council, 91
French, Ruth, 288

G

Gannie. *See* Graham, Elizabeth Elaine "Betty"
Gans, Danny, 439, 445
Gauthrat, Mrs. (teacher during seventh and eighth grade), 74
Glass, Butch, 205
Glick, Gary, 407
Goetsch, Bud, 168
Graf, John, 198, 224-25, 247, 277, 279
Graham, Alan, 225
Graham, Betty, 60, 145, 171, 200, 503
Graham, Brian, 225, 430
Graham, Bruce, 225
Graham, Catherine, 7, 25, 27-28, 33, 36, 50, 53, 55, 63, 73-74, 223, 246, 262-64, 535-36, 556-57, 559-60
Graham, Catherine Francis (daughter of Hannah Boyle and Robert Graham), 55, 63, 73, 246, 322, 469, 536, 538
Graham, Catherine "Kitty" (daughter of Catherine Boyle Alexander and Charles James Boyle), 28
Graham, Christian James, 60, 81, 141, 225, 288, 383, 512
Graham, Cindy, 200-203, 220-21, 230-31, 237-38, 267-68, 288, 298-300, 326-29, 407, 424-27, 434-36, 439, 501, 508-9, 519-21, 526-28
Graham, Elizabeth (mother of Mary Anne Graham), 27
Graham, Elizabeth (Mrs. James Kenneth Graham). *See*

Opalewski, Elizabeth Elaine "Betty"
Graham, George, 27, 105, 383, 398, 557
Graham, Hannah "Nan". *See* Boyle, Hannah "Nan"
Graham, James (Earl of Montrose), 21
Graham, James (First Marquess of Montrose), 19
Graham, James (uncle), 27, 36
Graham, James (Viscount of Dundee), 20
Graham, James Kenneth, 60, 70, 465, 469, 475, 484, 494-95, 502, 509, 536, 538
  admission into Michigan Bar Association, 98
  childhood, 63, 65, 74
  courtship with and marriage to
    Cynthia Elaine Dailey, 288, 323
    Elizabeth Opalewski, 106, 119
  education, 73, 79, 83, 94
  extracurricular involvement, 205-6
  favorite sayings, 415-16
  financial success, 303-4, 308, 318
  hobbies, 383-84, 387
  life principles, 461-63
  military service, 157, 161
  retirement, 283, 288
  thoughts on
    anti-Americanism, 398-99
    death, 245-47
    discipline, 389, 412
    friends, 223-24
    humor, 419-20
    loyalty, 395-96, 398-400
    luck, 403
    physical fitness, 405-7
    prayer, 392
    September 11, 2001, 400
    spiritual belief, 391
    strengths and shortcomings, 411-12, 415
  travels, 321-22, 326, 328-29
  working career, summary of, 167, 195
Graham, Jennifer Elaine (daughter of Elizabeth and James Kenneth Graham), 60, 119, 150
Graham, Jenny (daughter of Mary Anne and William Graham), 27
Graham, Jim, 28, 55, 59, 77, 111, 126, 131, 135, 141, 174-75, 181, 199, 218, 228-29, 232-34, 236
Graham, Kevin James, 223, 225, 399
  birth, 60, 115, 304, 480
  childhood, 328, 471
  education, 140
  fatherhood of, 517, 534
  first car, 385
  hobbies, 383
  marriage to Virginia Caradonna, 60, 141
Graham, Marianne, 63, 245, 469
Graham, Mary Anne McGovern, 27
Graham, May, 27
Graham, Michael, 27, 556, 559
Graham, Nan (niece of James Kenneth Graham), 47-48, 55, 96, 117, 225, 245, 248
Graham, Richard (viscount of Prestin), 20

Graham, Robert "Bob" (son of
William and Mary Anne
Graham), 38, 246, 248, 384,
534
  birth, 27
  death, 27, 245-46, 321
  as a father, 63, 415, 469, 471, 538
  immigration to America, 31
  involvement in scouting, 65, 321
  marriage to Hannah Boyle, 38
  at Plymouth and Dodge, 79, 93
Graham, Robert James "Bobby"
(son of Hannah and Robert
Graham), 55, 63, 73, 157, 246,
303, 322, 536
Graham, Rosina "Ena," 27
Graham, Samuel "Sammy," 27, 31, 38
Graham, Sarah, 27, 557
Graham, Thomas, 19
Graham, William (son of Elizabeth
and Michael Graham), 27
Graham, William (son of William
and Mary Anne Graham), 27
Graham, William Robert "Bill"
(son of Hannah and Robert
Graham), 7, 19, 55, 63, 65, 73,
106, 157, 166-67, 246, 303,
322, 469, 534, 536, 538
Graham family
  history, 27
  lineage, 19
  origin of name, 19-20, 549, 551-52
  tartan, 550
"Grandchildren," 60, 288, 518
Grant, Cary, 74, 198, 269
Grantham, William de, 549
Grattan, Ray, 74, 223, 229, 430
Greenfield Park Elementary School,
73

Grey, Modey, 157
Griffin, Sidney, 118
Guay, Ed, 425
Guttenberg, Sam, 63

H

"The Hair Studio," 494
Hanley, Andy, 239, 251, 289, 419
Haughey, Mike, 83
Herman, Bill, 329
Highland Park Post Office, 166
"Hollywood Trumps Foxwood," 474
Hook, Harold, 198
Hunt, William, 60, 106
Husak, Julie, 425, 436
Hutton, E. F., 392-93

I

"In Appreciation of Cath, Bill, and Bob," 536
"Irish Lilt," 465

J

James I (king of England), 20
James VI (king of Scotland), 20
John Paul II (pope), 200, 256
Jordan, Brian James, 223
Jordan, Jim, 246
Jordan, William "Bill," 55

K

Kaiser (president of the University of Detroit High School), 81
"Kevin and Jennifer," 480

Kosanke, Charles, 247
Krizan, Andy, 73
Kummer, Tom, 74, 79, 223, 439, 455, 493

L

Lacey, Jim, 224
"Lady," 471
"Lady of the Lake, The" (Scott), 20
Lauren, Ralph, 198, 269
Leach, Dave, 94, 224
Legal News, 305
Legatus, 203, 206
Leiberman, Bernard, 105
Lenahan (kindergarten teacher), 73
Lenin, 398
LeNoble, Ray, 326
Leslie, Joan, 74
Liberace, 326-27, 439, 448, 452
"Life," 537
Loesch, Bob, 167-68, 224
Lombardi, Vince, Jr., 391
Lombardi, Vince, Sr., 391
Longo, Charlie, 77, 79
Lord Protector. *See* Cromwell, Oliver
Lorigan, Danny, 224
"A Love Ode to Cindy," 508

M

MacDonald, Patrick, 425, 428
Machiorlatti, Joe, 87, 224
Maloney, Joe, 168
Marie Frances (teacher at St. Benedict Grade School), 74, 223
Marie Kathleen, Mother (principal at St. Benedict Grade School), 74

Markle, Bill, 224
Martin, Dean, 326, 423, 461
Maurer, Jerry, 87, 224, 233
McDevitt, Maureen, 322
McGoldrick, William, 114
McGovern, Catherine, 27
McGovern, William, 22, 27, 556, 560
McGrath, Bob, 247
McIsaac, Angus, 168
Michigan Bar Association, 98
Millen, Jerry, 223, 430
"Mom and Dad," 469
Monaghan, Thomas (Domino's Pizza founder), 203
"Monsignor Tony—'70' on July 11, 2009," 495
Mooney (cardinal), 73
Murphy, Eoin, 223, 225, 247, 425

N

Nateese, Anna, 326
Neider, Alan, 407
"The Neighborhood Growing Up—Hanging Out," 490
Nelson, Willie, 224
Neville, James B., 38
Nichols, Bob, 167
Nicklaus, Jack, 399
1984 Pearl Harbor, 198, 392
"Northern Michigan Tour," 472
Nykerk, Elizabeth Anne, 152, 288, 296, 458, 477, 512, 518, 530
Nykerk, Keely Noelle, 60, 152, 296, 520
Nykerk, Natalie Elaine, 60, 477, 512
Nykerk, Steven James, 60, 149, 477, 534

O

Oakland Athletic Club, 406
Obama, Barack Hussein, 399
Opalewski, Bruno "Brownie," 248
Opalewski, Elizabeth Elaine "Betty"
    (Mrs. James Kenneth Graham),
    7, 94, 166, 169, 200, 224, 471,
    502-3
    courtship with and marriage to
    James Kenneth Graham, 60,
    105-6, 114, 157, 223, 246,
    288, 304, 538
    death of, 60, 246-48, 288
    as grandmother, 60, 141
    as a mother to Kevin and Jennifer,
    119, 141, 480
    travels, 321, 323, 326, 328
Opalewski, Emily, 115, 131, 248
Opalewski, Erwin, 248
Oriental Provision Company, 165
Ortolan, Bob, 224, 232
O'Sullivan, John, 224

P

Palmer Park Bowling Alleys, 166,
    490
Pearce, Murray, 94
Pellino (James Graham's friend/
    college teacher), 223
Phillips, Bob, 169, 171, 198, 225,
    234-35, 247, 276, 305, 308,
    322, 498
Plymouth Motor Factory, 79, 93,
    166
Polo Store, 198
Poulos, Mike, 198, 224-25, 247,
    277, 279

Prebenda, Frank, 218, 224
Presley, Elvis, 328
Purcel, Stuart, 406

R

Ralston, Bella, 65
Ralston, Dan, 65, 119
Ralston, John, 224
Reedy, Bill, 224
Reilly, John, 224
Reilly, Kay Van Poppolen, 223
Rick (Cindy Graham's son), 94,
    297, 434, 458, 472, 509, 534
Robann, Roger, 385
Roche, Jim, 87, 224
Rodner, Harold, 406
Ron, Rudy, and Andy Trio, 425
Roskopp, Bob, 224
Ross Operating Valve, 166
Rozman, Virginia Philion, 223
Russo, Gianni, 198
Rutherford, Charlie, 224

S

Sacred Heart Major Seminary, 288
Savas, Vicki, 407
Schuster, Bob, 247, 277
Scott, Walter
    "Lady of the Lake, The," 20
Sebring, Jay. *See* Kummer, Tom
Siero (Hannah Graham's doctor),
    245
Sikora, Gene, 94, 224
Sisters of the Holy Eucharist, 203
Snyder, Jack, 166
State Farm Insurance Company,
    167-68, 303-4

St. Benedict Grade School, 73, 75, 87, 392
"St. Ben's Class Of 1952," 493
St. Edmund Parish, 114
Stefanson, Charlie, 65
Stefanson, Jim, 65, 223-24
Stefanson, Sophie, 65
Stefanson, Tony, 65, 223-24
St. Hugo of the Hills Catholic Church, 60, 141-42, 203, 206, 295, 458, 495, 517
Sullivan, Joe, 166
Sullivan, Tim, 224, 439

T

"Time," 476
Tocco, Anthony M., 225, 247, 295, 326, 328-29
"To Jennifer and Steve—Happy Anniversary," 477
Toner, George "Rose," 105
Top Hat Club, 87
Torre, Joe, 224-25, 383

U

"Uncommon Roscommon," 473

V

VALIC (Variable Annuity Life Insurance Company), 169, 195, 198, 273, 304, 498
Valli, Frankie, 328, 439
Vanderlinder, Mike, 73-74, 223, 228
Variable Annuity, 169, 195, 268, 304
Vigneron, Allen, 225

W

Walsh, Patrick, 406
Warwick, Dionne, 198-99
West, Mae, 389
Wisper, Joe, 166
Woodson, Woody, 181, 198
Wooten, Jack, 167
Wriggle, Pat, 55, 251, 538

We hope you enjoyed this
"Breathless Journey in Time"

Cindy and Jim